SART

Also available from Continuum:

Sartre: A Guide for the Perplexed, Gary Cox
The Sartre Dictionary, Gary Cox
Sex and Philosophy, Edward Fullbrook and Kate Fullbrook
The New Sartre, Nick Farrell Fox
Sartre's 'Being and Nothingness': A Reader's Guide, Sebastian Gardner
Sartre's Ethics of Engagement, T. Storm Heter
Sartre's Phenomenology, David Reisman

SARTRE AND FICTION

GARY COX

continuum

Continuum International Publishing Group

The Tower Building   80 Maiden Lane
11 York Road   Suite 704
London SE1 7NX   New York NY 10038

www.continuumbooks.com

© Gary Cox 2009

British Library Cataloguing-in-Publication Data
A catalogue record for this book is available from the British Library.

ISBN-10:   PB: 0-8264-2318-3
HB: 0-8264-4403-2
ISBN-13:   PB: 978-0-8264-2318-4
HB: 978-0-8264-4403-5

Library of Congress Cataloging-in-Publication Data
Cox, Gary, 1964-
Sartre and fiction / Gary Cox.
p. cm.
Includes bibliographical references (p.) and index.
ISBN 978-0-8264-4403-5
978-0-8264-2318-4
1. Sartre, Jean Paul, 1905-1980–Criticism and interpretation. I. Title.
PQ2637.A82Z62 2009
843'.914–dc22

2008036397

Typeset by Newgen Imaging Systems Pvt Ltd, Chennai, India
Printed and bound in Great Britain by MPG Books Ltd,
Bodmin, Cornwall

CONTENTS

PREFACE

I read Sartre's four novels and his collection of short stories as a teenager in the 1980s. Indeed, the first time I ever came across the name Jean-Paul Sartre was when friends recommended Sartre's *Nausea* to me along with Camus' *The Stranger*, Salinger's *Catcher in the Rye* and Hamsun's *Hunger*. My teenage propensity for iconoclasm inspired me to devour these radical writers, who in turn encouraged me to explore ideas and to experiment, as much as resources allowed, with alternative ways of living. All this was two or three years after Sartre's death in 1980, an event that bypassed me at the time as I was slightly too young and still imprisoned in school. What interest could an English schoolboy have in the death, or life, of a crusty old French philosopher; in philosophy generally? Back then I didn't know the meaning of the word.

Although I went on to study Sartre's philosophy at university and beyond – I'm still studying it – I confess to having seen or read only a few of Sartre's plays prior to reading them all between 2004 and 2007 for *The Sartre Dictionary*. My reading and rereading of all Sartre's fiction in a relatively short space of time led me to see this impressive body of work, not only as a whole, but as an absolutely integral part of a grand philosophical and political project that also includes philosophical treatises, psychological investigations, journalistic articles, diaries, biographies and one autobiography.

Sartre and Fiction was inspired by a desire to cohere and develop what *The Sartre Dictionary* provides in summary outline through its many cross-referenced entries: an exploration of all Sartre's published fiction, its key ideas, its recurrent themes, its historical significance and above all its intimate relationship with the 'straightforward' philosophy that he produced.

As *Sartre and Fiction* hopefully makes clear, the abiding themes of Sartre's philosophical works are also the abiding themes of his fiction: self-identity, mortality, the existence of others, freedom, responsibility, bad faith and authenticity. Sartre's philosophy can be understood to some extent without reading his fiction, just as his fiction can be enjoyed without any knowledge of his philosophy, but to really appreciate the subtlety, profundity and humanity of Sartre's fiercely honest existential assessment of the human condition the two must be taken together. The reasons for this are explored in Chapter 1, 'Sartre's Writing'.

I could perhaps have taken a thematic approach to Sartre's fiction in this book, as some previous commentators have done; with a chapter on freedom, a chapter on bad faith and so on. There would even be scope for a chapter on cowardice, a chapter on crustaceans as a symbol of malice, blind will, base nature and naked, absurd existence, or even a chapter on the moustache as a symbol of middle-class pomposity and superficiality, so fascinated is Sartre with all these themes. In the interests of accessibility, however, and in order to provide a relatively detailed assessment of each work separately, I have dedicated Chapter 2 to an overview of the main features of Sartre's existentialist philosophy before dedicating Chapters 3–5 to each of the three branches of his fiction: stories, novels, and plays.

Throughout Chapters 3–5 I strive to flag up and explore the broader philosophical and political concerns addressed by a particular fictional work, as well as the biographical and historical context of that work and the various associations it has with other Sartre works both fictional and factual. Structured in this way, the book serves readers who want to see the big picture of Sartre's fiction as well as readers who require a focused yet contextualized critical analysis of a particular story, novel or play.

In researching this book I discovered many things about Sartre that were entirely new to me, particularly regarding the intimate and all important relationship between the extraordinary life of the man and his extraordinary body of fictional work. I hope I have succeeded in dispelling a few myths and clichés to reveal the actuality of that relationship.

ACKNOWLEDGEMENTS

Many thanks to philosophers I have known personally at the universities of Southampton, Birmingham and Bristol, particularly, in recent years, Dr Jonathan Webber for all those stimulating Sartre discussions. Thanks also to friends and family, particularly Sharon, for their encouragement and support. For much of the biographical and anecdotal detail in this book I am hugely indebted to Annie Cohen-Solal for her magnificent biography of Sartre, *Jean-Paul Sartre: A Life*.

LIST OF ABBREVIATIONS

Works by Sartre are cited using the following abbreviations. See Bibliography for full bibliographical information.

Short Stories

CL	*The Childhood of a Leader*
E	*Erostratus*
I	*Intimacy*
R	*The Room*
W	*The Wall*

Novels

N	*Nausea*

Roads to Freedom trilogy:

AR	*The Age of Reason*
Re	*The Reprieve*
IS	*Iron in the Soul*

Plays

CA	*The Condemned of Altona (The Sequestered of Altona or Altona or Loser Wins)*
DG	*The Devil and the Good Lord (Lucifer and the Lord)*
DH	*Dirty Hands (Crime Passionnel)*
F	*The Flies*
IC	*In Camera (No Exit or Behind Closed Doors)*
K	*Kean, or Disorder and Genius*
MWS	*Men without Shadows (Death without Burial or The Victors)*
Ne	*Nekrassov, A Farce in Eight Scenes*
RP	*The Respectable Prostitute*
TW	*The Trojan Women*

Other Sartre Works Cited

AJ	*Anti-Semite and Jew*
BN	*Being and Nothingness*
EAH	*Existentialism and Humanism*
Im	*The Imaginary*
LS	*Life/Situations*
SG	*Saint Genet*
ST	*Sartre on Theatre*
TE	*The Transcendence of the Ego*
TEx	*Truth and Existence*
WD	*War Diaries*
WL	*What is Literature?*
Wo	*Words*

CHRONOLOGY:
SARTRE'S LIFE AND WORKS

1905   Born in Paris on 21 June, the only child of Jean-Baptiste Sartre and Anne-Marie Schweitzer.

1906   Death of father, Jean-Baptiste.

1915   Attends the Lycée Henri IV in Paris.

1917   Mother, Anne-Marie, marries Joseph Mancy, much to the distaste of her doting son.

1922   Attends the Lycée Louis-le-Grand in Paris and studies philosophy under Colonna d'Istria who introduces him to the ideas of Bergson. Progresses to the prestigious École Normale Supérieure to study philosophy.

1929   Starts lifelong friendship with Simone de Beauvoir who is in the year below him at the École Normale. Graduates from the École Normale at his second attempt, first among 76 finalists.

1931   Begins teaching in the Lycée François Ier in Le Havre, a post he will hold for five years. Continues drafting what will eventually become his first novel, *Nausea*.

1933   Introduced to the phenomenology of Husserl by Raymond Aron at a now legendary meeting in a Parisian café. Begins studying Husserl and Heidegger during a nine month sabbatical at the French Institute in Berlin after exchanging places with Aron.

1935   Experiments with the psychoactive drug mescaline under experimental conditions in order to research the phenomenon of hallucinations and has a bad trip.

1936   First published work, *Imagination: A Psychological Critique*.

1937   *The Transcendence of the Ego*, a critique of Husserl's philosophy of mind. Drafting of *The Imaginary*.

1938   *Nausea*, a philosophical novel exploring the themes of contingency, absurdity and nihilism. A seminal work of existentialism, *Nausea* establishes his reputation and celebrity.

1939   *Sketch for a Theory of the Emotions* and *The Wall*, an acclaimed collection of short stories. Conscripted into the meteorological section of the French military, he begins his extensive *War Diaries* (published posthumously, 1983).

1940   Captured by the Germans and detained in various prison camps. Spends his time in captivity writing plays and teaching the philosophy of Heidegger. *The Imaginary*, a phenomenological investigation of the imagination.

1941   Released by the Germans with the aid of a fake medical certificate declaring him unfit for military service, he returns to German occupied Paris and founds the resistance group, Socialism and Freedom.

1943   *Being and Nothingness*, a detailed exposition of his existential phenomenology and his major philosophical work. *The Flies*, his play based on the Greek legend of Orestes and an implicit commentary on the political situation, is performed in occupied Paris. Start of friendship with Albert Camus.

1944   *In Camera*, a play exploring the idea that 'hell is other people.'

1945   Founds the literary and political review, *Les Temps modernes*, with de Beauvoir and Merleau-Ponty. *The Age of Reason* and *The Reprieve*, the first two volumes of a trilogy of novels, *Roads to Freedom*, set before and during World War II.

1946   *Existentialism and Humanism*, a book originally delivered as a popular and controversial lecture the previous year; *Men Without Shadows,* a play about a group of resistance fighters facing torture; *The Respectable Prostitute*, a play about racism in the USA; the essay *Anti-Semite and Jew* and a psychoanalytical biography of the poet Baudelaire.

1948   His atheism and anti-authoritarianism leads the Catholic Church to place his entire works on the Vatican index of prohibited books. *What is Literature?,* a work of literary theory with political overtones, and *Dirty Hands*, a play about an assassin and his questionable motives.

1949   *Iron in the Soul*, the third volume of a trilogy of novels, *Roads to Freedom*, set before and during World War II.

1951   *The Devil and The Good Lord,* a play set in Medieval Germany considering various philosophical, theological and political issues.

1952   End of his friendship with Camus following a very public row on the pages of *Les Temps modernes*. *Saint Genet*, an extensive psychoanalytical biography of his friend and contemporary, the writer Jean Genet.

1954   First of many trips to the Soviet Union. Publication of *Kean*, a play about the actor Edmund Kean that explores questions of personal identity.

1956   *Nekrassov*, a darkly comical play satirising the French right-wing press.

1959   *The Condemned of Altona*, a play about Nazi collaborators and German post-war collective guilt.

1960   Signs the treasonable 'Manifesto of the 121' calling for insubordination by French troops in Algeria. Visits Castro in Cuba with de Beauvoir. *Critique of Dialectical Reason, Volume One* (*Volume Two* published posthumously, 1985), an ambitious attempt to amalgamate existentialism and Marxism and the most important philosophical work of his later years.

1961   Paris apartment bombed by the O.A.S., a terrorist organisation opposed to Algerian independence (bombed again the following year).

1964   *Words*, the acclaimed autobiography of his childhood. Declines the Nobel Prize for Literature on the grounds that writers must refuse to be transformed by institutions.

1965   Adopts Arlette Elkaïm, his close female friend of several years. *The Trojan Women*, a play commenting on the Algerian War and imperialism generally, adapted from the tragedy by Euripides.

1967   Heads a tribunal set up by Bertrand Russell to investigate US war crimes in Indochina.

1968   Lends support to the student riots and French General Strike whilst continuing to work on *The Family Idiot*, a vast, psychoanalytical and sociological biography of the writer Flaubert.

1971   The first and second volumes of *The Family Idiot*.

1972   The third volume of *The Family Idiot*.

1973   The health of his long abused body deteriorates rapidly. Hypertension causes his eyesight to fail, destroying his ability to write.

1974 Visits the terrorist Andreas Baader in Stammheim Prison, Germany.

1977 Claims he is no longer a Marxist but continues to actively support left wing political causes.

1980 Dies in Paris on 15 April of oedema of the lungs. Buried in Montparnasse Cemetery. Over fifty thousand people line the streets at his funeral.

CHAPTER 1

SARTRE'S WRITING

Jean-Paul Sartre dedicated his life and his extraordinary intellect to philosophical questions concerning the nature of existence, particularly human existence, and the meaning or meaninglessness of human life. Before he became famous and something of a worldwide celebrity he taught philosophy at a school in Le Havre and at various colleges in Paris. Later on he gave sell-out philosophical talks and lectures in places as far apart as Vienna, New York and Tokyo. His philosophy, his phenomenological ontology or existentialism, is put forward in the thousands of pages of non-fiction that he wrote, in great theoretical works such as *The Imaginary, Being and Nothingness* and *The Critique of Dialectical Reason*, and in psychoanalytical biographies of the writers Charles Baudelaire, Jean Genet and Gustave Flaubert. His philosophy is also put forward, clarified and taken to a far wider audience than would otherwise have been the case in an impressive accumulation of fictional writings that includes a collection of short stories, four novels and ten plays. This book examines each of these fictional works in detail.

Had Sartre only produced his fictional writings he would be a significant literary figure and a renowned playwright. He would probably have still been offered the Nobel Prize for Literature that he famously declined in October 1964 on the grounds that writers must not allow themselves to be transformed by institutions.[1] As it is, taken together, his achievements as a philosopher, biographer, novelist and dramatist, not to mention diarist and journalist, make him a figure unsurpassed in the history of ideas, certainly in terms of sheer volume and variety of output. He is what he set out to be as a child, a man of letters *par excellence*, seemingly as much at home crafting a short story as pouring out with the aid

of stimulants a long and complex treatise synthesizing existentialism and Marxism.[2] Certainly, with the exception of poetry, which
in his *War Diaries* he confesses to being not much good at (*WD*,
p. 314), he could manage it all with great skill and often to high
critical acclaim. His secretary Jean Cau recalls, however, that different kinds of writing put Sartre in different moods. Writing philosophy made him whistle, drafting a play could make him irritable
(Cohen-Solal 2005, p. 280). Presumably, he found writing philosophy easier, or rather, the rapidity with which he was able to write
philosophy made him feel most acutely what he once described as
'the speed of my soul' (*Wo*, p. 154); the free flight of his consciousness towards the future.

Unlike the vast majority of people, Sartre appears to have had
no real notion of intellectual difficulty and certainly no fear of it.
He was ridiculously clever and a tireless worker. He did, however,
find some kinds of writing trickier and more labour intensive than
others. He fairly dashed off *Saint Genet*, for example, his acclaimed
600-page biography of Genet, while he wrestled for several years
on and off with *Words*, a relatively short but beautifully crafted
autobiography of his childhood. His love of the kind of workload
that would crush most people meant that he was not inclined to shy
away when the going got tough. He loved a challenge and certainly
he loved the challenge of advancing his philosophy, his vision of
the human condition, in a variety of literary media. So, not least,
Sartre wrote fiction because he could. He was equal to the task and
enjoyed testing himself and advancing his theories on more than
one front.

As he tells in *Words*, his earliest intellectual passion apart from
reading was writing fiction. His early novels were trashy, globetrot-
ting tales of heroes and villains with contrived plots that he poured
out without rereading them.[3] He was not, he says, fascinated by
what he wrote once the ink had dried but by the act of writing itself
that allowed him both to create heroes and to create himself, the
writer, as a hero (*Wo*, p. 106). In *Words* Sartre writes, 'At the age of
eight...I embarked on a simple but insane operation which altered
the course of my life: I unloaded on to the writer the consecrated
powers of the hero' (*Wo*, p. 106). He tells of being bowled over by
the story of Charles Dickens' arrival in New York. A dense crowd
brimming with expectation, mouths open, caps waving, massed on
the quay as his ship approached '...to be so wildly acclaimed, men

of letters, I thought, must have to tackle the worst of dangers and render the most distinguished services to humanity' (*Wo*, p. 106).

When he later discovered philosophy and realized that he had an aptitude for it and a great deal to contribute to it, he did not as a consequence abandon his earlier aspirations to be a writer of fiction. Confronted by a choice between philosophy and fiction he could not bring himself to abandon either, so he chose to excel at both and to amalgamate them whenever possible. Each was made to serve the purposes of the other. He wrote philosophical works rich in descriptions of real life that read, in places, like literary fiction. He wrote short stories, novels and plays that are truly philosophical. Chapter 2 of this book considers the philosophical ideas that both underpin Sartre's fiction and are evolved in it.

Sartre wrote fiction to take his philosophy to a wider audience and to make himself world-famous in the process, to achieve his ultimate ambition of joining the pantheon of famous dead writers he so admired. But it is also true to say that only fiction, only literature, serves to fully convey the intricacies, the subtleties, the universal applicability, even the atmosphere, of Sartre's vision of reality and the human condition. Sartre is, as is so often said, an existentialist. To fully achieve his existentialist philosophical aims he has to reveal people as they really are, in the concrete, existential circumstances of their everyday lives, meeting its existential challenges or succumbing to its existential pressures, affirming their freedom or sliding into bad faith. With the possible exception of the kind of psychoanalytical biography Sartre favoured almost exclusively towards the end of his career, there is no better way to capture philosophically the existential realities of human life than through literary fiction. To take an example, Sartre's first and arguably greatest novel, *Nausea*, manages to convey a sense of the terrifying contingency and absurdity of existence. This sense, in which terror is very much a part of the philosophical picture, simply could not be conveyed by a straightforward philosophical explanation couched in formalized technical language. An understanding of Sartre's technical language does, thereafter, help the reader to fully appreciate what is and is not going on in *Nausea*, but it is the literary, even poetical tones of the novel that breathe real life and uncompromising truth and urgency into the philosophical theory.

Why, it is sometimes asked, didn't Sartre just stick to writing 'straightforward' philosophy like most philosophers? Well, actually, it is not true, certainly in the past, that most philosophers have stuck to writing straightforward, conventional philosophy. Plato wrote dialogues as did Berkeley and Hume, and Wittgenstein has his 'two voices'. Nietzsche often wrote in aphorisms – 'I approach deep problems like cold baths: quick into them and quickly out again' (Nietzsche 1974, 381, p. 343). And even when Nietzsche did not write in aphorisms the way in which he makes his case could hardly be described as straightforward and conventional. Voltaire wrote the story *Candide* partly to criticize a certain interpretation of Leibniz' 'best of all possible worlds' thesis, and Rousseau put forward his philosophy of education in *Emile*, a work that is part novel, part philosophical treatise. Among other philosophers who strayed from the straight and narrow, if indeed there is such thing, are Kierkegaard, Camus, de Beauvoir and Murdoch.

The more we think about so-called straightforward, conventional philosophy, as opposed to other ways of communicating philosophical ideas, the more vague the notion becomes. Sartre's major work, *Being and Nothingness*, for example, is often described as a work of philosophy as opposed to literary fiction, drama or biography. It is indeed a philosophical work but its style owes much to literary fiction, particularly its extended concrete examples and its rich turn of phrase, and when it first appeared in 1943 it was hailed as a new way of doing philosophy; as anything but conventional. As Cohen-Solal writes,

> ...once it gains notice, the appearance of such an enormous "bastard" takes the philosophical world by surprise. The treatise combines the classicism of its language, its reliance on other philosophical texts, its body of reference, its Cartesian logic, with a presentation that is revolutionary... At odds with the prevailing university tradition, here is a new philosopher who uses the "triviality" of daily life to explain his theories. (Cohen-Solal 2005, p. 188)

So-called straightforward, conventional philosophy must simply be the way or style of writing philosophy that has come to dominate academic philosophical journals in the twentieth century. That is, prose based, problem focused, highly abstract extended arguments with few examples. Analytical, technical, extremely specific, the next careful move in an important ongoing debate that may, for all that, be going nowhere. This style of philosophy is powerful and perfectly suited to addressing many philosophical issues, for others it is too narrow, too limiting. However obvious its merits, it does not have the right to claim the heart and soul of philosophy, relegating all other styles of philosophy to the margins. In countering those who go even further and claim that *logic* is the heart and soul of philosophy, it can be argued that while logic is undoubtedly the most important philosophical tool, studying logic and calling that philosophy is like studying a hammer and calling that carpentry.

So, in actual fact, we should say that *like* most great thinkers Sartre used various literary forms to convey his philosophical vision. His talent and his capacity for hard work allowed him not only to write theoretical works, stories, novels, plays and biographies, but to excel in all these areas. Each literary form he used made its own indispensable contribution to the integrated whole that is his complex, multifaceted philosophy. Had Sartre not written fiction the overall appearance, character and vibe of his philosophy would be almost unrecognizable. Would Sartre still be the Sartre we know had he not written *Nausea*, for example? Fiction, and particularly that work of fiction, cannot be taken out of the Sartre equation anymore than writing itself can be taken out of the Sartre equation. Sartre wrote, and had he been introduced to another form of writing he would have tried his hand at that too if he felt he could use it to make a worthwhile philosophical point.

He tried his hand at writing screenplays for example. He co-wrote the screenplay to the 1947 film *The Chips Are Down* and the screenplay to the 1957 film *The Witches of Salem*, an adaptation of Arthur Miller's play, *The Crucible*. Lastly, in 1958, he received a $25,000 advance from the legendary film director John Huston to write a screenplay about Sigmund Freud. He completed it but it became so watered down by the Hollywood machine that he eventually withdrew his name from it.

It may sound simplistic but Sartre wrote fiction because he wanted to and because he could. Fiction served the purposes of illustrating, enhancing and broadening his philosophy, especially when set alongside his articles, biographies and critiques. In short, Sartre wrote fiction because he wrote. As a child he wanted only to write fiction, but that was before he discovered philosophy and before he realized that the best fiction – literature – *is* philosophy. Can it be denied that the great writers, playwrights and poets are philosophers – Conrad,

Golding, Dostoevsky, Hardy, Lawrence, Shakespeare, Coleridge – a philosopher being anyone who ponders in a relatively structured and sustained way the fundamentals of the human condition: our being, our morality, our mortality.

We seem to have come up against a wall in exploring why Sartre wrote fiction and can go no further than saying: he wrote fiction because it was available to him as a powerful form of philosophical expression. As that great philosopher and stylist Wittgenstein once said, 'If I have exhausted the justifications I have reached bedrock, and my spade is turned. Then I am inclined to say: "This is simply what I do."' (Wittgenstein 1988, 217, p. 85). It seems that if we want to dig further into Sartre and find out what he was all about, and what ultimately his philosophy was all about, we should not be pondering why he wrote *fiction* – although that hopefully has yielded some interesting findings – we should be pondering why he wrote. 'Why did Sartre write?' is arguably the most interesting and productive question that can be asked about Sartre. It is certainly a question he gave a vast amount of thought to himself. Not only in *What is Literature?*, a work of literary theory, but also in the three biographies he published about writers and in his aptly titled autobiography, *Words*.

What is Literature? analyses from a philosophical and political perspective the nature and purpose of writing and reading and the relationship between writer and reader. One of its chapters is titled 'Why Write?'. As well as being Sartre's most significant contribution to the philosophy of aesthetics, the work is a political manifesto that identifies literature as a form of social and political action. What Sartre calls, 'action by disclosure' (*WL*, p. 14). What, in Sartre's view, sets literature apart from other, lesser forms of writing, such as mere storytelling for the purpose of entertainment, is the intention of the writer. To succeed in writing literature – as Sartre always aspires to do, even, arguably, in his factual works – a writer must engage with contemporary issues. He must be committed to asking relevant questions and to challenging current norms in a way that raises the awareness of his readership and inspires them to action. Literature reveals and challenges aspects of the contemporary world. A committed writer like Sartre does not, for example, write about political corruption in Ancient Argos unless it is to comment on political corruption in his own time. Writing literature heightens the social, political, historical and philosophical awareness of the writer, while reading literature raises these same forms of awareness in the reader.

The effect of literature on the reader should be liberating. Literature is nothing if it is not a liberating force. '...there is no "gloomy literature", since, however dark may be the colours in which one paints the world, one paints it only so that free men may feel their freedom as they face it' (*WL*, p. 47). For the reader to establish a genuine relationship with the writer's work is for the reader to redefine his relationship with his own situation. Perhaps he becomes aware of his alienation or his oppressed condition, perhaps he is inspired to question and actively reject the *status quo* that he has hitherto accepted without complaint.

For Sartre, the purpose of writing, the purpose of literature, is not to provide an apology for the way things are or to flatter the powers that be. Such writing is opposed to freedom and deeply inauthentic. Literature provokes rather than sedates, it is a stimulant that is capable of bringing an individual, a group, a whole social class, out of a state of alienation into an awareness of freedom. In liberating the reader through his successful efforts to create challenging and provocative works of art, the writer is in turn liberated by the reader and fully realizes his own freedom. As an engaged and committed writer of literature, Sartre wrote to respond to history and to shape history through his impact on his readership.

The view of literature that Sartre puts forward in *What is Literature?* is generally very sympathetic to Marxist theory. Nonetheless, he maintains that a writer, in his quest to liberate himself and others, should not be a slave to political ideology to the extent that he becomes nothing more than a mouthpiece of partisan dogma. Sartre felt that some of his intellectual contemporaries had become slavish in their support of the Communist Party. Sartre often supported the Communist Party but not always and he was never a member. Like his alter ego Mathieu Delarue in *The Age of Reason*, he resisted pressure to make his association official.

It is no mere coincidence that the three biographies Sartre published are all about writers. He was fascinated by what led Baudelaire, Genet and Flaubert to write, to choose a life of imagination. Many Sartre scholars argue with good reason that Sartre's ultimate aim in considering why these men wrote was to answer the question of why he himself wrote. Some scholars even argue that Sartre's vast biography of Flaubert, *The Family Idiot*, his last significant work, is really his autobiography in disguise, a sequel to his autobiography *Words*. It remains a matter of debate how much of himself Sartre projects onto Flaubert both intentionally and unintentionally, but what is certain is that his biography of Flaubert returns to the central theme of *Words*: writing as a choice of being. The thesis that *The Family Idiot* is Sartre's autobiography in disguise is not really credible, but it is a work in which Sartre is obsessed with the *choice* to be a writer, a choice of self that was very much his own.

In *Words* Sartre tells how his doting family treated him as a necessity, as a being that was meant to be. He even goes as far as to say that his grandfather, Charles Schweitzer, treated him as a gift from heaven, as an indicator of the sublime, as a solace to his fear of old age and death. The precocious Poulou (Sartre's pet name) was, however, never quite convinced that he was a necessary being. Instead, he felt vague and insubstantial, pointless, even superfluous. Sartre later gave the same feelings to Lucien Fleurier, the central character of his short story *The Childhood of a Leader*. Sartre saw himself as travelling on a train without a ticket; travelling through life without justification for his absurd existence, troubled by a ticket-inspector that was also himself. 'Stowaway traveller, I had fallen asleep on the seat and the ticket-inspector was shaking me. "Your ticket!" I was forced to admit that I had not got one' (*Wo*, p. 70). Realizing that he had no ticket, that nobody had or could have given him a ticket, how was he to justify his presence on the train?

One of the abiding themes of Sartre's philosophy is that there is nothing that a person is in the mode of being it. Whatever a person is he must *choose* to be it, he must constantly strive through his actions to *be* what he is without ever being able to fully and finally become it. Whereas a table, for example, is what it is, a being-in-itself, a person, a being-for-itself, can only ever aim at or play at being a banker, a waiter, a writer and so on. The ever-present possibility of an alternative choice of himself prevents him from simply *being* a banker, a waiter or a writer – a writer-*thing*.

From the age of seven Sartre *chose* writing as his ticket to life and his reason to be. His choice to be a writer was his fundamental choice of himself, a choice that influenced all his subsequent choices and so shaped his entire life and personality. 'I was born from writing: before that, there was only a reflection in a mirror. From my first novel, I knew that a child had entered the palace of mirrors. By writing, I existed, I escaped from the grown-ups; but I existed only to write and if I said: me – that meant the me who wrote' (*Wo*, p. 97).

Sartre claims in *Words* that it was his desire for heroic immortality as a writer, set alongside his early dismissal of Christian notions of salvation and the afterlife, that motivated him rather than any particular gift or genius. He is fond of arguing that genius is as genius does. 'The genius of Proust is the totality of the works of Proust' (*EAH*, pp. 41–42). Sartre deliberately set out from childhood to create himself as a 'genius' through sustained hard work and unflinching self-belief.[4] Constantly making himself a writer through the act of writing enabled Sartre to maintain an illusion of substance and purpose that effectively kept at bay those disturbing childhood feelings of pointlessness and superfluity. He maintained this grand illusion so well by his efforts, believed so strongly in his vocation, in his capacity to achieve his destiny, that as a young man he was, unlike his friends, untroubled by fears of an untimely death. 'I had forearmed myself against accidental death, that was all; the Holy Ghost had commissioned a long-term work from me, so he had to give me time to complete it' (*Wo*, pp. 123–124).

Towards the end of *Words* the ageing writer finally writes himself out of the grand illusion that has sustained him since childhood. He finally confronts what he has always known, what he has spent the greater part of his life striving to deny, that writing (or any other activity) cannot remove his superfluity and make him a necessary being at one with himself. Like everyone else he remains a ticketless traveller on a journey to nowhere. 'I have become once again the traveller without a ticket that I was at seven' (*Wo*, p. 157). Despite his monumental efforts he remains contingent and mortal, his immortal status as a writer existing only for future generations of equally contingent mortals. Nonetheless, even in his disillusionment, he claims to fear the cooling of the sun that will one day annihilate all people and with it his legacy (*Wo*, p. 155).

Despite the disillusionment with writing expressed in *Words*, Sartre continued to write copiously for another nine years until in 1973 he lost his sight and was no longer able to work. He had been blind in his right eye since the age of four. Hypertension resulting from stimulants, over work and his generally unhealthy lifestyle, caused the sight in his left eye to fail also.

My occupation as a writer is completely destroyed...The only point to my life was writing...What will no longer be accessible to me is something that many young people today are scornful of: style, let us say the literary manner of presenting an idea or a reality. This necessarily calls for revisions...I can no longer correct my work even once, because I cannot read what I have written. (*LS*, pp. 4, 5, 6, 10. Quoted in Cohen-Solal 2005, p. 489)

Sartre continued to write until darkness set in because, despite his many claims regarding freedom and choice, he felt compelled by long habit, by a 'worn exigency' (*Wo*, p. 104), to write for at least six hours everyday. 'My commandments have been sewn into my skin: if I go a day without writing, the scar burns me; and if I write too easily, it also burns me' (*Wo*, p. 104). Sartre continued to write because it was his profession. There was the vast sphere of Sartrean influence – the Sartre empire – to maintain and expand by further writing. He could have amassed a personal fortune, but there were many political causes to support and a fair number of people on the payroll who depended on the 'engine room' (Cohen-Solal 2005, p. 279) continuing to function. Not least, Sartre felt he had a moral duty to continue writing and to use his pen as a sword. His fame and influence were such that he could affect political outcomes with his polemics; embarrass governments, rescue lost causes, save lives. Perhaps, above all, Sartre wrote and continued to write because he simply loved doing what he was best at: playing the role of a smart-mouthed upstart, an agitator, troublemaker and firebrand with the insight and incisive wit to expose the pretensions, delusions and hypocrisy of Western, bourgeois society. 'I have renounced my vocation, but I have not unfrocked myself. I still write. What else can I do?' (*Wo*, p. 157).

CHAPTER 2

SARTRE'S EXISTENTIALISM

Sartre's existentialist philosophy, or more specifically some of his specialist terminology, can appear difficult. After a bit of jargon busting, however, I am confident you will see Sartre's reputation for complexity and obscurity as largely undeserved. Anyway, it is enough at this stage to grasp the general gist of it. Sartre's ideas will certainly become clearer over time as you assimilate them, especially if you revisit certain key passages in this chapter as you go. To read philosophy is often to have to *reread* it, all the while taking time to sit back and reflect. Sartre's ideas will certainly become clearer in subsequent chapters when revealed in the context of his fictional writing. The main aim of Sartre's fictional writing is, after all, to give real substance to his abstract philosophical ideas, to explore, develop and explain those ideas in real-life, existential situations. Though I do not recommend it, as subsequent chapters assume to some extent that this chapter has been read, you can skip this chapter for now and read it, if you desire, *after* reading subsequent chapters. After all, many people enjoy Sartre's fiction and learn from it without having any prior knowledge of his philosophy. Familiarity with his philosophy does, however, amplify appreciation of his fiction, just as familiarity with his fiction enhances understanding of his philosophy.

Sartre's grand philosophy, as put forward in his many fictional and non-fictional writings, amounts to a detailed description of the human condition. It provides an integrated, holistic account of the central and often inescapable features and phenomena that comprise human reality or *existence* – hence the name *existentialism*. Although the complex sounding terminology Sartre sometimes employs to get deep beneath the skin of these phenomena and expose their significance will be unfamiliar to the newcomer to his philosophy, the phenomena themselves are certainly not unfamiliar. Whether or not a person likes to confront them, these phenomena are the hard facts of our everyday lives, the uncompromising existential truths of what a major influence on Sartre, Martin Heidegger, refers to as our *being-in-the-world*: abandonment in a godless universe; the accidental, contingent, even absurd nature of our existence; the relentless passage of time that prevents us from ever being at one with ourselves; the unavoidable reality of others who judge us; desire, freedom, responsibility, anxiety and death. It is a grim list no doubt, but that, Sartre argues, is the way it is. To seek to live in denial of these hard existential truths is what Sartre calls *bad faith*. To confront them, on the other hand, to live in a manner that affirms rather than denies them, is to achieve what Sartre refers to as *authenticity*. Authenticity, for Sartre, is the overcoming of bad faith.

Sartre is often characterized in shallow, flippant accounts as a nihilist, as a man advocating despair in face of a cruel and meaningless universe. Although he certainly explores this attitude, particularly in his 1938 novel, *Nausea*, his philosophy is in fact ultimately positive and constructive. Like Friedrich Nietzsche, who is also often mistaken for a nihilist, Sartre actually has an anti-nihilist agenda. Like Nietzsche, his aim is to show that a worthwhile life is still possible within the reality dictated by the existential truths. Indeed, his ultimate aim is to show that a life is *more* worthwhile, interesting, creative, dignified, noble and authentic for being lived in face of the existential truths than a life characterized by a cowardly evasion of them, a life characterized by bad faith.

The person in bad faith fools himself that his existence is necessary, that he has fundamental rights, God given or otherwise, that his actions are determined by circumstances rather than by his free choices and so on. The person in bad faith is irresponsible; he treats his choice not to choose as though it were not a choice. He acts as though he cannot choose or does not have to choose. The person in bad faith may act as though he is immortal, believing that he will always be as he is now or that he will live on in an afterlife cleansed of all inconveniences and acrimony. His life, according to Sartre, is a fake, a lie. By failing to confront reality for what it is he fails to realize his full potential as a person capable of creating himself and his destiny by positively affirming his freedom.

Sartre's main justification for his bold claims about the human condition, the value of freedom and authenticity, the nature of bad faith and so on, is the very coherence of his integrated, holistic account of them; his systematic revealing of the fact that every essential aspect of human reality is intimately related to every other. For Sartre, one essential phenomenon of human reality directly and logically implies another. He shows, for instance, that consciousness is essentially temporal, that freedom is an inalienable feature of consciousness, that bad faith is a direct possibility of freedom and that authenticity is the antithesis of bad faith. This integrated, holistic account must be examined more closely and described in some detail if it is to make complete sense; if it is not to appear as the mishmash of ill-formed ideas that some critics accuse it of being. The easiest and best way to do this is to trace the main lines of argument put forward in Sartre's major philosophical work, *Being and Nothingness*, considering other associated works as required. *Being and Nothingness* is the nearest thing to a bible of existentialism; to fathom its apparent complexities is to get more or less to the bottom of what existentialism is really all about.

BEING-IN-ITSELF AND BEING-FOR-ITSELF

There are two related terms at the very heart of Sartre's entire philosophical theory: *being-in-itself* and *being-for-itself*. These related terms underpin virtually everything Sartre says about everything else, so much so that if a newcomer to Sartre can gain even a basic grasp of the meaning of these two terms he or she will have already made significant progress towards understanding his existentialism. For reasons that will become apparent it is best to begin unfolding an account of Sartre's philosophy from the starting point of being-in-itself.

Most philosophers have a view about what exists in the most general or fundamental sense. René Descartes, for example, thinks that there is mind, matter and God. Sartre thinks that fundamentally there is being-in-itself. All that can really be said about being-in-itself is that it *is*. It is its own foundation. That is, it is founded upon itself and not upon anything else. It is that which exists fundamentally, *in itself*, in its own right, rather than being that which does not exist in itself and is dependent upon something else for its existence. It is self-sufficient, uncreated and unchanging. It is tempting to suppose that it has always been and will always be, but it is eternal only in the sense of being timeless. There is no past or future for being-in-itself. It is also tempting to suppose that the existence of being-in-itself is necessary, but to describe it as necessary is to characterize it as that which cannot not be, when, according to Sartre, it has no characteristics whatsoever other than *being*. Being-in-itself exists utterly, yet its existence is not necessary. It *is*, yet it need not be. This is the contingency, superfluity or even absurdity of being-in-itself. It exists without reason or justification. The fact that being-in-itself has no characteristics leads Sartre to describe it as *undifferentiated being*. Not only is it timeless and unnecessary, it is non-spatial. It should not be thought of as an infinite block of stuff – although Sartre does sometimes refer to physical objects as 'in-itself', in contrast to persons who are 'for-itself'. If being-in-itself were spatial it would be differentiated in the sense of having different regions, here and there and so on, but being-in-itself has no regions or parts just as it has no past or future. It contains no differences or contrasts, it has no distinguishing features; it just *is*.

To think accurately of this featureless existence seems to be to think of nothing at all. If I try to imagine being-in-itself I end up giving it some attribute like dimension or colour that it does not have. Interestingly, the German philosopher George Hegel argues that being (he does not use the term being-in-itself) is so undifferentiated and featureless that it is in fact indistinguishable from non-being or nothingness. For Hegel, being and non-being are only abstract concepts produced by philosophical reasoning. In reality, there is neither being nor non-being but only *becoming*. Sartre disagrees with Hegel, insisting that being-in-itself *is* while non-being or nothingness *is not*. For Sartre, being-in-itself is logically primary. All else – that is, non-being – is logically subsequent to it, dependent upon it and derived from it.

Non-being, or what Sartre calls *being-for-itself*, does not exist fundamentally; it does not exist in its own right. Only being-in-itself exists in that way. Being-for-itself exists only as a denial or negation of being-in-itself, only as a *relationship* to being-in-itself. It borrows its being from being-in-itself, existing as a lack or absence of being-in-itself. Sartre refers to being-for-itself as a *borrowed being*. Like a shadow or a reflection its borrowed being is entirely dependent on something other than itself.

Although Sartre says that being-in-itself *is* and non-being *is not*, the phenomenon of non-being or being-for-itself is crucially important in his philosophy. Indeed, his entire philosophy is essentially an exhaustive investigation and description of the phenomenon of being-for-itself. It is vital to note that being-for-itself refers to the essential nature or way of being of consciousness or personhood. Every consciousness or person is essentially a being-for-itself. So, in many contexts, the terms 'consciousness', 'person' and 'being-for-itself' can be used interchangeably. Sartre's investigation into the nature of being-for-itself amounts to an investigation into the essential, existential features of human consciousness and reality. Sartre's view of consciousness as non-being, as being-for-itself, is considered in detail in due course.

It is tempting to suppose that being-in-itself gave rise to being-for-itself, as though giving rise to its negation was a project that being-in-itself undertook at some point in time. Being-in-itself, however, because it is what it is and can never be other than what it is, cannot have projects or conceive of possibilities. Sartre insists, though not all scholars agree with him, that it is impossible to answer the question of where being-for-itself came from. In his view, any attempt to account for what he describes as the *upsurge* of being-for-itself from being-in-itself produces only speculation that cannot be confirmed as true or false. For Sartre, the emergence or upsurge of being-for-itself is an unfathomable mystery, just as the existence of being-in-itself is an unfathomable mystery.[1]

As said, being-for-itself is not a non-being in itself, its own non-being, it is the non-being or negation of being-in-itself. In not being its own non-being, being-for-itself always has to strive to be its own non-being without ever being able to become it. Being-for-itself always has to be both the project of negating being-in-itself in order to realize itself as the negation of being-in-itself, and the project of negating itself in order to avoid a coincidence with itself that would be its own annihilation. Being-for-itself is a paradoxical, ambiguous, indeterminate being that always lacks identity both with being-in-itself and with itself. It is perpetually not what it is (being) and what it is not (non-being) and can only exist in this way, as a flight or escape from any kind of self-identity.

The easiest way to understand the paradoxical, ambiguous, indeterminate nature of being-for-itself is in terms of time or temporality, as a temporal view of it brings to mind ideas everyone is familiar with from their own experience. After all, each of us is a being-for-itself on a lifelong temporal journey. Being-for-itself exists as a temporal flight or *transcendence* away from its past towards its future. It is both its past which is no longer, and its future which is not yet. If it could ever be fixed in the present it would cease to exist, but the present does not exist anymore than being-for-itself can be fixed in the present. Being-for-itself is always not what it is (past) and what it is not (future). We all know what this means if we think about it because we all live this paradox all the time. I am my past which is no longer, and all my actions in a world which is the result of the past aim at a future which is not yet. As for the present, there is no such moment as the present, for when being-for-itself reaches the future at which it aims that future does not become the present but rather immediately becomes the past. The present, argues Sartre, is actually the *presence* of being-for-itself to being-in-itself as a temporal flight from being-in-itself towards the future.[2]

Being-for-itself is not in the world as objects are. Being-for-itself transcends the world and it does so by constantly escaping it towards the future. It is what Sartre calls a *temporal transcendence* – it transcends temporally. Being-for-itself, however, because it is only the negation of being-in-itself, is an escaping that continues to require the being it seeks to escape. It is an escaping that cannot finally escape. It is a transcendence that is constantly re-captured by the physical world, precisely because the physical world is the ground of its transcendence. To be a transcendence towards the future, being-for-itself must have something to transcend. What being-for-itself transcends is the human body, what Sartre calls its *embodiment*, and the wider situation or circumstances of the body. Sartre refers to all this – embodiment and the wider situation – as the *situatedness* or *facticity* of being-for-itself. What being-for-itself transcends is facticity; what Sartre describes as, 'The coefficient of adversity of things' (*BN*, p. 503). In short, being-for-itself is not a transcendence-in-itself, a pure transcendence, but the transcendence of its facticity. Being-for-itself *is* the transcendence of facticity and nothing beyond that.

In everyday terms, it is human projects that constitute the transcendence of being-for-itself. A person's projects always aim at a future in which he will have overcome something presently lacking or absent, a future in which he hopes and desires to be more satisfied, fulfilled and at one with himself. Sartre argues that ultimately being-for-itself always aims at coinciding with itself, at being its own foundation, at being what he calls a *being-for-itself-in-itself.* In so far as God is conceived as a being-for-itself-in-itself, as a consciousness that is nonetheless identical with itself, Sartre argues, somewhat controversially, that the fundamental project of every being-for-itself is to be God.[3] Being-for-itself, however, can never achieve this state of self-supporting self-identity because it exists only as the negation of being-in-itself and as such is grounded upon it rather than upon itself. It is destined always to be grounded upon a being that it is not and as such can never be its own foundation. Sartre's examination of the impossibility of being-for-itself becoming being-for-itself-in-itself provides an explanation of why complete satisfaction and self-fulfilment are unachievable, why, in Sartre's view, 'Man is a useless passion' (*BN*, p. 636). Incidentally, it is largely because he holds that being-for-itself-in-itself is an impossible state of being that Sartre is an atheist. He denies the existence of God, a divine consciousness, on logical grounds.

Being-for-itself is nothing in itself, therefore it must constantly make itself be something, or rather, it must constantly aim at being something without ever being able to become it once and for all. A person can 'become' a banker, for example, but this does not mean that he has become a banker-*thing* in the way that a table is a table. He has to constantly choose to play the role of a banker and can always choose to do otherwise. Being-for-itself aims at being something through choice and action. This is what Sartre has in mind, when he argues along the lines that to be is to do. By doing, however, a person does not become his being absolutely; his being is rather a constant becoming. Being-for-itself is burdened with always having to choose itself, with always having to choose its responses to its situation. It has to constantly choose its way of being. It cannot not do so because not to choose is still a choice – a *choice* not to choose. Sartre's views on choice and action are considered in more detail in due course.

CONSCIOUSNESS AND INTENTIONALITY

As we have seen, consciousness is or exists as being-for-itself and each conscious human being is essentially a being-for-itself in relation to being-in-itself. To focus in a rather abstract way on the logic of the relationship between being-for-itself and being-in-itself, as we have done so far, produces what Sartre calls an *ontological* description of the relationship. To focus in a less abstract way on the concrete, existential relationship between consciousness and the world produces what Sartre calls a *phenomenological* description of the relationship. It is basically the same relationship that is being described, what is different is the level or focus of the description. If an ontological description reveals or comprises the bones of Sartre's philosophy (his *phenomenological ontology,* as it is formally known) a phenomenological description puts flesh on those bones. At the heart of Sartre's phenomenological description of the relationship between consciousness and the world is the notion of *intentionality* or *aboutness.*

Consciousness does not exist as a thing, it is not any kind of object. It is not a mental substance, as the philosopher Descartes supposes, existing in its own right and then entertaining thoughts. In fact, it is nothing in itself. It exists only in relation to what it is consciousness of. If it were not conscious of anything it would not exist. Sartre sums this view up with the maxim: consciousness is consciousness of __. As he writes in *Being and Nothingness,* 'To say that consciousness is consciousness of something means that for consciousness there is no being outside of that precise obligation to be a revealing intuition of something' (*BN,* p. 17). Sartre did not invent the theory of intentionality, the theory that consciousness exists only in so far as it intends something or is about something. Sartre's biggest single philosophical influence, the German philosopher Edmund Husserl, inherited it from another German, the philosopher and psychologist Franz Brentano, who introduced the idea in a book called *Philosophy from an Empirical Standpoint.* Brentano writes:

> Every mental phenomenon includes something as object within itself, although they do not all do so in the same way. In presentation something is presented, in judgement something is affirmed or denied, in love loved, in hate hated, in desire desired and so on. This intentional inexistence is characteristic exclusively of mental phenomena. No physical phenomena exhibit anything like it. We can, therefore, define mental phenomena by saying that they are those phenomena which contain an object intentionally within themselves. (Brentano 2004, pp. 88–89)

The theory of intentionality implies that because consciousness is always of or about something and nothing beyond that, any attempt to investigate consciousness must always lead immediately to an investigation of whatever consciousness is of or about. The philosophy of Brentano, Husserl, Sartre and others, formally known as *phenomenology*, seeks to understand consciousness by investigating the way in which different *phenomena*, different *intentional objects*, appear to consciousness. An intentional object is whatever consciousness is about, be it perceived, imagined, believed or felt. Hatred, for example, is an intentional object, a collection of appearances to consciousness. John's hatred of George does not exist as such, it is an intentional object (in this case an intentional psychic object) comprised of John's anger when he sees George, his feelings of aversion when he thinks of him, the negative things he says about him, his wish or intention to harm George and so on. These appearances are not manifestations of an underlying hatred, they are the hatred. There is no hatred in itself beyond the various appearances that we collectively describe as John's hatred for George.

A physical object is also an intentional object, a collection of appearances to consciousness. Far away, a pebble, for example, appears small. Close up it appears large. When turned, different sides appear and disappear. Its shape appears differently as its orientation changes, its colour alters with the light. It makes a sound as it is thrown back on the beach. The same things can be said of the pebble as was said for hatred. There is no pebble in itself beyond the various shifting appearances that we collectively describe as this pebble.

Phenomenologists talk of reducing things to their appearances, or of there being nothing beyond appearances. They want to get away from a distinction that has often been made in philosophy between appearance and reality, the view that what is real is somehow hidden behind appearances. Phenomenology does not equate a physical object with a supposed underlying ground or substratum that never appears, but with a set of appearances, actual and possible. Actual appearances, Sartre argues, do not indicate an underlying thing-in-itself, but rather an infinite series of possible appearances that could appear. He refers to these possible appearances as *transphenomenal*. Transphenomenality is the mark of the real. An object is real not because there is a hidden thing-in-itself underlying what appears, but because it has an infinite series of transphenomenal aspects which are not presently appearing but which could appear. The notion of transphenomenality allows Sartre to distinguish between a real object and an imagined object. An imaginary rotating cube, for example, does not reveal, as it rotates, sides that were transphenomenal. The sides that appear were not hidden before they appeared, they simply did not exist. What appears to emerge is only what is added by the rotating cube intending consciousness concerned.[4]

When Sartre argues as he does above, there seems no doubt that he is a realist about appearances. Appearances are not distinct from reality, they are reality. They appear to us, but they exist as they appear to us independently of us. At other times, and this is an inconsistency in his philosophy, he is less of a realist about appearances, insisting that appearances must appear to someone in order to have any reality as appearances. 'Relative the phenomenon remains, for "to appear" supposes in essence somebody to whom to appear' (*BN*, p. 2). When Sartre argues like this he presents himself less as a realist and more as a so-called *transcendental idealist*, somewhat in the style of the great German philosopher, Immanuel Kant. Sartre clearly argues for an undifferentiated being-in-itself which is differentiated into distinct phenomena by consciousness. Consciousness, Sartre argues, is a negation that places particular negations or negativities into being that, so to speak, carve being up into particular phenomena – this as distinct from that, this as not that, this as external to that, here as not there, then as not now and so on.

Sartre's transcendental idealism is more deeply rooted in his philosophy than his realism. It is unavoidably implied by his view of the ontological relationship between being-in-itself and being-for-itself that is at the very heart of his system. He clearly holds, as we have seen, that being-in-itself is completely undifferentiated. Phenomena can only arise through the negation of being-in-itself that is being-for-itself, they can exist only from the point of view of being-for-itself.

Sartre's most deeply held view is that being-for-itself or consciousness is grounded upon being-in-itself, while differentiated being, the richly varied world of phenomena we all inhabit, is grounded upon consciousness, or at least, upon the negations that consciousness places into being. Sartre argues that phenomena are not grounded upon being but upon particular privations or lacks of being. Particular privations of being occur when, for example, being is questioned. The relationship of consciousness to the world is primarily characterized by a questioning attitude. This attitude is not just the capacity to judge that something is lacking but the constant expectation of a disclosure of non-being. If I look to see if my steak is cooked, for example, it is because I consider it possible that it is *not* cooked. Even supposing there are steaks apart from consciousness of them, a steak can only be 'not cooked' for a consciousness that experiences the steak in the mode of not yet being what it will be in future. The steak does not lack being cooked for itself, it lacks being cooked for a consciousness that has desires and expectations with regard to it.

Consciousness constantly introduces non-being, negation, negativities, lack, absence into the world in order to make sense of it and to act purposefully within it. In abstract ontological terms we might say, phenomena are grounded not upon being but upon non-being, they arise for being-for-itself when being-for-itself places particular negativities into undifferentiated being thus giving rise to differentiated being. In slightly more down to earth phenomenological terms we might say, a situation is always understood not in terms of what it is but in terms of what it lacks for the consciousness encountering it. In itself a situation is a fullness of being, it lacks nothing, but in itself it is precisely not a situation because to be a situation it must be a situation for something, the situation of something. The lacks that make it a situation, that give it future possibilities and so on, are given to it by the consciousness, the person, for whom it is a situation.

In Sartre's view a person interprets every situation according to his desires, hopes, expectations and intentions. Every situation a person encounters is understood as presently lacking something desired, expected, intended or anticipated. As said, the situation in itself does not lack anything; it lacks something for the person whose situation it is. For Sartre, consciousness is always predisposed to find something lacking. Indeed, he maintains that lack is intrinsic to the very meaning of every situation for any particular consciousness.

Every situation, he argues, is a situation for consciousness. Consciousness, as that which exists by negating the situation, must be situated in order to be. Consciousness, for which the situation is a situation, is not part of the situation, but the negation of the situation. It transcends the situation in order to realize the situation. Every situation is understood not in terms of what it is but in terms of what it lacks, and what every situation lacks is precisely consciousness or being-for-itself. Being-for-itself is those particular lacks that determine the situation as a situation. Sartre explores the phenomenon of lack in *Being and Nothingness* with the example of judging that the moon is not full (*BN*, pp. 110–111).

In itself a crescent moon is neither complete nor incomplete, it is simply what it is. In order to understand it as a partial appearance of the full moon it must be judged in terms of the full moon that is presently lacking. The meaning of the crescent moon is founded upon the non-being of the full moon as that which the crescent moon lacks. The crescent moon itself does not lack the full moon. The crescent moon lacks the full moon for a consciousness that is the temporal surpassing of the being of the crescent moon towards the non-being of the full moon. It is the non-being of the full moon that gives the crescent moon its meaning for consciousness. For consciousness the crescent moon exists in the mode of being the non-being of the full moon. As that which is given the crescent moon is what it is. As a meaningful phenomenon, the crescent moon is understood as what it is by virtue of what it lacks.

In so far as consciousness is those particular lacks that determine the situation, it is itself a lack. Recall that being-for-itself, unlike being-in-itself, is that which can never achieve identity with itself. Being-for-itself is that which lacks identity with itself, or, to put it simply, being-for-itself is that which lacks itself. This is not to say that being-for-itself is a lack in itself. If it were a lack in itself it would be identical with itself as lack, whereas it is that which cannot achieve identity with itself either as being or as non-being. Its being is to be what it is not and not to be what it is. Being-for-itself has rather *to be* its own lack. As the negation of being, being-for-itself is a lack of being, but as the negation of itself as a lack of being it is that which strives in vain to lack itself as nothing in order to be being, in order to be a being-for-itself-in-itself. As said, this Godlike state of self-identity and self-fulfilment is impossible to achieve. In short, complete satisfaction is impossible. In Sartre's view 'Man is a useless passion' (*BN*, p. 636) because being-for-itself is always constituted as a lack. 'If I could just win the lottery,' sighs the gambler, 'I would never want anything again,' fooling himself that by winning the lottery he would achieve the impossible and become a permanently fulfilled lack. Constituted as a lack that it has to be, being-for-itself cannot be completely fulfilled. As the negation of being it must surpass any particular obtained object of desire towards a further unobtained object of desire.

Closely linked to the phenomenon of existential lack is the phenomenon of existential absence. Sartre outlines existential absence by describing the experience of discovering that his friend is absent from a café where he has arranged to meet him (*BN*, pp. 33–35). 'When I enter this café to search for Pierre, there is formed a synthetic organisation of all the objects in the café, on the ground of which Pierre is given as about to appear' (*BN*, p. 33). Pierre, as the person Sartre expects to find, is existentially absent. This *existential absence* is distinct from an abstract and purely *formal absence* that is merely thought. 'Wellington is not in this café, Paul Valéry is no longer here, etc.' (*BN*, p. 34). The distinction between existential and formal absence emphasizes that non-being does not arise through judgements made by consciousness after encountering the world, but that non-being belongs to the very nature of the world as it is for consciousness. Pierre's absence from the café is not merely thought. His absence is an actual event at the café that characterizes the café as the place from which Pierre is absent.[5]

A person's entire world can exist in the mode of the negative; in the mode of not being the presence of whatever is desired. The misery of missing someone or something is rooted in this negating of the world. The misery of losing a lover, for example, lies not so much in the loss of the pleasure the lover gave, but in the reduction of the whole world to a dull background that has no other significance or value than to be the perpetual affirmation of the lover's absence.

BEING-FOR-OTHERS

Every person is a being-for-itself, but according to Sartre this is not all they are. There is another aspect of every person's being that is not for-itself but for-others. Every person has a *being-for-others*. Every person exists for other people and is subject to the judgements of other people. Being-for-others is manifested as shame, embarrassment, pride and all those other emotions and dispositions that are essentially other-related and without which a person would be incomplete. Sartre argues that nobody can, for example, be ashamed alone. Even what he calls 'the religious *practice* of shame' (*BN*, p. 245) is not wholly private but shame before an imagined other person. It is a derivative form that still involves considering oneself from the point of view of another person (the Other).

A person is his being-for-others – his shame, his pride – but he is it over there for the Other. The Other possesses part of what a person is and is free to judge him; free to admire, respect or despise him. Having aspects of his being belong to others, aspects that he is nonetheless held responsible for, makes a person uncomfortable. A good deal of most people's behaviour is directed towards seeking to influence their being-for-others, if not to gain control over it. People generally desire to impress and certainly go to great lengths to encourage others to love, respect or fear them. Try as they might, however, they can never be sure they are creating the desired impression that others are not freely choosing to adopt an opinion contrary to the opinion they wish them to have. Even if they are pretty sure others are impressed, that others love them and so on, they can never be certain it will last. Each person's freedom is subject to the freedom of the Other, the transcendence of the Other. The mere gaze of the Other fixes a person as an object in the world of the Other. As an object for the Other, a person is a *transcendence-transcended* by the transcendence of the Other. He ceases to exist primarily as a free subject for himself and exists instead primarily as an object for others.

To make better sense of this switch from transcendent subject to transcended object Sartre gives us the example of a voyeur at a keyhole (*BN*, pp. 282–284). Until the voyeur is caught in the act he remains a free being-in-the-world, a transcendence. He is a subject absorbed in what he is doing and does not judge himself. He is free to transcend the meaning of his act and does not have to define himself as a snoop. Later on, if he reflects on his act, he can avoid branding himself a voyeur by telling himself his act was simply an aberration and so on. Suddenly, however, he realizes he is seen. All at once the meaning of his act has escaped him. It now belongs to the Other for whom he has become an object. In catching him in the act the Other has caught his freedom and is at liberty to judge him as he pleases, to inflict meanings upon him – spy, sneak, pervert.

In *Saint Genet*, a biography of the writer Jean Genet, Sartre tells how the young Genet first realized he had a being-for-others when he was caught in the act of stealing. Hitherto he had genuinely thought of himself as saintly. Suddenly, others were judging him and forcing the label 'thief' upon him.

It must always be kept in mind when considering being-for-others that a person is Other for the Other and is therefore able to alienate the freedom of the Other in turn by transcending his transcendence. Controversially, Sartre characterizes human relationships as a ceaseless power struggle for transcendence, arguing that the basis of all human relationships is conflict. This conflict, and the suffering that results from having a being-for-others that is beyond a person's control, is explored most thoroughly in Sartre's play, *In Camera*. Garcin, one of the central characters of that play, famously exclaims, 'There's no need for red-hot pokers. Hell is – other people!' (*IC*, p. 223).[6]

THE BODY – SUBJECT AND OBJECT

There is a common fallacy known as dualism, the most famous proponent of which is Descartes, that a person is a non-physical subject, a mind, riding around inside a physical object, a body, which it steers like a pilot steering a ship. The philosopher Gilbert Ryle refers to dualism with 'deliberate abusiveness' as 'the dogma of the Ghost in the Machine' (Ryle 1990, p. 17). Dualism supposes that two radically different substances, mind and body, though they happen to be found together and somehow interact, are so fundamentally distinct that the mind survives the destruction of the body and can exist without it. Sartre offers a view of mind and body that does away with dualistic thinking and the various intractable problems it presents: the problem of how mind and body interact, for example, or the problem of how a mind can exist without a body. Sartre does not *solve* the problems of dualism, they are, as said, intractable, rather he circumvents them with an alternative description of the way things are in which dualism and its problems have no place.

His description centres on what he calls the 'double property of the human being' (*BN*, p. 79), who is not a subject inside an object, but wholly subject or wholly object depending upon point of view. To some extent, the double property of the human being has already been revealed in the account of being-for-others given above. From his own point of view, as a being-for-itself, a person is a free transcendence, a being-in-the-world. His body for him is not primarily an object alongside other objects to be acted upon, but himself acting in the world towards his intended future. He does not know his body, he is it. On the other hand, from the point of view of the Other, as a being-for-others, a person is a transcendence-transcended, a facticity, what Heidegger calls a *being-in-the-midst-of-the-world*. His body for the Other is an object alongside other objects that can be acted upon like any other object. Summarizing his opposition to mind-body dualism Sartre writes:

> ...these two aspects of the body are on different and incommunicable levels of being, they can not be reduced to one another. Being-for-itself must be wholly body and it must be wholly consciousness; it can not be *united* with a body. Similarly being-for-others is wholly body; there are no 'psychic phenomena' there to be united with the body. There is nothing *behind* the body. But the body is wholly 'psychic'. (*BN*, p. 329)

A person can, of course, take the point of view of the Other with regard to his body. He can, for example, look at his eye in a mirror and see it as an object. The example of a person looking at his eye in a mirror illustrates very well the phenomenon of double property and the distinction that exists between the body as it is for oneself and the body as it is for the Other. The fact that the eye in the mirror is the same eye that is seeing this reflection cannot be inferred directly from the eye in the mirror. To infer that the eye in the mirror is the eye seeing its reflection a person must know about mirrors and the phenomenon of reflection. If a person had never seen a mirror before he would initially mistake his reflection for another person. However, even when a person knows from experience that the eye in the mirror is the eye seeing the eye in the mirror, the eye in the mirror and the eye seeing the eye in the mirror remain ontologically distinct – they belong to fundamentally different categories of reality. The eye in the mirror, though he knows it is nobody's eye but his own, remains other. It is an object in the visible world and he sees it only as an object. He cannot and does not see the eye seeing.[7]

> I am the *Other* in relation to my eye. I apprehend it as a sense organ constituted in the world in a particular way, but I can not 'see the seeing;' that is, I can not apprehend it in the process of revealing an aspect of the world to me. Either it is a thing among other things, or else it is that by which other things are revealed to me. (*BN*, p. 328)

The body is either an object in the world among other objects or it is a person acting in the world. A person's own body is not an object that he acts upon in order to act upon the world. To suppose that a person utilizes his body as an instrument in order to utilize the world is to suppose, as Cartesian dualists suppose, that a person is a non-physical subject riding around inside a physical object that he manipulates. Sartre strives to get away from this kind of dualistic thinking. If I walk to the shops it is *I* who walk to the shops, I do not go to the shops in my body as I might go to the shops in my car. Sartre explains the instrumental status of the body as it is for oneself with an example of a person engaged in the task of writing. From the point of view of others, a person who is writing utilizes his hand as an instrument in order to utilize a pen. For himself, however, he does not utilize his hand, he utilizes a pen in a hand that is himself. His hand is not acted upon by the for-itself; it is the for-itself acting in the world and as such is surpassed as an object-hand by the project of writing. 'I am not in relation to my hand in the same utilising attitude as I am in relation to the pen; I *am* my hand.... The hand is only the utilisation of the pen' (*BN*, p. 347).

The world can be viewed as an infinity of potential systems of instrumentality. For a potential system of instrumentality to become an actual system of instrumentality there must be an 'arresting of references' (*BN*, p. 347) to which the entire system refers. Every system of instrumentality must refer back to that for which it is a system of instrumentality. In the case of a person writing, the hand is not an instrument in the system, but that to which an entire system of instrumentality refers. The system of instrumentality emerges by virtue of its orientation towards the hand in action. That is, the for-itself in action. The hand in action arrests the system, determines it, orientates it, gives it meaning and so on. At the same time the system gives meaning to the activity of the hand.

> In this sense the hand is at once the unknowable and non-utilisable term which the last instrument of the series indicates ('book to be read – characters to be formed on the paper – pen') and at the same time the orientation of the entire series (the printed book itself refers back to the hand). But I can apprehend it – at least in so far as it is acting – only as the perpetual, evanescent reference of the whole series...my hand has vanished; it is lost in the complex system of instrumentality in order that this system may

exist. It is simply the meaning and the orientation of the system. (*BN*, p. 347)

What Sartre says of the hand also applies to consciousness. A person's consciousness, which for others is amid the instrumentality of the world, is, for the person himself, the meaning and orientation of the system of instrumentality that he discloses through his purposeful activity.

Just as the for-itself transcends the hand and makes it vanish as an object, so it can transcend the tool the hand is manipulating and make it vanish also. When a person has learnt to use a tool skilfully the tool is forgotten while in use, it is surpassed towards the task. It exists in the mode of what Sartre and Heidegger refer to as *ready-to-hand*. The tool becomes an extension of the body as it acts towards its future goals: '...my body always extends across the tool which it utilises: it is at the end of the cane on which I lean and against the earth; it is at the end of the telescope which shows me the stars' (*BN*, p. 349).

A person's body *is* his consciousness in the sense that he is not in the world as a passive awareness, but as a being that acts towards the future. It can be said that his body is absorbed by his consciousness, although this tends to suggest that consciousness and body are two distinct phenomena that could exist separately but happen to be united. To say that consciousness is embodied is not to say that consciousness happens to ride around inside the body, but that embodiment is consciousness' way of being-in-the-world and its only way. Given that a person exists, it is absolutely necessary that he be embodied.

FREEDOM AND RESPONSIBILITY

Perhaps the best-known fact about Sartre is that he was a great advocate of human freedom. Certainly, during and after World War II he campaigned tirelessly in defence of individual liberty, lending his support to a variety of left-leaning political movements around the world opposed to the oppressive forces of colonialism, capitalism and middle class values.[8] The racist, nationalistic, narrow-minded bourgeois attitudes that surrounded Sartre, particularly as a child, became a lifelong pet hate that inspired much of his writing. At times he naively defended totalitarian regimes, most notably in

China and the Soviet Union, which proved to be brutally oppressive. His support for these regimes was a product of a well-meaning over-optimism about what political movements can achieve. (Sartre kept faith with politics on the grounds that if politics can't change the world for the better then nothing can.) He showed no embarrassment about his support for these regimes whenever the accumulated evidence of atrocities obliged him to withdraw it. He was slow to accept the evidence because of his deep mistrust of the right-wing press that thrives in Western, capitalist countries. His contempt for the right-wing press in postwar France is most clearly expressed in his 1956 play, *Nekrassov.*

Sartre's advocacy of human freedom is not only a political stance, a desire to promote liberty and justice around the world, it is deeply philosophical. Sartre holds on considered philosophical grounds that all people are fundamentally, necessarily and inalienably free regardless of their circumstances or the level of political, social and economic oppression they suffer. Although civil liberty became increasingly important to Sartre, his philosophy of freedom is not primarily concerned with liberty. For Sartre, freedom is not essentially about what people are at liberty to do, about what they are able to do and so on, but about each person's *responsibility* for whatever they do or do not do in every circumstance in which they find themselves. It is vital to a proper understanding of Sartre's theory of personal freedom to realize that it is just as much a theory of personal responsibility. For Sartre, freedom is not freedom from responsibility, freedom is having to make choices and therefore having to take responsibility.

Sartre's theory of freedom is rooted in his theory of choice and action which in turn is rooted in his theory of human consciousness and temporality – his theory of being-for-itself. In arguing for free will Sartre does not simply make room for it by offering various refutations of determinism – the view that all events and states are necessitated by prior events and states. He offers a positive account of free will showing not only that free will is possible, but that it is necessary given the nature of being-for-itself. As seen, being-for-itself is a paradoxical and indeterminate being that is never at one with itself, never identical with itself. As the negation of being-in-itself it is not founded upon itself but upon what it is not, and is therefore nothing in itself, nothing in the present. Being-for-itself is never in the present. It exists only as a perpetual temporal transcendence away from the past towards the future. As a temporal transcendence it stands outside the causal order. The causal order, that which cannot be other than it is once it has come to pass, belongs to a past that being-for-itself realizes by constituting itself as the future of that past. The past exists only for a for-itself that transcends it towards the future. The for-itself exists only as a transcendence of the past towards the future. The for-itself is the future of the past, which is to say, it is the future *possibilities* of the past. As nothing but a being towards the future, as nothing but the future possibilities of the being that it transcends, the for-itself has to be these possibilities. It cannot not be an opening up of possibilities.

The freedom of the for-itself consists in the perpetual opening up of the possibilities of being. The for-itself discovers itself in a world of possibilities that it creates by being a temporal transcendence towards the future. The for-itself is not *in* the future, the future exists only as the 'not yet' towards which the for-itself flees. Furthermore, the future can never be reached because to 'reach' the future is to immediately render it past. Hence, Sartre describes the future as a *future-past* and the past as a *past-future*. Nonetheless, it is in the future at which the for-itself aims that the for-itself is free, free in the sense of having future possibilities which it realizes for itself, possibilities among which it must choose by its actions. The for-itself projects itself through bodily action towards its chosen possibilities, transforming those possibilities – the possibilities that are the for-itself as a being towards the future – into actuality. The transformation of possibility into actuality is the transformation of future-past into past-future, the transformation of the possibilities that constitute the for-itself into a past being for further transcendence.

The fact that being-for-itself has to be a temporal transcendence in order to exist at all, the fact that it cannot not be an opening up of possibilities, implies that it cannot not be free. It is a necessary attribute of the existence of the for-itself that it is not free to cease being free. People are necessarily free, or, as Sartre puts it, people are 'condemned to be free'.

> I am condemned to exist forever beyond my essence, beyond the causes and motives of my act. I am condemned to be free. This means that no limit to my freedom can be found except freedom itself or, if you prefer, that we are not free to cease being free. (*BN*, pp. 461–462)

The for-itself can never surrender its freedom. It can never render itself an object causally determined by the physical world, for the very project of surrender, the very attempt to render itself causally determined, must be a free choice of itself. The for-itself cannot render itself determined by the world, for whenever or however it attempts to do so, it must choose to do so. The for-itself can never not choose because, as Sartre says, 'Not to choose is, in fact, to choose not to choose' (*BN*, p. 503). A person's freedom does not consist in a complete detachment from all obligation, it consists in the constant responsibility of having to choose who he is through the actions he chooses to perform in response to the facticity, adversity and resistance of his concrete situation. For Sartre, there is no end to the responsibility of having to choose.

Just as freedom is necessary, so it is also limitless. Not limitless in the sense that a person is free to do anything, fly unaided etc., but limitless in the sense that his obligation to be free, his obligation to choose a response in every situation, is unremitting. Even if a person is disabled and unable to walk, for example, his freedom is nonetheless unlimited. He is not free to walk in the sense of being at liberty to walk, but he is nonetheless free to choose the meaning of his disability and therefore responsible for his response to it.

> I can not be crippled without choosing myself as crippled. This means that I choose the way in which I constitute my disability (as 'unbearable,' 'humiliating,' 'to be hidden,' 'to be revealed to all,' 'an object of pride,' 'the justification for my failures,' *etc.*). (*BN*, p. 352)

If he considers his disability the ruination of his life then that is a choice he has made for which he is responsible. He is free to choose his disability positively. To strive, for example, to be a successful para-athlete or to spend the time he used to spend playing football writing a book.

Sartre's view, which is certainly uncompromising, seems harsh and even politically incorrect in our contemporary excuse culture that undervalues individual responsibility and overvalues the blaming of circumstances. Sartre's view should, however, be seen as empowering and very much politically correct in terms of the respect it shows people. To tell a disabled person that he is, existentially speaking, responsible for his disability, is not to insult him or to show him a callous lack of consideration, it is to inspire him and to offer him the only real hope available if his disability is incurable. Any disabled person who is not wallowing in self-pity – *choosing* to wallow in self-pity as Sartre would have it – would surely embrace Sartre's description of his situation. No disabled person wants to be reduced to their disability, considered as 'just a person in a wheelchair' and so on. Sartre is saying precisely that a disabled person is not his disability but instead his freely chosen response to his disability.

Sartre argues that a person's awareness of his unlimited freedom can be a source of anxiety or anguish. It makes a person anxious to know that there is nothing that he is in the mode of *being* it, that whatever he does is his choice and that there is nothing to stop him doing whatever he thinks of doing that it is possible for him to do, other than his choice not to do it. Our freedom makes us anxious because there is nothing but our freedom to stop us from performing destructive, dangerous, embarrassing or disreputable acts at any moment. You could choose right now to tell your boss, if you have one, to go to hell, or you could destroy your respectable reputation in an instant by choosing to go naked in the street. In his 1937 book, *The Transcendence of the Ego,* Sartre gives an example of a young bride who is deeply anxious about summoning passers-by from her window like a prostitute. Her anxiety is rooted in the fact that she is free to behave in this way, that it is quite possible for her to do so. She suffers what Sartre describes as 'a vertigo of possibility' (*TE*, p. 100). 'She found herself monstrously free, and this vertiginous freedom appeared to her *at the opportunity* for this action which she was afraid of doing' (*TE*, p. 100).

By the time Sartre wrote *Being and Nothingness* in 1943 he had refined his idea of what can be called *freedom-anxiety* by distinguishing it from fear. Working more literally with the theme of vertigo, he takes the example of a man walking along a narrow precipice (*BN*, pp. 53–56). The man fears he might fall but he also suffers anxiety, which manifests itself as vertigo, because he is free to jump. 'Vertigo is anguish to the extent that I am afraid not of falling over the precipice, but of throwing myself over' (*BN*, p. 53).

In order to avoid freedom-anxiety people often adopt strategies to convince themselves and others that they are not free, that they need not or cannot choose, or have not chosen when in fact they have. In the case of the precipice walker, he quite understandably strives to ignore the freedom to jump that menaces him by absorbing himself in the task of picking his way cautiously along the path as though his movements were physically determined by the demands of the situation rather than by himself. He imagines himself compelled to act as he does by survival instincts and so on. To deny the reality of freedom and choice, perhaps as a means of avoiding anxiety, perhaps as a coping strategy, perhaps with the aim of relinquishing responsibility, is what Sartre refers to as *bad faith*. Bad faith is not the opposite of freedom, it is freedom that gives rise directly to the possibility of bad faith in so far as bad faith is a project of freedom whereby freedom aims at its own suppression and denial.

BAD FAITH

Bad faith is often described as self-deception because superficially it appears to be self-deception, but this description is at best an oversimplification and at worst misleading and incorrect. Bad faith cannot be self-deception for the simple reason that self-deception, in the sense of lying to oneself, is impossible. A person can no more succeed in lying to himself than he can get away with cheating while playing himself at chess. He simply cannot cheat without knowing he is doing so. Whenever a person lies he knows he is doing so. 'The essence of the lie implies in fact that the liar actually is in complete possession of the truth which he is hiding' (*BN*, p. 71). A lie involves a deliberate attempt to mislead and relies on the fact that a person's own consciousness is a consciousness of which the Other is not directly conscious. Lying requires that there be two externally related consciousnesses, a duality of deceiver and deceived. Sartre argues that such a psychic duality cannot exist within the unity of a single consciousness. Consciousness, he says, is *translucent*, it is consciousness through and through and thoughts exist only in so far as a person is conscious of them. In being translucent consciousness cannot be compartmentalized with thoughts concealed from each other in different compartments.[9]

In rejecting the existence of a psychic duality within the unity of a single consciousness Sartre rejects the Freudian distinction between conscious and unconscious. In trying to show the absurdity of Freud's position Sartre argues that consciousness would not be able to repress certain unwanted thoughts and imprison them in the unconscious without actually *knowing* what it was repressing.

'If we reject the language and the materialistic mythology of psychoanalysis, we perceive that the censor in order to apply its activity with discernment must know what it is repressing' (*BN*, p. 75).

Sartre explains as forms of bad faith the attitudes and behaviours that Freud explains as products of a psychic duality within the individual. Bad faith does not require a psychic duality within the individual and it does not involve self-deception. As will be seen, bad faith is more akin to an ongoing project of self-distraction or self-evasion than to self-deception. As bad faith is not an abstract concept but a concrete, existential phenomenon – the attitude, disposition and way of behaving of particular persons in particular situations – it is best to construct an account of it on the basis of specific, concrete examples of people in bad faith. This is certainly Sartre's approach, not least in his philosophical writing. As for his fictional writing, as will be seen in subsequent chapters, it is replete with characters in bad faith, some of them striving to overcome it and achieve authenticity, many of them not.

Sartre opens the detailed account of bad faith that he provides in *Being and Nothingness* with the example of the flirt and her suitor (*BN*, pp. 78–79). The flirt, a young woman, takes her suitor's compliments and polite attentions at face value ignoring their sexual background. Finally the suitor takes the young woman's hand establishing a situation that demands from her a decisive response, but she chooses to flirt, neither withdrawing her hand nor acknowledging the implications of holding hands. She treats her hand as though it is not a part of herself, as though it is an object for which she is not responsible, and she treats her act of omission of leaving her hand in the hand of the man as though it is not an action. The flirt knows her hand is held and what this implies yet somehow she evades this knowledge, or rather she is the ongoing project of seeking to evade it and distract herself from it. She distracts herself from the meaning of her situation and the disposition of her limbs by fleeing herself towards the future. Each moment she aims to become a being beyond her situated self, the meaning of which would not be her current situation. She aims to become a being-for-itself-in-itself. Such a being would not be subject to the demands of the situation. It would not be obliged to choose and to act. She abandons her hand, her whole body, to the past, hoping to leave it all behind her. Yet, in the very act of abandoning it, she re-apprehends the situation of her body as a demand to choose. To take the man's hand willingly or to withdraw, that is the choice. But she fails to meet this demand by choosing herself as a being that would-be beyond the requirement to choose. It is this negative choice that exercises and distracts her and stands in for the positive choice she knows her situation demands. She avoids making this positive choice by striving to choose herself as a person who has transcended her responsibility for her embodied, situated self; she strives to choose herself as a being that has escaped its facticity.

As we have seen, every human being is both an object and a subject, a facticity and a transcendence, or to be more precise, the transcendence *of* his facticity. There are various related forms of bad faith as revealed by the various concrete examples Sartre provides and all of them manipulate the 'double property of the human being' (*BN*, p. 79) in some way. Essentially, bad faith is the project of seeking to invert and/or separate facticity and transcendence. The flirt treats the facticity of her situation, in terms of which her choices of herself should be exercised, as though it has a transcendent power over her body. That is, she treats her facticity as though it is a transcendence. At the same time, she treats her transcendent consciousness as though it is its own transcendence; as though it is a transcendence-in-itself rather than the transcendence of the facticity of her situation. That is, she treats her transcendence as though it is a facticity.

Another example from *Being and Nothingness* of a character in bad faith is that of the waiter (*BN*, pp. 82–83). Sartre paints a vivid picture of the waiter in action. The waiter walks with a robotic stiffness, restraining his movements as though he were a machine. He steps a little too rapidly towards his customers, he is a little too eager and attentive. He is playing at being a waiter. One view of Sartre's waiter is that he is in bad faith for striving, through his performance, to deny his transcendence and become his facticity. He overacts his role as a waiter in order to convince himself and others that he is a waiter-*thing*. As a waiter-*thing* he would escape his freedom and the anxiety it causes him. He aims to become *for himself* the transcendence-transcended that he often is for others in his role as waiter. He strives to be at one with his own representation of himself, but the very fact that he has to represent to himself what he is means that he cannot be it.

Striving to be a thing so as to escape the responsibility of being free is certainly an identifiable form of bad faith. However, against this view of Sartre's waiter it can be argued that although the waiter does indeed strive to be a waiter-*thing*, he is not in bad faith because the purpose of his striving is not to escape his freedom. Arguably, he is no more in bad faith for trying to be a waiter than an actor is in bad faith for trying to be Macbeth. A closer reading of Sartre's description of the waiter reveals that, just like an actor, there is a definite sense in which he knows what he is doing. He acts with ironical intent, consciously – though not self-consciously – impersonating a waiter. It is a good impersonation that has become second nature to him. To claim that acting like a waiter is second nature to him is not to claim that he believes he has become a waiter. Rather, it is to claim that he has become his performance in the sense that when he is absorbed in it he does not reflect that he is performing. Sartre says that the waiter 'plays with his condition in order to *realize* it' (*BN*, p. 82). He does not mean that he plays with his condition in order to become it, but that his condition is only ever realised as a playing with his condition. As seen, being-for-itself cannot achieve identity with itself. The waiter can never *be* what he is, he can only play at being it.

It can be argued that, far from being in bad faith, the waiter is *authentic*, the very antithesis of bad faith. Unlike the flirt he does not evade what he is, the transcendence *of* his facticity, by striving to treat his facticity as a transcendence and his transcendence as a facticity. Instead, he strives to take full responsibility for the reality of his situation, choosing himself positively in his situation by throwing himself wholeheartedly into his chosen role. He strives to embrace what Sartre calls his 'being-in-situation' (*WD*, p. 54). A waiter in bad faith would be a reluctant, rueful waiter; a waiter who thought, 'I am not really a waiter'; a waiter who chose to wait at tables while wishing he were someone else somewhere else. The distinction between bad faith and authenticity is considered further in the final section of this chapter.

One further example from *Being and Nothingness* worth considering, as it reveals further important dimensions of the phenomenon of bad faith, is the example of the homosexual (*BN*, pp. 86–88). The homosexual does not deny his homosexual desires and activities. Instead, he denies that homosexuality is the meaning of his conduct. Rather than take responsibility for his conduct he chooses to characterize it as a series of aberrations, as the result of curiosity rather than the result of a deep-seated tendency and so on.

He believes that a homosexual is not a homosexual as a chair is a chair. This belief is justified in so far as a person is never what he is but only what he aims to be through his choices. The homosexual is right that he is not a homosexual-*thing*, but in so far as he has adopted conduct defined as the conduct of a homosexual, he is a homosexual. That he is not a homosexual in the sense that a chair is a chair does not imply that he is not a homosexual in the sense that a chair is not a table. Sartre argues that the homosexual 'plays on the word *being*' (*BN*, p. 87). He slyly interprets 'not being what he *is*', as 'not being what he is not'.

The homosexual attempts to deny he is his facticity, when, in fact, he is his facticity in the mode of no longer being it. That is, though he is not his facticity – his past – in the mode of being it, he is his facticity in so far as it is a past that he affirms as his by having to continually transcend it towards the future. He assumes in bad faith that he is a pure transcendence; that his facticity, being past, has vanished into the absolute nothingness of a generalized past that has nothing whatsoever to do with him. In truth, far from being a pure transcendence, he is and must be the transcendence of his facticity. In his project of bad faith the homosexual attempts to create within himself a rift between facticity and transcendence. A character that in many ways resembles the homosexual described in *Being and Nothingness* is Daniel Sereno, a central figure in Sartre's *Roads to Freedom* trilogy.

The homosexual has a friend, a champion of sincerity, who urges him to come out and admit that he is a homosexual. In doing so, he urges him to consider himself a facticity rather than a pure transcendence. In urging the homosexual to consider himself a facticity the champion of sincerity aims to stereotype him as 'just a homosexual'. It is easier for him to achieve this aim if he can persuade the homosexual to apply the label 'homosexual' to himself. His motive in seeking to stereotype the homosexual is to deny him the freedom that makes him an individual; it is to transcend him, thereby reducing him to a transcendence-transcended. Once again we discover the struggle for transcendence that Sartre argues is the basis of all human relationships.

Ordinarily, sincerity is seen as a form of honesty or good faith. Sartre, however, exposes sincerity as a form of bad faith. If the homosexual took his friends advice to be sincere and admitted he was a homosexual, if he declared, 'I am what I am', he would not overcome his bad faith. He would simply exchange the bad faith of considering himself a pure transcendence for the bad faith of considering himself a facticity. We have already seen that the person who considers himself a facticity is in bad faith for seeking to evade the truth that he is the transcendence *of* his facticity. To declare, 'I am what I am,' is to assert the fallacy that I am a fixed entity while at the same time evading the existential truth that I am an indeterminate being who must continually create myself through choice and action. In short, it is to declare myself a facticity when in reality I am the transcendence of my facticity – it is bad faith.

The sincerity identified above is relatively unsophisticated. Sartre also identifies a more sophisticated and devious form of sincerity. This more sophisticated form of sincerity still involves a person declaring, 'I am what I am,' but here his aim is not to be what he is, rather it is to distance himself from what he is through the very act by which he declares what he is. In declaring himself to be a thing he aims to become that which declares he is a thing rather than the thing he declares himself to be. He posits himself as a thing in order to escape being that thing; in order to become that which contemplates the thing he has ceased to be. Unlike a person who adopts the simpler form of sincerity, he does not aim to be his facticity by denying his transcendence, he aims to be a pure transcendence divorced from his facticity. Sartre identifies confession as an instance of this more sophisticated form of sincerity.

The person who confesses a sin, for example, renders his sin into an object for his contemplation that exists only in so far as he contemplates it and ceases to exist when he ceases to contemplate it. Believing himself to be a pure transcendence he believes he is free to move on from his sin and to abandon it to the past as a disarmed sin that is neither his possession nor his responsibility. Confession that aims at absolution is bad faith.

In *Truth and Existence* Sartre returns once again to the subject of bad faith. In this work he explores the strategies of evasion and self-distraction people employ to avoid the truth and remain ignorant of their real situation, arguing that at heart bad faith is a wilful ignorance that aims at the avoidance of responsibility. Ignorance, Sartre notes, is in fact a mode of knowledge. To choose to ignore reality is to affirm that it is knowable. '...ignorance itself as a project is a mode of knowledge since, if I want to ignore Being, it is because I affirm that it is knowable' (*TEx*, p. 33). Ignorance is motivated by fear and anxiety that knowledge of stark reality is always possible, always lurking. In Sartre's view, to know the truth, to know the way things are and to see life as it is, does not require great intelligence but rather honesty and courage in face of reality.

Sartre takes the example of a woman with tuberculosis (*TEx*, p. 33–35). The woman refuses to acknowledge that she has tuberculosis despite having all the symptoms. She views each symptom in isolation, refusing to recognize their collective meaning. She engrosses herself in pursuits that do not afford her time to visit the doctor, pursuits that distract her from making the choices required by her situation. Her symptoms place her at the threshold of new knowledge, but she chooses ignorance because she does not want the responsibility of dealing with her tuberculosis, of seeking a cure for it and so on, that new knowledge would call for. In her refusal to face her situation, in her self-distraction and her evasion of responsibility, she is similar to Sartre's flirt considered above.

For Sartre, to dispense with such wilful ignorance and irresponsibility and instead to courageously affirm the existential truths of the human condition – abandonment, freedom, responsibility, contingency, mortality, etc. – is to overcome bad faith in favour of authenticity.

AUTHENTICITY

Unlike the other phenomena considered so far in this chapter, Sartre does not discuss authenticity in *Being and Nothingness*. He only promises at the close to dedicate a future work to it 'on the ethical plane' (*BN*, p. 647). This promise was never fully realized, though not for want of trying. Sartre made extensive notes on the ethics of freedom, responsibility and authenticity between 1945 and 1948, nearly 600 pages of which were published posthumously as *Notebooks for an Ethics*. Sartre certainly says enough about authenticity in various places in his writings, not least in his *War Diaries*, for us to construct a clear picture of it. What Sartre makes abundantly clear is that bad faith is synonymous with inauthenticity, that authenticity is the antithesis of bad faith and that sincerity, as a mode of bad faith, is distinct from authenticity.

Sartre's examples of people in bad faith reveal that the most blatant feature of inauthenticity is the attempted evasion of responsibility. The flirt and the woman with tuberculosis refuse responsibility for their current situation, the homosexual refuses responsibility for his past deeds. Each strives to become a pure facticity or a pure transcendence, a being that no longer has to choose what it is because it has become what it is – a for-itself-in-itself. Yet the fact remains that these characters *are* responsible. Unable to be a pure facticity or a pure transcendence, every person must perpetually choose himself as the transcendence of his facticity, as the transcendence of his past deeds and his current situation. A person cannot relinquish responsibility for his past deeds or his current situation because he is responsible for any attempt to relinquish responsibility. In other words, a person who behaves as though he cannot choose to respond to his current situation or need not choose himself as the future of his past is choosing to do so and is therefore responsible for doing so. As seen, being-for-itself must perpetually choose what it is as it is unable simply to *be* what it is. The unlimited freedom and responsibility of being-for-itself lies in the fact that it cannot not choose what it is. It is 'condemned for ever to be free' (*AR*, p. 243) because it is condemned to a lifetime of choosing itself.

In Sartre's view, inauthenticity is the denial and avoidance of the basic existential truth that we are free and responsible, whereas authenticity, as the antithesis of inauthenticity, is the acceptance and affirmation of this basic existential truth. Sartre argues that authenticity involves a person confronting reality and facing up to the hard truth that they are a limitlessly free being that will never obtain coincidence with itself as a for-itself-in-itself. Whereas the inauthentic person seeks to avoid recognizing that this is the fundamental truth of his being, the authentic person not only recognizes it, he strives to come to terms with it and even to treat it as a source of values. The authentic person responds fully to the demand to accept reality for what it is that pervades Sartre's existentialism.

Sartre argues that authenticity 'consists in adopting human reality as one's own' (*WD*, p. 113). It involves a person accepting and affirming what in truth he has always been: a free and responsible being lacking coincidence with himself. Instead of acting in bad faith, exercising his freedom in order to deny his freedom, instead of choosing not to choose, the authentic person assumes his freedom. Assuming his freedom involves assuming full responsibility for himself in the situation in which he finds himself. It involves accepting that this and no other is his situation; that this situation is the facticity in terms of which he must now choose himself. A person can, of course, flee his present situation if he is not physically constrained but this still involves a choice. A choice, moreover, that gives rise to new situations and to new demands to choose. Above all, assuming his freedom involves realizing that because he is nothing in the mode of being it he is nothing but the choices he makes in his situation.

In his *War Diaries* (*WD*, p. 112) Sartre describes a soldier friend of his as inauthentic for failing to assume his freedom as described above. Sartre's friend is not a soldier as a table is a table, he is not a soldier-*thing*, but in so far as he serves in an army, 'soldier' is the meaning of his conduct. Nonetheless, he denies he is a soldier, describing himself as a civilian in disguise. This declaration reveals he is not taking responsibility for his choices. 'He thus stubbornly continues to *flee* what he's *making of himself*' (*WD*, p. 112). He flees what he is making of himself – a soldier – towards the non-existent civilian-*thing* he wishes to be. In Sartre's view, he has not accepted his being-in-situation. Rather than accept that he is only ever his response to his facticity, he chooses to see himself as a facticity, as a fixed entity swept along by circumstances. It is in ceasing to be like Sartre's soldier friend and accepting his being-in-situation that a person overcomes bad faith and achieves authenticity.[10]

An authentic soldier, like Mathieu in Sartre's novel *Iron in the Soul*, recognizes that accepting his being-in-situation requires him to play to the full the role of a soldier. This does not mean that he pretends to be a soldier. To pretend would be to inauthentically consider himself a civilian in disguise. Rather, in playing to the full the role of a soldier he aims at being a soldier to the best of his ability, immersing himself wholeheartedly in the military situation in which he finds himself and making it his own. He does not believe he is a soldier-*thing*, but neither does he disbelieve he is a soldier in the sense of believing that he is really something other than a soldier; something other than his present role. Like Sartre's waiter, he absorbs himself in his performance to the extent that he does not reflect upon the fact that he is performing. He has become his performance and his attitude towards himself involves a suspension of disbelief.

Authenticity is not simply a matter of a person recognizing that there are no excuses for his actions, he must resist by an act of will any desire for excuses. 'Of course, it's a question not just of *recognising* that one has no excuse, but also of *willing* it' (*WD*, p. 113). An authentic soldier, for example, not only recognizes that in his current situation there are no excuses not to play at being a soldier, he does not want there to be any excuses. To be truly authentic, a person must fully realize his being-in-situation without regret. If he does not want to be where he is he will leave (desert) without regret and face the consequences of doing so without regret. If he stays, he will assume responsibility for his staying and throw himself into the spirit of things.

Authenticity involves a person coming to terms with the fact that he will never achieve the substantiality of a for-itself-in-itself. It does not, however, involve abandoning the desire for substantiality and foundation. The desire to be its own foundation is fundamental to being-for-itself and so it cannot abandon this desire. '...the first value and first object of will is: to be its own foundation. This mustn't be understood as an empty psychological desire, but as the transcendental structure of human reality' (*WD*, p. 110). Attempting to completely abandon the desire for foundation can collapse into a project of nihilism whereby a person strives to be his own nothingness. He strives to escape the desire to be a for-itself-in-itself by aiming at being a non-being-in-itself, an equally impossible and unachievable state of being. Arguably, Roquentin, the central character of Sartre's novel *Nausea*, adopts this project of nihilism.

The project of authenticity is still motivated by the search for substantiality and foundation, but it differs crucially from bad faith in that it 'suppresses that which, in the search, is *flight*' (*WD*, p. 112). The authentic person does not aim at substantiality by means of a futile flight from his freedom. Instead, he aims at substantiality by continually founding himself upon the affirmation of his freedom. The affirmation of his inalienable freedom is assumed as his basic principle or ultimate value. He seeks to identify himself with his freedom rather than flee it in the vain hope of identifying himself with being-in-itself. The project of authenticity is actually more successful at achieving a kind of substantiality than any project of bad faith because the project of authenticity reconciles a person to what he really is, an essentially free being, whereas bad faith is only ever a flight from what a person really is towards an unachievable identity with being-in-itself. In fleeing freedom a person does not establish a foundation, but in assuming his freedom he establishes freedom itself as a foundation. In assuming his freedom he 'becomes' the free being that he is, rather than failing to become the unfree being that he can never be.

It must be stressed that the form of substantiality arrived at through authenticity is not a fixed state of being. As seen, it is logically impossible for being-for-itself to obtain a fixed state of being by any means and all attempts to do so function in bad faith. The substantiality obtained through authenticity is not achieved once and for all, it is a substantiality that has to be continually re-assumed. A person cannot simply *be* authentic, he *has to be* authentic. To assume that I am authentic, an authentic thing, as a spade is a spade, is to fall back into bad faith. Authenticity is not a fixed and stable foundation that a person can establish for always at a particular time, but a shifting and inherently unstable foundation that he must maintain by constantly choosing authentic responses to his situation. Authenticity is the continued task of choosing responses that affirm freedom and responsibility rather than responses that signify a flight from freedom and responsibility. The authentic person takes on the unending task of resisting the slide into bad faith that threatens every human project.

EXISTENTIALISM, ETHICS AND MARXISM

Although the philosophical positions considered so far in this chapter are Sartre's best known, he did not simply reach them then stop. Like all great philosophers he continued to develop and refine his ideas as he grew older in light of new knowledge and experience. Even a brief account of Sartre's thinking is very incomplete, therefore, if it does not consider the *progress* of his existentialism beyond 1945; the direction his thinking took as a profound response to the earth-shattering events of World War II.

The overall direction and character of Sartre's postwar philosophy can be summed up by saying that it steadily acquired a far greater appreciation of the social aspects of human existence; of ethics, politics and history. He was, as we have seen, interested in the Other long before 1945, but his focus then had been very much on the dynamics of personal encounter; on how encountering the Other involves various ontological modifications to the consciousness, freedom and being-in-the-world of an individual being-for-itself. Sartre did not abandon his theories of consciousness, freedom and being-for-others as he moved forward. Instead, he integrated them into a broader theory of the human condition that seeks to make coherent the claim that people are both inalienably free individuals *and* products of their economic, sociological, political, historical and cultural context. He also integrated a somewhat modified notion of authenticity into his broader postwar vision. Unlike Merleau-Ponty, who identified authenticity as far too evocative of a romantic, unattainable individualism to be credible, Sartre refused to reject the notion.

Merleau-Ponty holds that the complexities and ambiguities of the human condition are such that it is impossible to distinguish a striving for personal authenticity from a response to social demands and expectations. Arguably, his position shows a failure to appreciate what Sartre came to recognize: that the project of authenticity is not always or essentially about striving for an unattainable individualism and freedom from social demands and expectations, but about an individual taking full responsibility for his situation and his responses to his situation. As most situations are to some extent human social situations, meeting the demands of most situations requires a degree of social conformity. As Sartre acknowledges in his later writings, for a person to take full responsibility for his being-in-situation, and hence be authentic, he may well have to determine himself to comply with the demands and expectations that result from his social and historical circumstances.

In his 1946 work, *Anti-Semite and Jew*, for example, Sartre argues that it is authentic for a person raised in the Jewish culture to conform to the expectations of that culture by choosing himself as a Jew. He argues that it would be inauthentic for the same person to choose not to be a Jew because this choice of himself would be a denial of his situation and the 'Jewish reality' (*AJ*, p. 137) that constitutes his ethnic, cultural and historical facticity. Sartre's transition towards this point of view began during and because of World War II. In his novel, *The Reprieve*, written during the German occupation of Paris and completed in late 1944, there is a wealthy Parisian Jew, Birnenschatz, who initially rejects his Jewishness, refusing to identify himself with Jews who are suffering under Nazi tyranny. Historical events eventually move him to feel ashamed of his inauthentic stance and to become an authentic Jew.

Sartre's project of giving authenticity a social dimension reflected his growing concern with ethics generally and was part of a broader move towards establishing an existentialist moral theory. As said, he never fully realized the promise he made in *Being and Nothingness* to produce a work 'on the ethical plane' (*BN*, p. 647), but he did produce several hundred pages of notes on ethics between 1945 and 1948 that were later published posthumously as *Notebooks for an Ethics*. These notes must be treated with caution as they are, as their title suggests, working notes. Nonetheless, as present day Sartre scholars are increasingly discovering, they constitute some of Sartre's most interesting and thought-provoking postwar material.

What is clear in the *Notebooks* is that Sartre sees ethics as an Other-related phenomenon, as a feature of being-for-others. He argues that no action is unethical until another person judges it to be so. An ethical state of affairs is one in which people respect and affirm each other's freedom. His difficulty is to accommodate this claim with his view that the freedom of the other always negates my freedom; that his being-for-itself always transcends my own, thereby reducing me to an object, to a transcendence-transcended. Sartre takes the position that the objectification and alienation of a person by others, although unavoidable on a mundane level, need not result in active oppression as it has done historically. Although people will always experience themselves as objects for others, they need never be *mere* objects for others. Although the *Notebooks* do not clarify how people will succeed, Sartre insists that they have the potential to recognize on all occasions that the human object before them is also a person and a free transcendence, what Merleau-Ponty refers to as an *embodied consciousness*. For Sartre, to recognize and affirm ones own freedom is to be authentic, while to affirm the freedom of others is to be ethical.

It appears to follow from this that a person must be authentic to be ethical, he must affirm his own freedom in order to affirm the freedom of others. That is, he must fully recognize freedom in himself in order to achieve full recognition of freedom in others. In short, a person must be authentic to affirm the freedom of others. To be authentic is to recognize and embrace the inescapable existential truths of the human condition, such as mortality, freedom, responsibility, being-for-others, the being of others and so on. One of these existential truths is the existence of the freedom of others. Therefore, not only must a person be authentic to affirm the existential truth of the freedom of others, to affirm the freedom of others *is* to be authentic. Arguably, ethics is other-related authenticity.

An existentially ethical world would be one where a history driven by human freedom has realized an end to the exploitation and oppression that results when one freedom does not respect and affirm another. For Sartre, how this world is to be achieved is unclear. For Kant, it is to be achieved by every person adhering unerringly to the universal moral principle of the *categorical imperative* and acting towards others only on maxims that can be universalized without contradiction. Sartre, however, will not help himself to Kant's categorical imperative because he refuses to base his ethics on *a priori* moral principles. For Sartre, it appears that behaving ethically is a matter of acting authentically in any given, concrete situation involving others, rather than a matter of adhering to the same abstract universal principle in all situations involving others. Sartre's ethical world is surely very similar to Kant's *kingdom of ends*, a world in which every person treats every other person as a self-determining end-in-himself, rather than as a mere means lacking freedom, as an object acted upon. In advocating something similar to Kant's kingdom of ends, Sartre's ethics are somewhat Kantian. In wanting to make his ethics a matter of authentic responses to concrete situations, responses that depend on the authentic assessment of situations rather than upon adherence to a universal moral principle, Sartre is not a Kantian deontologist but arguably the advocate of a form of *virtue ethics*. Like the virtue ethics of Aristotle, Sartre's ethics is not about following abstract moral rules, but about achieving one's full potential and flourishing as a free human being alongside other free human beings.

Notebooks for an Ethics also considers the problem of history. As we do not presently have a world where every freedom fully respects and affirms every other freedom then this ethical state of affairs can only be achieved, if it is achievable, via an historical process. Sartre explores Hegel's philosophy of history. He accepts Hegel's view that history is a coherent dialectical process in which people develop their world and are in turn developed by their world, but he rejects any suggestion that inevitable deterministic forces drive this historical dialectic. History, Sartre argues, must be driven by human freedom, otherwise human freedom and responsibility are illusory. Sartre returned to this key problem years later, considering it in great detail in his ambitious two volume work, *Critique of Dialectical Reason*. The first volume, *Theory of Practical Ensembles,* was published in 1960, while the unfinished second volume, *The Intelligibility of History*, was posthumously published in 1985.

From the late 1940's onwards Sartre's ethical considerations, indeed his existentialism as a whole, were increasingly absorbed into his Marxism. Sartre had no misgivings about placing existentialism at the service of Marxism. He identified Marxism as the dominant philosophy of the age and existentialism as a subordinate theory meant to function within Marxism positively influencing its future development towards the realization of a possible but not inevitable classless and harmonious society. The later Sartre became know above all else for his Marxism; for his Marxist inspired political activities and for the epic intellectual effort to synthesize existentialism and Marxism that is his *Critique of Dialectical Reason*.

Sartre's pro-existentialist critics argued that he should abandon his newfound Marxism as incompatible with his existentialism, while his pro-Marxist critics argued that he should abandon his existentialism as incompatible with his newfound Marxism. Few thinkers besides Sartre seemed to think that the two theories were, or could be made to be, compatible. The tension grew until by the late 1950s Sartre felt compelled to show his critics on all sides, as well as prove to himself, that existentialism and Marxism were not contradictory philosophies. The *apparent* incompatibility concerns freedom. As seen, existentialism maintains above all else that human freedom is inalienable, whereas, according to many Marxists of Sartre's time, Marxism is a deterministic theory of human history at the centre of which is the notion of dialectical materialism.

For Marx, mankind is a product of his dialectical relationship with the material world. Since his earliest evolution mankind has constantly shaped and been shaped by his environment. What mankind has been, is and will become is the result of an historical process. Hegel, Marx's major influence, identifies this historical process with the dialectical development of ideas towards perfect rationality – thesis versus antithesis produces synthesis. Marx, turning Hegel's idealism on its head, identifies this historical process with the dialectical development of matter by mankind and mankind by matter. What is all-important in this historical process as Marx sees it is *production*. Mankind acts purposefully on the world – *praxis* – with the means available to him, means that are a product of earlier *praxis*, to produce new materials, tools and technologies. These new products change man by changing the way people interact with the world and with each other. The telephone, for example, a product of many earlier developments, enabled many new productive activities to emerge while rendering others obsolete, and it allowed if not forced people to interact with each other in new ways. Marx recognizes that every technological revolution, every change in what he calls 'the means of production', brings about a social revolution, changes in what he calls 'the relations of production', changes in who has effective power and control over what and who.

Sartre agrees with Marx. What he does not agree with is what some Marxists have seen as the main implication of Marx's theory, namely, that it is deterministic and that there is no place in it for human freedom. Sartre's reading of Marx is that his theory of dialectical materialism gives an all-important role to human consciousness and, by implication, human freedom because freedom is an essential characteristic of consciousness. Sartre argues that it is a misreading of Marx to suppose that his materialism is a reductionist theory that proposes the development of matter by matter with humans being nothing more than a material product of the process. Of course, humans cannot play a role in the development of matter without having material bodies, but this is not to say that they are merely material. The reductionist view of dialectical materialism is more properly called mechanical materialism. Sartre felt obliged to respond to those post-Marxists who endorsed mechanical materialism by accusing them of maintaining a simplistic dialectic that did not involve free, conscious people as such. Sartre treats 'dialectical materialism', with its reductionist connotations, as a corrupted term, preferring instead the term 'historical materialism' which reflects more accurately the materialism Marx actually proposed.

So, Sartre begins to synthesize existentialism and Marxism by arguing that it is a misunderstanding of Marxism to view it as utterly materialistic and deterministic, as fundamentally opposed to any theory of human freedom, individuality or even consciousness. Sartre goes on to argue that Marxism can accommodate the existentialist view of human freedom and indeed must do so if it is to make sense. A person is a part of the material world by virtue of his body but he could not exist in a dialectical relationship with matter unless he was able to distinguish himself from matter and be a point of view on it. By 'matter' Sartre and Marx do not mean raw matter. They both note that the material world people encounter is almost always worked matter, the product of earlier *praxis*.

As the negation of being, consciousness remains rooted in matter and could not exist without matter. Nonetheless, as a negation it is never at one with the matter it negates. Consciousness transcends matter towards the future and in so doing realizes the future possibilities of matter, possibilities that are none other than the future possibilities of a consciousness existing in relation to matter. In *Being and Nothingness* Sartre denies the possibility of dialectical processes existing in nature apart from consciousness. In the *Critique* he allows that they might exist, only then to argue that the historical dialectic, the development of matter through man and man through matter, cannot be accounted for in terms of blind, mechanical dialectical processes that do not involve consciousness. Man is made by history, but it is also man that *makes* history by responding practically to his present historically derived situation. Through *praxis* man projects himself beyond the present situation towards *his* future situation, towards future possibilities that will be realized when a future state of matter is produced. This future state of matter will, in turn, provide the conditions for further projection; for further projects of production.

Marx argues that it is upon the basis of prior conditions that men make their history. He does not mean, as some Marxists take him to mean, that men are mechanisms conditioned by circumstances to act in a certain determined way, but that men make their history by *choosing* their *response* to their conditions. Man is the product of his own productive activity but he is never just a product among products because he is the only product capable of realizing that he is product. Sartre argues that Marxism is not only a theory of history that requires a notion of human consciousness and therefore freedom, Marxism *is* history become conscious of itself. In this respect Marxism is comparable to Darwinism – evolution become conscious of itself.

Marx famously advocates that people should strive for their political freedom. 'The proletarians have nothing to lose but their chains. They have a world to win' (Marx and Engels 1985, pp. 120–121). This presupposes that people are at least psychologically free in the Sartrean sense. What value or meaning could political freedom have for beings that were entirely subject to deterministic laws? In the *Critique* Sartre recognizes far more than he does in *Being and Nothingness* that an individual person or a whole social class of people can be without freedom in any real practical sense as a result of political and economic oppression. A person's existential freedom remains inalienable, he cannot not choose, but his freedom does not amount to much if his only choice is, for example, to endure drudgery and exploitation in a factory for a subsistence wage or die of starvation. This view is, in a sense, a development rather than a departure from views expressed in *Being and Nothingness* in so far as Sartre recognizes in that work that the most serious threat to a person's freedom is the freedom of the Other. Just as one person can transcend another and reduce him to an object, to a transcendence-transcended, so one social class can, through economic and social exploitation, transcend another social class and reduce its members to objects. In this way the Sartre of the *Critique* develops his existentialist theory of being-for-others into a *Marxist* theory of man's alienation by man.

CHAPTER 3

SARTRE'S SHORT STORIES

As Sartre tells in his autobiography, *Words*, he wrote many short stories as a child. In his career, however, he published only five short stories, a collection that appeared in 1939 entitled *The Wall* which he dedicated to the capricious Olga Kosakiewiecz.[1] The collection was also repackaged some years later with the alternative title *Intimacy*.[2] Both these titles are also those of individual stories in the collection. Before Gallimard published them as a collection some of the stories appeared individually in Gallimard's journal, *La Nouvelle Revue Française,* around the time of the publication of Sartre's first novel, *Nausea*, in 1938. These few short stories, of undoubted literary excellence, are an integral and significant part of the philosophical project and existentialist vision of the early Sartre.

The novel and the stories together met with huge critical acclaim and through the Parisian whirlwind of interest they generated they quickly established Sartre as a major new force in French literature. After reading *The Wall* in *La Nouvelle Revue Française* in 1937, the great French writer André Gide, then in his 70s, asked the editor of the journal, 'Who is this new Jean-Paul?' He added, 'I think we can expect a great deal from him. As for his short story, it's a masterpiece' (Letter from Gide to Paulhan, 27 July 1937. Quoted in Cohen-Solal 2005, p. 120). The critic Gaëtan Picon wrote, '*Nausea* had been last year's revelation; *The Wall* is far from disappointing us as to the rare talent of its author...the language is pure, naked and full...With his meditation on existence, Sartre brings a new theme into our literature' (quoted in Cohen-Solal 2005, p. 121).

Sartre, the new *enfant terrible* of French literature, brilliant, unconventional and forthright, soon found himself overtaken by events and conscripted into the French Army. He was still winning prizes for *The Wall* as he launched weather balloons near the French-German border in the 'Phoney war' of 1939–40.[3] Crucially, he continued to write; an estimated one million words in the ten months he served to June 1940 before the Nazis took him prisoner. Flushed with success, inspired by momentous events, confident that he could deliver on the great expectations of Gide and others, Sartre had plunged himself into a creative frenzy that was to last more than three decades.

THE WALL

The Wall is set during the Spanish Civil War. In so far as it explores the psychology of prisoners of war facing execution it is comparable to Sartre's 1946 play, *Men without Shadows*. A captured prisoner, Pablo Ibbieta, is condemned without trial along with many others to be shot at dawn. He spends the night locked in the cold, draughty cellar of a disused hospital with two fellow prisoners, Tom Steinbock and Juan Mirbal, two guards and a Belgian doctor who is there to observe the prisoners' physiology and behaviour as they await death. Told from Ibbieta's point of view, the story explores the thoughts, feelings and actions of men who believe they have only a few hours to live. 'I was determined to die cleanly and I only thought of that. But ever since the doctor told us the time, I felt time flying, flowing away drop by drop' (*W*, p. 13).

Juan, who is only a young man, cries and looks for reassurances from the doctor.

> 'Does it hurt – very long?'
> 'Huh? When – ? Oh, no,' the Belgian said paternally. 'Not at all. It's over quickly.' He acted as though he were calming a cash customer. (*W*, p. 7)

As the night progresses Juan sinks into deep self-pity and in the morning has to be carried to his execution. Ibbieta unsympathetically identifies Juan's self-pity as a kind of bad faith, a distraction from reality, as fever is a kind of distraction from illness. '...he was like a sick man who defends himself against illness by fever. It's much more serious when there isn't any fever' (*W*, p. 13).

Tom, who is older than Juan, has more composure but nonetheless urinates in his trousers involuntarily. He becomes philosophical and talks to Ibbieta of his inability to contemplate oblivion even though he is a materialist who doubts there is an afterlife. 'I tell myself there will be nothing afterwards. But I don't understand what it means. Sometimes I almost can – and then it fades away and I start thinking about the pains again, bullets, explosions' (*W*, p. 8). Again Ibbieta is unsympathetic. He sees Tom's talk as another kind of bad faith, a distraction from reality. Ibbieta feels no attachment to Tom or Juan and as the night passes he ceases to feel any attachment to anything, his past or even those he has loved. The love and desire he felt for his girlfriend Concha only the night before has vanished.

> Concha would cry when she found out I was dead, she would have no taste for life for months afterwards. But I was still the one who was going to die... I knew it was over: if she looked at me *now* the look would stay in her eyes, it wouldn't reach me. I was alone. (*W*, p. 12).

Emotions become painful, disgusting, they are for those who believe they have a future. Ibbietta does not want to think or feel anything. He wants to 'stay clean' (*W*, p. 14); to die a clean death without any display of fear or emotion. He struggles to maintain control of his body that sweats profusely despite the cold. He feels so damp that he wonders if, like Tom, he has wet himself. He is calm but it is a 'horrible calm' (*W*, p. 12) in which he feels utterly detached from his own body. He is concerned to give the doctor as little as possible to observe. He looks upon the doctor as alien, as a representative of the living. The doctor has faith in science, plans, hopes; he has control of himself because the world still makes sense to him. 'I watched the Belgian, balancing on his legs, master of his muscles, someone who could think about tomorrow' (*W*, p. 10). The world has ceased to make sense to Ibbieta. Objects appear withdrawn and lacking in density, they are absurd and have no other significance than to indicate his approaching death. 'I too found that objects had a funny look: they were more obliterated, less dense than usual. It was enough for me to look at the bench, the lamp, the pile of coal dust, to feel that I was going to die' (*W*, p. 12).

A deep nihilism sets in. Ibbieta sees his whole life as meaningless, valueless and absurd now that he is about to die; so many unfinished, pointless projects premised on the illusion of immortality. 'I took everything as seriously as if I were immortal... I had spent my time counterfeiting eternity' (*W*, p. 11). He identifies those who have condemned him, with their vain aspirations and earnest political opinions, as equally absurd. As they will eventually die too, their lives, like all lives, are no more meaningful than his. He views them in much the same way, with much the same contempt, as Roquentin views the *salauds* (swine or bastards) in Sartre's novel *Nausea*, a work written around the same time.

> These men dolled up with their riding crops and boots were still going to die A little later than I, but not too much. They busied themselves looking for names in their crumpled papers, they ran after other men to imprison or suppress them; they had opinions on the future of Spain and on other subjects. Their little activities seemed shocking and burlesqued to me; I couldn't put myself in their place, I thought they were insane. (*W*, p. 15)

Here Sartre is emphasizing the existential truth that under the aspect of eternity, in light of our mortality, nothing that people do really matters. Arguably, people reveal the ultimate absurdity and pointlessness of their causes and concerns precisely when they fool themselves that a cause can be sufficiently important to justify violence and oppression; a further increase in the already vast sum of pointless human misery. Of course, by the same nihilistic argument, human misery does not really matter either.

Clearly, *The Wall* explores such familiar existentialist themes as despair, death, absurdity, meaninglessness and nihilism. Above all, it explores the existential truth that life has no meaning other than the relative meaning given to it by our finite projects. Believing that his time has run out, Ibbieta can have no projects, other than dying with dignity, and as a result all objects and all human endeavours appear to him as absurd and futile.

The wall in the title of the story is the unyielding wall against which prisoners stand to be shot, the wall they push against with their backs and would like to get inside to escape the bullets. 'Someone'll holler "aim!" and I'll see eight rifles looking at me. I'll think how I'd like to get inside the wall, I'll push against it with my back --- with every ounce of strength I have, but the wall will stay, like in a nightmare' (*W*, p. 8).

The wall is also a symbol of death in so far as it presents an absolute limit. For Sartre, as for other atheistic existentialists, death is an unyielding wall offering no compromise that every person must come up against sooner or later. However, as he argues elsewhere, disagreeing with one of his major influences, Heidegger, people do not experience their finitude as such. Unless, like Ibbieta, they have been condemned to death they do not experience what Heidegger calls *being-towards-death*; they do not experience themselves as *progressing* towards an encounter with death. Indeed, Sartre argues that a person who in ordinary circumstances views his death as nearer today than yesterday is mistaken. He will, of course, live for a certain number of days, but he is mistaken if he thinks that with each day that passes he is using up a predetermined quota. It is inevitable he will die eventually, but the time of his death is not predetermined. When he is dead others will total up his years, but this total was not fixed in advance while he was alive and his life was not a process of fulfilling it. Only a condemned person has a quota of days or hours, but even a condemned person can be reprieved or killed unexpectedly before reaching the firing squad. The closeness or apparent closeness of death changes with circumstances.

> Sudden death is undetermined and by definition can not be waited for at any date; it always, in fact, includes the possibility that we shall die in surprise before the awaited date and consequently that our waiting may be, *qua waiting*, a deception or that we shall survive beyond this date; in the latter case [Ibbieta's] since we were only this waiting, we shall outlive ourselves. (*BN*, p. 557)

Ibbieta is close to death circumstantially and views his life accordingly, but at the end of the story his circumstances radically change and he unexpectedly 'outlives himself'. Having courageously and authentically accepted his mortality and mastered his fear of death, he stubbornly refuses to betray a comrade, Ramon Gris, in exchange for his life. 'I could save my skin and give up Gris and I refused to do it. I found that somehow comic; it was obstinacy. I though, "I must be stubborn!" And a droll sort of gaiety spread over me' (*W*, p. 16). Amused by his posturing captors and the absurdity of their worldly concerns Ibbieta gives them what he believes is false information simply to perpetuate their farcical behaviour. The information turns out to be correct, however, and his life is spared, or, existentially speaking, his death is indefinitely postponed.

THE ROOM

The robust and practical M. Charles Darbédat troubles and tires his sick wife, Jeannette, with his growing concerns about their daughter, Eve. He wants Eve to commit Pierre, her obsessive, deluded, paranoid husband, to a sanatorium for the insane and to make a fresh start in life, but Eve refuses to do so. She loves Pierre and cannot bear to be parted from him. She prefers his company to that of normal people like her father who are shallow, insensitive and lack imagination. She spends most of her time in the room that Pierre never leaves, a room that is always darkened against the daylight and smells heavily of incense. 'Eve quietly turned the doorknob and they entered the room. M. Darbédat's throat tightened at the heavy odour of incense. The curtains were drawn' (*R*, pp. 24–25).

Much to the annoyance of her father, who agrees with the professional opinion of his friend, Dr Franchot, that 'One must never enter the delirium of a madman' (*R*, p. 26), Eve allows herself to be drawn into Pierre's private, irrational world and to be captivated by his fantasies, rituals and fears. She seeks to understand the purpose of his strange rituals, helping him to perform them, and though she is sane, she strives to share in his madness by striving to feel the fear he feels when his imaginary flying statues arrive and buzz about the room.

Pierre's deepest moments of mental crisis are indicated by the arrival of the statues. From a physiological point of view he suffers a kind of fit or seizure. He sweats, his pupils dilate, his breathing becomes heavy and he cries out in distress. '*I'm afraid of the statues*, she thought. It was a violent, blind affirmation, an incantation. She wanted to believe in their presence with all her strength' (*R*, p. 38). For Eve, however, fearing the statues remains only a game. 'Eve felt exhausted: *a game*, she thought with remorse; *it was only a game. I didn't sincerely believe it for an instant. And all that time he suffered as if it were real*' (*R*, p. 39). In not being able to experience Pierre's fear as he experiences it, Eve feels cut off from him, excluded from his bizarre world, alone. As Pierre says to her, ' "There is a wall between you and me. I see you, I speak to you, but you're on the other side" ' (*R*, p. 35).

Far deeper and far more genuine than Eve's make-believe fear of Pierre's flying statues is her fear, her knowledge, that his condition is growing worse, that finally he will lose his mind completely and sink into a permanent stupor. She intends to relieve him of his suffering before that happens. 'One day his features would grow confused, his jaw would hang loose, he would half open his weeping eyes. Eve bent over Pierre's hand and pressed her lips against it: *I'll kill you before that*' (*R*, p. 40).

M. Darbédat and his friend Dr Franchot label Pierre *insane* so as to reduce him to a stereotype and dismiss him as a person. '...he'd get along much better with people of his own type. People like that are children, you have to leave them alone with each other; they form a sort of freemasonry' (*R*, p. 20). For Sartre, the attitude of Darbédat and Franchot reflects not only that of ordinary people but also that of traditional psychiatry which views insanity as a general condition, a product of various impersonal processes that is suffered as an illness. In his theory of existential psychoanalysis which he developed sometime after writing *The Room*, Sartre offers an alternative view in which insanity is identified as an expression of a person's unique response to the world, a response that can only be understood through a thorough exploration of his personal history. This approach to insanity was taken up and developed by the psychiatrist R. D. Laing and detailed in his ground breaking work, *The Divided Self: An Existential Study in Insanity and Madness.*

For Laing, the task of the psychiatrist is not to curb or control a patient's schizophrenic behaviour but to provide safe and non-judgemental circumstances in which his behaviour is allowed full expression in the hope that a process of self-discovery will enable him to resolve his insanity and move beyond it. Eve acts as something of a non-judgemental existential psychoanalyst towards Pierre, allowing his unusual behaviour free reign and even indulging in it.

We are given to understand that, unfortunately, Pierre has a degenerative condition and that there is no hope of his moving beyond his insanity. He is, in a sense, mentally *ill* after all, although his illness, as lived by him, is not simply a disease of the brain but a unique personal journey. Eve's indulgence, her genuine love for him, helps Pierre to take this journey with a level of personal dignity. Her father would have Pierre treated as less than a person, as an unclean object unworthy of respect to be placed in an asylum away from ordinary, healthy, decent people.

Going down the stairs he thought: we should send out two strong-arm men who'd take the poor imbecile away and stick him under a shower without asking his advice on the matter... Pierre is no longer a human being. (R, p. 29).

M. Darbédat is suspicious, disapproving and ashamed of Pierre's condition, he believes it is something his daughter ought to rid herself of in order to return to the bright, respectable, predictable, secure world of well-balanced, practical people – the family of mankind. 'He watched the faces of the passers-by with sympathy; he loved their clear, serious looks. In these sunlit streets, in the midst of mankind, one felt secure, as in the midst of a giant family' (R, p. 29).

Eve is intensely aware that Pierre is still a person despite his condition, that for him his delusions are real and meaningful. She can partially comprehend their power and significance when she plays his games and uses her imagination to enter into his make-believe world. Indeed, to her, Pierre is more of a person than people who are sane. He has a rich and complex inner life and a certain awareness of the mystery of being, whereas the people she sees from the window talking and laughing so thoughtlessly as they hurry about their business seem to her to be two dimensional, having no real inner life or sense of mystery at all. 'An old lady crossed the street with mincing steps; three girls passed, laughing. Then men, strong, serious men carrying briefcases and talking among themselves. *Normal people*, thought Eve, astonished at finding such a powerful hatred in herself' (R, p. 30).

Apart from exploring different attitudes to insanity and to some extent the phenomenon of insanity itself, *The Room* explores the familiar Sartrean themes of authenticity and bad faith. Through his insanity Pierre has achieved a kind of authenticity, he is genuine with a view of reality and an approach to life that is all his own. Normal people like M. Darbédat, on the other hand, lack his unique vision, they share in a collective view of reality, they have faith – bad faith – in the predictability of the word, the certainty of their perceptions and the soundness of their narrow ideas. The story exhibits Sartre's usual contempt for bourgeois attitudes – primarily, in this story, bourgeois attitudes to insanity – and for ordinary, well-adjusted, narrow-minded people who go about their daily lives exercising bad faith in an attempt to avoid giving the terrifying contingency and absurdity of their existence any consideration whatsoever. Certainly M. Darbédat's narrow-mindedness is akin to that of the *salauds* (swine or bastards) of Bouville in Sartre's 1938 novel, *Nausea*. Pierre and Eve, on the other hand, are more akin to Antoine Roquentin, the alienated and all too open-minded central character of that novel. Pierre and Eve are alienated from ordinary, normal people. Pierre by his insanity, Eve by her choice to be with Pierre and share his peculiar world. Like Roquentin, Eve chooses to be an outsider looking in on society. 'Suddenly she thought with a sort of pride that she had no place anywhere. *Normal people think I belong with them. But I couldn't stay an hour among them. I need to live out there, on the other side of the wall. But they don't want me out there'* (*R*, p. 31).

The Room also bears certain similarities to Sartre's 1959 play, *The Condemned of Altona*. Both works feature a reclusive, inspired madman who confines himself to darkened quarters where his irrational obsessions create a private, fantasy world that captivates a lover.

EROSTRATUS

Erostratus enters the mind of a psychopath, Paul Hilbert, detailing, from his own point of view, the relentless progression of his obsessive misanthropy from fantasy to violent action. Hilbert tells his story in a sparse, matter of fact way, offering us little or no insight into the past that may have shaped him. He tells us only that he was born hating the human spirit that most men love and has no idea why he is like he is. With no authorial voice passing judgement on Hilbert the reader is left to draw his or her own conclusions about him from an analysis of his words and deeds.

Hilbert is a resentful, alienated, cold-hearted, misanthropic, loner with dangerous psychotic and sociopathic tendencies. His particular schizophrenia, the fact that he is cut off from his own humanity, is revealed early on in the story when he says, 'I have placed myself above the human within me and I study it' (*E*, p. 41). Hilbert has no interest in people on a personal level. He despises them and finds them physically repulsive. 'But I tell you I *cannot* love them. I understand very well the way you feel. But what attracts you to them disgusts me' (*E*, p. 48). Nonetheless, he wants to impress mankind with an act of infamy for which, like Erostratus, he will always be remembered. Erostratus was an Ancient Greek who, lacking the talent to immortalize his name in any other way, burnt down the Temple of Artemis at Ephesus in 356 BC, one of the seven wonders of the ancient world. The Ephesians sought to eradicate his fame by imposing a death sentence on anyone who spoke his name. Unfortunately, this law served only to fuel his notoriety. Hilbert's educated colleague, Masse, who first tells him about Erostratus, is of the opinion that nobody knows the name of the person who *built* the temple. Hilbert is further encouraged by the thought that the creator is forgotten while the destroyer is remembered (*E*, p. 46). In fact, it is known that the temple was conceived around 550 BC by the architect Chersiphron and his son Metagenes.

Hilbert decides that he will go out into the streets of Paris and indiscriminately kill six people with a revolver. Just buying a gun makes him feel powerful and superior and he is sexually aroused by walking the streets with a heavy penis-substitute in his pocket.

> I walked with a certain stiffness, I looked like a man with a hard-on, with this thing sticking out at every step. I slipped my hand in my pocket and felt the *object*. From time to time I went into a *urinoir* – even in there I had to be careful because I often had neighbours – I took out my revolver, I felt the weight of it, I looked at its black checkered butt and its trigger that looked like a half-closed eyelid. (*E*, p. 42)

Hilbert's masturbatory playing with his heavy, potent revolver reminds us of the psychology and symbolism of contemporary gun culture in general. Gangster Rap in particular incessantly associates the loaded pistol with the ready penis.

Not unlike Hugo Barine in Sartre's 1948 play, *Dirty Hands*, who says, 'I wanted to hang a crime round my neck, like a stone' (*DH*, Epilogue, p. 113), Hilbert wants to perform a decisive act the consequences of which cannot be undone. He believes that the supremely decisive act of killing will make him a less indeterminate, more substantial person who is universally feared and respected. He believes killing will allow him to overcome his former self, allow him to completely transcend his past inadequacies.

> It would possess me, overturning my all-too-human ugliness --- a crime, cutting the life of him who commits it in two. There must be times when one would like to turn back, but this shining object is there behind you, barring the way. I asked only an hour to enjoy mine, to feel its crushing weight. (*E*, p. 50)

Clearly, Hilbert's crushing weight and the stone Barine wanted to hang round his neck are phenomenologically the same. In the same category as Barine and Hilbert we might also place Franz Gerlach, the central character of Sartre's 1959 play, *The Condemned of Altona*. Franz tortures Russian prisoners to death, not for the Nazi cause but in an attempt to overcome his sense of powerlessness and inadequacy through a decisive act of evil. These characters all aspire through the irreversible act of homicide to become what Sartre refers to in *Being and Nothingness* as a being-for-itself-in-itself – an impossible Godlike entity that is a substantial and self-supporting consciousness rather than a mere negation founded upon the world of which it is conscious. In short, these characters want to *be*, rather than be mere relations to being.

Hilbert becomes obsessed with his plan. He fantasizes, often sexually, about shooting people or blowing them up with a bomb. 'I tied her to a pillar and after I explained at great length what I was going to do, I riddled her with bullets. These images troubled me so much that I had to satisfy myself' (*E*, p. 51). He neglects his office job until he is dismissed. He sends letters to 102 French writers explaining what he is going to do and why.

> Soon I am going to take my revolver, I am going down into the street and see if anybody can do anything to *them*. Goodbye, perhaps it will be you I shall meet. You will never know then with what pleasure I shall blow your brains out. (*E*, p. 49)

He lives expensively, ordering deliveries of hot food from a local restaurant, intending to carry out his shooting spree when all his money is spent.

With only a few francs left he takes his revolver and leaves his room in a highly charged emotional state intending to kill. He is both fearful and anxious in face of what he plans to do.

His anxiety is suffered in face of his overwhelming freedom to do the deed. It is at one with his realization that there is nothing, except choosing not to, to stop him (or anyone else) from committing such a terrible crime. Describing freedom as 'vertiginous freedom' (*TE*, p. 100), Sartre refers to the anxiety people experience whenever they seriously consider a dangerous experiment in freedom as the 'vertigo of possibility' (*TE*, p. 100). Overcome by confusion in the large crowd, by an intense fear and anguish that is too much to bear physically, Hilbert is unable to carry out his scheme. He returns to his room and stays there for three days without eating or sleeping, psyching himself up for 'the execution' (*E*, p. 51).

Angry, excited and delirious with hunger he returns once again to the street. Again he is overcome by fear and anxiety, he hardly knows where he is going or what he is doing, but finally he manages to shoot a big man three times in the belly. There is at least the suggestion that as he shoots he feels compelled to act *against* his will by his hysteria and his broader insane desires. 'Then I *knew* I was going to start screaming. I didn't want to: I shot him three times in the belly' (*E*, p. 53). Sartre is often criticized for arguing that people are always responsible for what they do, but arguably, in the way he has Hilbert describe his own mental state at this critical moment in his personal history, he acknowledges a degree of diminished responsibility – the hallmark of insanity generally accepted by both psychiatry and the law. Alternatively, it is possible to draw the less problematic conclusion that Hilbert is bound to be conflicted, that he is bound to have misgivings and second thoughts about what he nonetheless *wants* to do just before he does it, particularly as what he wants to do is so momentous. That our fears and anxieties inspire doubts and reservations about what we are doing just as we take the plunge does not imply that suddenly we are not *choosing* to do it. Even less problematic is the reading that Hilbert shoots the man to stop himself from screaming; what he didn't want to do was scream. However, the use of a colon linking 'I didn't want to: I shot him...' seems to suggest otherwise.

Hilbert runs away in a direction opposite to that he had planned, firing two more shots to disperse the crowd. He locks himself in the lavatory of a café as a crowd gathers outside. It seems to him that the crowd are waiting fearfully outside the door for him to shoot himself. He resents this. 'But they were in no hurry; they gave me all the time in the world to die. The bastards, they were afraid' (*E*, p. 54). With his usual resentment and self-importance he prefers to see the crowd as cowardly rather than himself. He puts the barrel of the gun in his mouth but lacks the courage even to put his finger on the trigger. The story ends with him throwing down the revolver and opening the door.

Hilbert's loathing of other people, the focus of all his thoughts, is a distraction from the deep self-loathing that is at the root of his mental condition. Symptomatic of his self-loathing is the fact that he only likes to view people from above, where he can look down on them and they do not look at him. Similarly, he will not allow the prostitutes he hires to touch him or pay him any attention.

> I was in heaven: there I was, calmly sitting in an armchair, dressed up to my neck, I had even kept my gloves on and this ripe woman had stripped herself naked at my command and was turning back and forth in front of me. (*E*, p. 44)

He wants, by the way he looks at women and the way he makes them move, to reduce them to mere objects, to their being-in-the-midst-of-the-world. He meticulously avoids running the risk that they will transcend his transcendence and reduce him to an object, to a transcendence-transcended. He cannot abide others because he cannot abide his being-for-others. He wants to annihilate others so as not to exist as a being for them. Furthermore, because he knows he cannot annihilate all others, he wants to take final and complete control of his being-for-others by defining himself as one of the 'black heroes' (*E*, p. 46), as an infamous villain, a definition he believes others will accept and never question.

Modern times have seen a huge increase in the number of indiscriminate shootings and bombings conducted for personal and/or political motives. The reasons for this trend are complex but undoubtedly the emergence of a global mass media has made an enormous contribution to it. Any psychopath can achieve instant, worldwide recognition for himself or the cause he identifies himself with if he slaughters enough innocent people. In light of this, *Erostratus* has particular contemporary resonance. Hilbert's fantasies, his delusions of grandeur, are comparable to those of Jihadist suicide bombers or to any of the increasing number of violently psychotic students who conduct indiscriminate shootings in mainly American schools.[4]

> I felt a strange power in my body when I went down into the street. I had a revolver on me, the thing that explodes and makes a noise. But I no longer drew my assurance from that, it was from myself: I was a being like a revolver, a torpedo or a bomb. I too, one day at the end of my sombre life, would explode and light the world with a flash as short and violent as magnesium. (*E*, p. 47)

INTIMACY

Set in Paris in the 1930s, *Intimacy* tells the story of Lucienne Crispin's half-hearted and ultimately unsuccessful attempt to leave her dull, oafish, impotent husband, Henri. The story is Sartre's most sexually explicit piece of writing and would have been considered quite scandalous at the time it was published.

Lucienne (Lulu) is young, physically attractive, irresponsible, indecisive and sexually repressed. She likes to be seen with handsome men and to be admired by them for her good looks but she does not like to be sexually aroused by them; to exist for them sexually.

> Of course, he did manage to bother me with all his feeling around, he knows how; I have a horror of men who know how, I'd rather sleep with a virgin. Those hands going right to where they want, pressing a little, not too much – they take you for an instrument they're proud of knowing how to play. I hate people to bother me. (*I*, p. 77)

It is repeatedly suggested in Lulu's internal monologue that her sexual preference is for women.

> Then I stretched out on my back and thought about priests and pure things, about women, and I stroked my stomach first, my beautiful flat stomach, then I slid my hands down and it was pleasure; the pleasure only I know how to give myself. (*I*, p. 58)

Lulu's upbringing, her conformity, her romantic ideas about men, the value she places on being a Madame, all serve to prevent her from acknowledging her lesbian tendencies. Though her fantasies often return her to her sexual preference she evades seeing her fantasies as anything more than silly daydreaming. She certainly never explores the implications that actively indulging her sexual preference would have for the way she lives her life. She remains a frustrated daydreamer, denying herself the sex she really wants, repulsed by the sex she allows herself. She recalls being 'miserable' when her friend Rirette was in love with Fresnel, that it 'worried' her to think of him making love to Rirette (*I*, p. 61), yet she avoids concluding that she was jealous and would like to have been in Fresnel's place.

I wonder what her face must look like when she's stretched out like that, all naked under a man, feeling hands on her flesh. I wouldn't touch her for all the money in the world, I wouldn't know what to do with her, even if she wanted, even if she said, 'I want it!' I wouldn't know how, but if I were invisible I'd like to be there when somebody was doing it to her and watch her face…and stroke her spread knees gently, her pink knees and hear her groan. (*I*, p. 61)

Partly to relieve her boredom, partly because she thinks it is the socially acceptable thing to do (more acceptable than being a lesbian) and partly because she is too weak-minded to resist, Lulu allows herself to be drawn into love affairs with dominant, decisive men whose virility both intrigues and intimidates her. Her current lover, Pierre, is such a man. Rirette, more than Lulu, recognizes that he is 'a real man', that 'he's intelligent', that 'he has money', that he knows 'how to command', that he has a 'dominant personality' (*I*, p. 63). Pierre wants Lulu to run away with him to Nice, but she is reluctant to leave the mundane, predictable, domestic, slightly squalid intimacy she has with Henri.

Throughout the story Lulu equates intimacy with men with a certain grubbiness, but she draws a distinction between the grubby intimacy with Pierre she finds threatening and the grubby intimacy with Henri she finds reassuring. After sex with Pierre she thinks, 'I'm defiled. It doesn't surprise me that he's pure now that he left his own dirt here, in the blackness, there's a hand towel full of it and the sheet's wet in the middle of the bed' (*I*, p. 75). In contrast, her attitude towards Henri is far more tolerant.

…he wasn't very clean, he didn't change his underwear often enough; when Lulu put it in the dirty laundry bag she couldn't help noticing the bottoms were yellow from rubbing between his legs. Personally, Lulu did not despise uncleanliness: it was more intimate and made such tender shadows. (*I*, p. 55)

So, it is not really filth that Lulu finds disgusting but sex itself. Dirt is tolerable, even endearing, when it is impotent Henri's yellowed underpants but not when it is potent Pierre's semen.

Henri's impotence, his physical inertia particularly in bed, the lack of challenge he presents both sexually and as a person generally makes Lulu feel safe and secure. She particularly likes his impotence as she finds erect penises frightening. She finds Henri's impotence, his flaccid penis that she can touch without it becoming hard, charming and feminine, 'like a big flower' (*I*, p. 58).

> The trouble is you can never really hold it in your hands, if it would only stay quiet, but it starts moving like an animal, it gets hard, it frightens me when it's hard and sticking up in the air, it's brutal...I loved Henri because his little thing never got hard, never raised its head...I always took his soft little thing between my fingers...but it didn't move, it behaved itself in my hand... (*I*, p. 58)

For Lulu, Henri is not so much a man, a person in his own right, as a big comfort-doll or baby that she finds it soothing to take care of. Lulu believes she cannot have children because of her 'constitution' (*I*, p. 56). Lacking children she treats Henri rather like a baby. Lazy and inert with no other desire than to be coddled and pampered Henri is happy to go along with this. Certainly her feelings towards Henri are more those of a mother than a woman, although again there is a repressed sexual element in them.

> If he could only stay like that, paralysed, I would take care of him, clean him like a child and sometimes I'd turn him over on his stomach and give him a spanking, and other times when his mother came to see him, I'd find some reason to uncover him, I'd pull back the sheet and his mother would see him all naked. (*I*, pp. 55–56)

It is at least suggested that Lulu's sexual desire for Rirette is reciprocated, but like Lulu, Rirette will not fully acknowledge her feelings. She distracts herself from her real feelings by being shocked at Lulu's 'obscene body' and the sexy way she dresses, but notably she is unable to take her eyes of Lulu as she moves.

> Rirette followed her, almost falling several times because she didn't watch her step: she had eyes only for the slender silhouette of blue and canary yellow dancing before her! It's true, she does have an obscene body...She's supple and slender, but there's something indecent about her, I don't know what. She

does everything she can do to display herself, that must be it. (*I*, p. 70)

Rirette indulges her obsession for Lulu by interfering in her personal life. She wants to make Lulu leave Henri, ostensibly because Henri is impotent and not as good a man as Pierre and because Lulu no longer loves Henri, but her true motivation is that she enjoys exercising power over Lulu. Also, interfering in Lulu's intimate relationships compensates Rirette a little for the fact that she is not involved in an intimate relationship of her own; meddling in Lulu's affairs gives her an emotional life by proxy.

Encouraged by Rirette, Lulu manages to leave home with a packed suitcase, but even while she prepares to run away to Nice she deliberately shops with Rirette where Henri will see her. Sure enough, much to Rirette's annoyance, Henri sees Lulu and demands that she return to him, not because he loves her but because she is his wife and his property. ' "She is my wife," he said, "she belongs to me, I want her to come back with me." ' (*I*, p. 73). Rirette and Henri struggle over Lulu who herself is as 'limp as a bag of laundry' (*I*, p. 73). Rirette finally manages to get Lulu into a taxi and away from Henri. The split, however, is only temporary as Lulu returns to Henri that night after Pierre leaves her alone in a hotel room. 'I'll go. They can't make me leave him like a dog' (*I*, p. 77). She spends the remainder of the night with Henri before returning to the hotel in the morning. Finally, she is retrieved from the hotel by friends, the Texiers, and taken back to Henri before Pierre returns. She sends Pierre a letter telling him that she is staying with Henri because he is so unhappy, but that she will continue to meet with Pierre as usual. Her letter speaks of her passion for Pierre. 'I wish you could be here, I want you, I press myself against you and I feel your caresses in all my body' (*I*, p. 82). Yet we know that when they are together this passion frightens and disgusts her. We leave Lulu as we find her, dithering, dishonest, flirtatious, sexually confused, refusing to take possession of her inalienable freedom and determine her own destiny.

Intimacy is a brilliant study of the complexity and confusedness of sexuality and sexual relationships within a society that brings morality, shame, gender expectations and sexual taboos to bear on every natural emotion and desire. More specifically, *Intimacy* is a study of the socially influenced sexual psychology and broader personality of a physically attractive, irresponsible, passive yet manipulative young woman who is in bad faith in various ways.

Lulu is indecisive, apparently incapable of making important decisions or of committing herself to a clear course of action. At the end of the story she decides not to choose between Henri and Pierre and to persist with a life of deception and double standards. Of course, as Sartre notes in *Being and Nothingness*, 'Not to choose is, in fact, to choose not to choose' (*BN*, p. 503). To choose not to choose is to make a negative choice that fails to confront the reality of the situation. For Sartre, choosing not to choose, acting as though one had no choice and made no choice, is a central feature of bad faith. Lulu not only chooses not to choose, she views her actions as though others are responsible for them, as though she is a facticity acted upon from outside rather than a free transcendence acting in the world. She views life as an 'enormous wave' breaking on her, 'tearing her from the arms of Henri' (*I*, p. 79). 'You never, never do what you want' she thinks, 'you're carried away' (*I*, p. 79). And again, 'The flood carries you away; that's life; we can't judge or understand, we can only let ourselves drift' (*I*, p. 80). She stays because Henri and the Texiers want her to; she planned to leave because Pierre and Rirette wanted her to. She is what Sartre describes in his *War Diaries*, written soon after, as a 'buffeted consciousness' (*WD*, p. 112). That is, a person who sees herself as a fixed entity buffeted and swept along by circumstances, a person who believes she cannot really help what she does. 'We shall designate this state buffeted human reality, for it realises itself as buffeted amid the possibles, like a plank amid the waves' (*WD*, p. 111).

In bad faith Lulu believes that everything happens *to* her. In reality, relying largely on her physical attractiveness to others, she *makes* herself the passive centre around which others gather and scheme with regard to her. As others want her as an object for their own ends she is ultimately able to manipulate circumstances in her favour by being the object that they want her to be. Lulu's bad faith is comparable in certain respects to the bad faith of Sartre's flirt (*BN*, p. 78) who attempts to avoid taking responsibility for her situation and her actions in her situation. Both women choose to suppose that they have no choice, exercising their freedom in a self-defeating manner as they attempt to make themselves synonymous with being-in-itself. Lulu is certainly a flirt. With no real commitment to doing so she flirts with the idea of leaving Henri for the sake of a would-be romantic love affair with Pierre that is itself a mere flirtation, a self-indulgent hobby that she finds far more upsetting than exciting when she cares to reflect on it.

> My God, to think that's life, that's why you get dressed and wash and make yourself pretty and all the books are written about that and you think about it all the time and finally that's what it is, you go to a room with somebody who half smothers you and ends up by wetting your stomach. (*I*, p. 77)

She does not want to commit herself emotionally to Pierre and is not capable of doing so, partly because she prefers women and partly because she is lazy, timid and unadventurous. She craves only the dull, unemotional, domestic intimacy she has with Henri. She craves it because it is predictable and reassuring and places no demands on her. 'They went to bed and Lulu was shaken with enormous sobs because she found her room and bed clean and the [familiar] red glow in the window' (*I*, p. 78).

Some critics have accused Sartre of misogyny and Lulu is certainly the first of several very negative, inauthentic female characters that appear in his writings – Estelle and Inez in *In Camera* being the most notable and certainly the most loathsome. In Sartre's defence, it must be noted that Lulu is not *all* women but only one woman, although she does typify a particular kind of flirtatious, flighty, female personality that many people, men and women, can recognize to some degree from their own experience of others. To argue otherwise one would have to argue that Lulu is not a well drawn or credible character when surely she is. It can also be argued in Sartre's defence that most of his male characters are negative and inauthentic also. He is undoubtedly far harder on most of his male characters than he is on most of his female characters. Paul Hilbert in *Erostratus*, Lucien Fleurier in *The Childhood of a Leader*, The Autodidact in *Nausea*, Jacques Delarue in *Roads to Freedom*, Joseph Garcin in *In Camera*, Senator Clarke in *The Respectable Prostitute*, Hugo Barine in *Dirty Hands* and Gerlach Senior in *The Condemned of Altona* would make a very unpleasant gathering indeed. Sartre has his heroes and heroines but he is nonetheless merciless in his analysis of our all-too-human failings, with his most constant theme being the widespread if not universal human frailty and lack of self-discipline that disposes most people, men and women, to diverse projects of bad faith in which they fail miserably to affirm their being-in-situation. As a writer Sartre is far better described as a misanthrope than a misogynist. That is, a misanthrope who distrusts people and is disappointed by them rather than one who simply hates them.

THE CHILDHOOD OF A LEADER

Extremely detailed yet brilliantly concise, *The Childhood of a Leader* traces the emotional, psychological, social, sexual and moral development of a privileged bourgeois from infancy to adulthood. It is by far the longest short story in the collection and arguably the most sophisticated in terms of the range of complex philosophical ideas it explores. It is unfortunate that it has been somewhat overlooked by recent Sartre scholars as it is a major piece of work, an integral part of Sartre's early philosophy.

The central character of *The Childhood of a Leader*, Lucien Fleurier, is a sensitive, intelligent, imaginative child given to fantasizing and inventing games. Even as an infant he worries about his self-identity and the nature of reality. When made to wear an angel costume he worries that he might become a girl or be permanently mistaken for one. He wonders if he is real, if anything is real, if his parents and other adults are just pretending to be who they appear to be. He often feels he is asleep, that his thoughts are just mist or that he is nothing but mist himself, and he wishes he could wake up to a reality that is clear, certain and solid.

> 'What am I, *I* – ?' There was this fog rolling back on itself, indefinite. 'I!' He looked into the distance; the word rang in his head...Lucien shuddered and his hands trembled. 'Now I have it!' he thought, 'now I have it! I was sure of it: *I don't exist!*' (*CL*, p. 99)

As he grows he tries various strategies to overcome his troubling sense of unreality.

As an adolescent Lucien becomes close friends with Berliac, a Jewish youth who is very mature and well informed for his age. Lucien and Berliac share confidences, each admitting to a childhood desire for his own mother. This is the *Oedipus complex* as defined by the Jewish Austrian psychiatrist, Sigmund Freud. According to

Freud, every male child envies his father's intimacy with his mother. He desires to kill his father and sleep with his mother. Thus, Berliac introduces Lucien to Freudian psychoanalysis, which Lucien then studies avidly. Psychoanalysis appears to hold the answer to Lucien's worries about his identity. It seems he has been unable to find the true Lucien and his lifelong search for him has been misguided because the true Lucien is hidden in his subconscious. 'The true Lucien was deeply buried in his subconscious; he had to dream of him without ever seeing him, as an absent friend' (*CL*, p. 104). He decides, like Berliac, that all his worries are just complexes as diagnosed by Freud.

Much to Berliac's annoyance, Lucien becomes acquainted with Berliac's mentor, Bergère, a surrealist artist in his thirties whose intentions towards Lucien are sexual. Bergère finally succeeds in seducing Lucien who, nervous but consenting at the time, is left feeling disgusted and ashamed of himself. He fears what will become of his respectable, middle-class reputation and his destiny to lead if he 'becomes' a homosexual.

> 'But suppose I get in the habit?' he thought with anguish. 'I could never do without it, it'll be like morphine!' He would become a tarnished man, no one would have anything to do with him, his father's workers would laugh when he gave them orders. (*CL*, p. 118)

His reaction is to have nothing more to do with Bergère, Berliac or Freud. Raised in an anti-Semitic environment it is easy for him to convince himself that the dangerous, perverted, Jewish ideas of Berliac and Freud temporarily corrupted his mind and his moral health and led him to the episode with Bergère.

In an attempt to convince himself that he is heterosexual he finds a girlfriend, Maud, and loses his virginity, but it is clear that he does not really enjoy heterosexual sex. '...she always wanted to sleep with him, it was tiresome; their confused flesh giving off an odour of scorched rabbit stew in the torrid heat of springtime' (*CL*, p. 143). He embraces the security and respectability of his family, looking forward to the day when he will inherit his father's factory, assert his bourgeois rights and be respected by his workers as a leader of men. He adopts his father's positive view of capitalism, his nationalism and above all his anti-Semitism. He is encouraged to join the French Fascist movement by André Lemordant, a fellow student with a moustache and a mature manner. He helps his Fascist brothers, the *camelots*, to beat up an immigrant in the street in a random, unprovoked, racially motivated attack.

At Pierrette Guigard's eighteenth birthday party Lucien proudly refuses to shake hands with Weill, a Jew. Lucien leaves the party immediately, his pride melting as he reaches the street. He starts to worry that the Guigard's will never speak to him again, but the next day, to his surprise and relief, Pierrette's brother apologizes for having introduced him to a Jew. '"My parents say you were right and you couldn't have done otherwise because of your convictions'" (*CL*, p. 140). Lucien is transformed by the thought that he has convictions that other people respect. For the first time in his life he feels as though he has real substance. He feels powerful and threatening and clearly defined. 'Now Lucien felt clean and sharp as a chronometer' (*CL*, p. 141).

The finishing touch to the transformation and solidification of Lucien's self-image is added when, dissatisfied with his pretty, childish face, he decides to grow a moustache. '...he would have liked to find on his own face the impenetrable look he admired on Lemordant's. But the mirror only reflected a pretty, headstrong little face that was not yet terrible. "I'll grow a moustache," he decided' (*CL*, p. 144).

The Childhood of a Leader was conceived during the same period as Sartre's seminal 1938 novel, *Nausea*. The two works complement each other in that they explore many of the same philosophical ideas – contingency, indeterminacy, self-identity and bad faith. Both Lucien Fleurier and Antoine Roquentin, the central character of *Nausea*, are haunted by issues of self-identity and bewildered by existence generally. Their existential anxieties are largely the same. They differ in terms of their response to their anxieties, with each choosing himself as the kind of person the other detests. Antoine detests those who, like Lucien, seek to fool themselves that their existence is necessary, while Lucien comes to detest those who, like Antoine, think and question too much and dwell on their contingency and superfluity. Lucien suppresses his anxieties by striving to *be* something, and eventually becomes a superficial, bourgeois *salaud* (swine or bastard) steeped in bad faith, very much like one of the *salauds* described in *Nausea* that Antoine so despises. For his part, Antoine sees through the deluded posturing of the *salauds* and in opposition to them thoroughly indulges his anxieties. Rather than strive to *be* something, he strives instead to be nothing. Arguably, his project of nihilism, as an attempt to *be* his own nothingness, is a last desperate attempt to escape his indeterminacy and as such is as much a project in bad faith as Lucien's. Antoine, however, remains a far more sympathetic character than Lucien because he strives with a brutal honesty that is genuinely admirable to confront certain existential truths that Lucien, as he grows older, strives to evade. Also, Antoine's way of being, his way of being in bad faith, harms only himself, where as Lucien's bigotry is harmful to others.

Like the young, precocious Sartre himself, Lucien Fleurier is troubled by questions of identity and reality throughout his childhood.[5] Lucien's childhood and adolescence are characterized by a quest to understand who he is, to find and define himself, to give himself a solidity and reality that replaces the vagueness, indeterminacy and insubstantiality he usually feels. In feeling indeterminate and contingent he is recognizing the existential truth that there is nothing that he is in the mode of being it, that, like everyone else, he must play at being what he is because he cannot simply be what he is. Like many people, Lucien does not like to have a sense of his own indeterminacy and contingency, it makes him uncomfortable and anxious. Hence, as he grows up, he is increasingly motivated to ease his anxiety in any way he can. He eventually chooses to think and act in profound bad faith, creating the illusion of his own necessity and determinacy and forcing himself to believe in it. The crucial episode in the development of Lucien's bad faith is his homosexual relationship with Bergère. His journey into extreme bad faith is largely an aversion reaction to this episode.

Bergère awakens homosexual desires in Lucien, but partly as a result of his naivety and partly as a result of bad faith Lucien refuses to acknowledge his own homosexual tendencies or the true meaning of Bergère's advances. 'He had no luck; twenty times, these last few days, he had almost discovered what Bergère wanted of him and each time, as if on purpose, something happened to turn away his thought' (*CL*, p. 115). In this respect Lucien is comparable to Sartre's flirt in *Being and Nothingness* who relinquishes responsibility for herself and her situation, refusing to acknowledge the sexual background of her suitors' attentions (*BN*, pp. 78–9). Lucien escapes the burden of his responsibility for himself by allowing himself to exist for Bergère as a flattered, pampered object, a doll. He has fantasized since childhood in a vaguely sexual way about being treated like a doll. Unable to determine himself, Lucien allows himself to be determined as the object of Bergère's homosexual desires. 'Lucien slowly removed his slippers and dressing gown and slipped under the covers without a word...he told himself, "I'm his little doll!"' (*CL*, pp. 116–117).

Though Lucien is a homosexual in so far as he practices homosexuality, he nonetheless shares the deep-rooted homophobic prejudices of his social class. He reacts strongly against his homosexual encounter with Bergère, against his own homosexuality, by making a radical conversion to extreme bad faith. He strives to deny the true meaning of his sexual encounter by treating it as an unfortunate aberration to be blamed on circumstances and other people. In time, he treats it as an aberration to be blamed on the traditional and convenient scapegoat of Jews and their supposedly dangerous, corrupting ideas. Lucien's anti-Semitism is a distraction from his homosexual desires. What he really fears and therefore hates are these desires, but to hate them would be to recognize that he has them, so instead he hates Jews and what he comes to identify as Jewish intellectualism. 'And how much he preferred the unconscious, reeking of the soil, which Barrès gave him, to the filthy, lascivious images of Freud' (*CL*, p. 131).[6]

One of the central aims of *The Childhood of a Leader* is to show that the slide into anti-Semitism, into any kind of racism, is not first and foremost a political journey but a personal journey into the self-evasions, the inauthenticity, of bad faith. The story explores a set of personal circumstances – one set among many possible sets – that results in the adoption of bigotry as a means of imposing an illusion of certainty on a morally confused and confusing world. The story was published just prior to World War II and was a timely response to the increasing hatred and suspicion that was being directed towards Jews in France and throughout Europe. By the late 1930s Sartre would certainly have know about the systematic persecution of Jews that was taking place in Nazi Germany, but like most people, he would have been unaware of the true scale and horror of the problem.[7]

Lucien's membership of the French Fascist movement, an aggressive, macho, anti-intellectual tribe, makes him feel strong and proud and gives him a sense of belonging. He had formerly searched for his personal identity, but now he is happy to take on an identity granted and confirmed by the group; happy to be nothing more than his being-for-others. '"First maxim", Lucien said, "not to try and see inside yourself; there is no mistake more dangerous." The real Lucien – he knew now – had to be sought in the eyes of others' (*CL*, p. 142). In fiercely despising Jews, his badge of honour among his fellow fascists, he not only finds a scapegoat for his past actions, he sees himself as important and substantial in comparison to those he despises. He prides himself that he is not a member of a despised or humiliated race, but a Frenchman with a good French name and respectable ancestry. His anti-Semitism, unreasonable and unfounded though it is, transforms him into a man of conviction. His racist convictions define him and give him solidity; like religious beliefs they demand the respect of others. 'Lucien's anti-Semitism was of a different sort: unrelenting and pure, it stuck out of him like a steel blade menacing other breasts. "It's – sacred," he thought' (*CL*, pp. 142).

Throughout the story, and in other Sartre works such as *Nausea*, the moustache marks out those serious minded bourgeois who command respect for their convictions; their belief that whatever they choose to believe is true. These men of apparent substance have fooled themselves and others that they exist by right, that they are what they are in the mode of being it – a being-in-itself rather than a being-for-itself. It is not surprising then that Lucien completes the construction of his false object-self by growing a moustache.[8]

Primarily, *The Childhood of a Leader* details one person's slide into the kind of chronic, cowardly, morally repugnant bad faith that, for Sartre, typifies the French (or any) bourgeois. That is, the faith that his existence is not accidental but essential and that he has sacred rights granted by God and his nation, such as the right to have unquestionable opinions and prejudices and the right to have his necessary existence confirmed by the respect of others, especially the social inferiors he is destined to lead. In *Nausea*, as said, Sartre refers to the bourgeoisie as *salauds* (swine or bastards). *The Childhood of a Leader* complements *Nausea* in being about a *salaud*, or more specifically, in being about the evolution of a *salaud*. That is, a pillar of the community who has learnt to deny his inner life by becoming nothing more than a *posturing* before others, a poser. 'So many people were waiting for him, at attention: and he was and always would be this immense waiting of others. "That's a leader," he thought' (*CL*, p. 143). We can easily imagine that, like the *salauds* in *Nausea*, Lucien will go on to have a portrait of himself painted in which he appears grander, more significant, more substantial and infinitely less contingent than he really is. 'The power of art is truly admirable. Of this shrill-voiced little man, nothing would go down to posterity except a threatening face, a superb gesture, and the bloodshot eyes of a bull' (*N*, p. 136).[9]

CHAPTER 4

SARTRE'S NOVELS

Sartre published four novels, all of them before 1950. This is not many given the length of his writing career, his huge output generally and the great value he attached from childhood onwards to the novel as a form of expression. We can only conjecture as to the reasons.

The reason is surely not that he did not have another novel in him, that he was overawed and felt unable to follow what he had achieved with *Nausea* and the *Roads to Freedom* trilogy. Of course, by his own philosophical principles, he did not have another novel in him because he did not produce another novel. He argues in various places that genius is as genius does: 'Why should we attribute to Racine the capacity to write yet another tragedy when that is precisely what he did not write?' (*EAH*, p. 42). A novel or any other artefact does not pre-exist its creation. Sartre certainly attempted further novels, most notably an abandoned fourth volume of *Roads to Freedom* titled *The Last Chance* and an abandoned novel set in Italy titled *Queen Albemarle and the Last Tourist*.[1]

The fact is that Sartre's career is littered with unfinished works. An unfinished work on ethics: *Notebooks for an Ethics*, an unfinished biography of the French poet Stéphane Mallarmé, an unfinished second volume of *The Critique of Dialectical Reason*, an unfinished fourth volume of *The Family Idiot* (due to blindness) and so on. It always seems ungenerous to raise the issue of Sartre's unfinished works as many of them are substantial and important despite being incomplete, but the fact remains that they are incomplete. One great irony about Sartre is that he was often too busy writing and too full of idea to polish off his current project. He was frequently enticed away from one project by his enthusiasm for the next. It seems that he always had so much to say that particularly in his later years he did not always afford himself the huge investment of time that is generally required to revise, edit and craft a work into a well-rounded whole. The most notable exception among the works of the later Sartre is *Words*, which is painstakingly crafted and beautifully rounded off. No wonder it is the most acclaimed work of the mature Sartre and the one that finally led to an offer of the Nobel Prize for Literature. Sartre certainly knew how to craft a work, his short stories and his first novel, *Nausea*, written and rewritten while he was striving to establish himself prove this. But it seems that once the demands of fame, political engagement and travelling the world as France's anti-ambassador began to devour his time he was usually too busy to undertake the meticulous, time-consuming final revision that is required to fully wrap a work up.

It is revealing that Sartre managed to wrap up ten plays. Arguably, this is because it is possible to write a play quite quickly. Plays are relatively short and by definition do not require the writer to create long passages of descriptive narrative. Above all, they can be refined in rehearsal, as Sartre's plays often were. Novels, on the other hand, are by definition relatively long. Refining descriptive narrative is often time consuming, not least because it is a very open-ended practice. Unlike a factual work, which grows logically of its own accord as the writer pursues a thesis, a novel must generate a world *ex nihilo*. There are inevitably huge considerations of continuity, as well as issues of character consistency and credibility, for the novelist to take care of. For all these reasons Sartre never saw his way to completing another novel. After 1949 he simply chose not to afford himself the considerable time and mental space required to adequately indulge his imagination and his craft as a storyteller. This is a great pity as he is, judging by the four novels he completed, a highly accomplished and entertaining novelist. It is those four *completed* novels – four more than most people ever write – to which this chapter is dedicated.

NAUSEA

In 1929 Sartre graduated from the prestigious École Normale Supérieure, first of 76 candidates. He was among France's academic elite but he was destined for a long period of obscurity. After a break of a few months he began a compulsory period of military service with the meteorological corps, a post he returned to nearly a decade later when World War II broke out. Once he had been trained to handle meteorological equipment the authorities decided he would serve his time better as a teacher and he was duly posted to the Lycée François Ier in Le Havre to cover for a teacher who had had a nervous breakdown. The star of the École Normale who had shown so much promise found himself in provincial exile. He made the most of this exile, however, and even maintained it by choice until 1936, returning there in 1934 after spending a few months in Berlin studying the phenomenology of Husserl.

The Le Havre years were an important period of personal and philosophical development for Sartre. Though publishers rejected his early manuscripts and the easy fame he had naively expected as an undergraduate eluded him, he continued to refine and develop his ideas. No longer the student show-off and prankster surrounded by bright young things he became more serious and more genuinely introspective. The atmosphere of Le Havre pervaded his moods. The coastal light and the sea breeze made the filthy slums, the seedy red light district, the huge, stark windswept docks and the smart bourgeois district above the cliffs with its villas, gardens and churches emerge with excruciating sharpness. Le Havre became Bouville, the town in which *Nausea* is set. The insight Sartre indulged and pondered during his solitary walks, the anxious realization that reality is inexorable and overwhelming yet elusive, unnecessary and superfluous (contingent), became 'the nausea', the terrifying and loathsome revelation that lies at the heart of the novel.

Sartre first outlined his ideas on contingency as early as 1926 while studying Nietzsche. He continued incubating these ideas during his military service and they went with him to Le Havre in the form of an ever increasing collection of notes and passages he nicknamed his 'factum on contingency'; 'factum' being a term he had adopted to describe any form of ruthless analysis. *Nausea* is set in 1932 and it was from late 1931 onwards that the factum, by absorbing the character and detail of Sartre's new situation, began to grow into something resembling the novel we know today. The work became Sartre's constant companion for six years as no less than three successive complete versions underwent continuous revision and refinement, always under the scrupulous eye of Simone de Beauvoir. He poured in his thoughts and experiences while at the same time ruthlessly cutting anything that struck him or de Beauvoir as unnecessary. The result is a highly polished and refined text, Sartre's most accomplished work of fiction; a work rivalled, possibly, only by *Being and Nothingness* as his greatest work of all. There are no wasted words in *Nausea* and as a result even its English translation has a sublime, poetic quality reminiscent of T. S. Eliot at his best.[2] 'What kind of book is *La Nausée?*' asks Iris Murdoch in *Sartre: Romantic Rationalist*, concluding that 'It seems more like a poem or an incantation than a novel' (Murdoch 1968, p. 19).

> I liked yesterday's sky so much, a narrow sky, dark with rain, pressing against the window-panes like a ridiculous, touching face. This sun isn't ridiculous, quite the contrary. On everything I love, on the rust in the yards, on the rotten planks of the fence, a miserly, sensible light is falling, like the look you give, after a sleepless night, at the decisions you made enthusiastically the day before, at the pages you wrote straight off without a single correction. (*N*, p. 27)

Nausea is a stylistic masterpiece that achieves a seamless marriage of fiction and philosophy; a *tour de force* that advances a distinctive and profound philosophical vision without ever falling short of being a pure and genuine novel. It is, as many commentators including Iris Murdoch have noted, a rare example of a truly *philosophical novel*. Unlike, for example, *Sophie's World* or *Zen and the Art of Motorcycle Maintenance* (both excellent philosophical books in their own way), it does not repeatedly depart from its core narrative to make excursions into philosophical reflection. Its core narrative, which is its entire narrative, is philosophical.

In considering the claim that *Nausea* is Sartre's most accomplished and sublime piece of fiction, a stylistic masterpiece etc., it is worth briefly comparing its merits with those of his other works of fiction.

Sartre's plays largely lack the aesthetic qualities of *Nausea*. They are often quite ugly, so many depressing, claustrophobic rooms. Mary Midgley says of existentialism, 'Life shrinks to a few urban rooms; no wonder it becomes absurd' (Midgley 2002, p. 19). This has some truth, certainly with regard to Sartre's plays. His plays are above all utilitarian and functional, vehicles for making important, intelligent, philosophical and political points. They amount to what some commentators have described as Sartre's 'thesis theatre'.

Sartre's *Roads to Freedom* is increasingly a period piece, with *The Reprieve* and *Iron in the Soul* – though not *The Age of Reason* – as much identifiable as historical testaments as novels exploring personal freedom and bad faith. *Roads to Freedom* is always preoccupied above all else with the situational tensions between its diverse characters; with Sartre's notion that 'The essence of the relations between consciousnesses is not the *Mitsein* [being-with]; it is conflict' (*BN*, p. 451). Although it is a philosophically thought-provoking series of novels, it does not attain the same timeless philosophical and ontological depth as *Nausea*. As Iris Murdoch writes: 'It [Nausea] is his most densely philosophical novel' (Murdoch 1968, p. 11).

Sartre's short stories are brilliant psychological examinations written with great style and refinement. Conceived during the same years as *Nausea*, they point the way to *Nausea* stylistically and aesthetically – particularly *The Childhood of a Leader* – but being only short stories they cannot hope to rival the power of *Nausea*; the breadth of its vision, its poignancy and beauty, its darkly melancholic mysticism. Arguably, only Sartre's biographies achieve anything approaching the same aesthetic. Certain passages in *Saint Genet*, for example, or his autobiography, *Words*.

Sartre's first published novel, *Nausea* firmly established his reputation as both a writer and a philosopher, and it remains his best known and most widely read work. It is undoubtedly the pinnacle of his achievements as an artist, though not as a philosopher, and had he written nothing else he would still be a major figure of world literature. Indeed, had he written nothing else his cult status would have attained the heights of cool reserved for those who write just one timeless classic before taking a vow of silence. If *Nausea* is at all true, there is surely nothing left to say that is worth saying anyway.

The basic plot of *Nausea* is simple. In terms of events relatively little happens. This is quite deliberate on Sartre's part. He is at pains to present a slice of ordinary life and to avoid doing what novels usually do, which is to impose on ordinary life the features of an adventure with clear cut beginnings that portend clear cut endings where characters are reconciled to themselves and to each other and above all fulfilled.

This is what I have been thinking: for the most commonplace event to become an adventure, you must – and this is all that is necessary – start *recounting* it. This is what fools people: a man is always a teller of tales, he lives surrounded by his stories and the stories of others, he sees everything that happens to him through them; and he tries to live his life as if he were recounting it. (*N*, p. 61)

Antoine Roquentin, the central character of the novel, in his self-destructive attempt to live free from all comforting misapprehensions, strives to avoid living life as if he were recounting it. He sums up his stark, nihilistic view of life, as lived rather than recounted, with these chilling, exquisitely negative words:

When you are living, nothing happens. The settings change, people come in and go out, that's all. There are never any beginnings. Days are tacked on to days without rhyme or reason, it is an endless, monotonous addition...There isn't any end either: you never leave a woman, a friend, a town in one go. And then everything is like everything else: Shanghai, Moscow, Algiers, are all the same after a couple of weeks. (*N*, pp. 61–62)

Antoine, and therefore the novel itself, walks a thin, ironical line between telling a story and striving not to tell a story. When Antoine slips into turning his life into an adventure, into literature, he catches himself and pulls back. 'I have no need to speak in flowery language. I am writing to understand certain circumstances. I must beware of literature' (*N*, p. 85).

Although *Nausea* seeks not to have a plot and treats the whole business of plots, stories, recounting and literature as deeply suspect, there is nonetheless a succession of events unavoidably resembling a plot that needs to be summarized if this examination of the novel is to proceed.

Antoine Roquentin, tall and red haired, is a rootless young man with no personal ties. He has returned to France after six years of travelling the world. His travels have left him with nothing but a few vague, unreliable memories. 'But I can't *see* anything any more: however much I search the past I can only retrieve scraps of images and I am not sure what they represent, nor whether they are remembered or invented' (*N*, p. 52). He is for us, as he is for himself, a man more or less without a past, his past being just a few scraps of thought. He does not earn his living and we are not told how he pays for his basic needs including the cheap hotel room in which he lives. He lives very simply with very few possessions and has no interest in acquiring more. He does nothing with his time that might ordinarily be described as constructive apart from write, and he is more or less bored with that. Apart from his vague ideas about one day finishing a book he does not think about the future beyond what he might do later that day or the following day. Unless obliged to do so by the few people he comes into personal contact with, he avoids making plans, and as such he has no future. He knows that the future does not exist, that belief in it, the belief that it will complete us and remove our indeterminacy, is one of many illusions that makes life tolerable for ordinary people. The future, he recognizes, cannot be joined. To 'reach' the future is for it to immediately become the past. As is so often the case, Antoine's ontological revelations foreshadow theories that Sartre went on to explore more formally and thoroughly in *Being and Nothingness* and other works. In *Being and Nothingness*, as part of his exploration of the phenomenon of temporality (*BN*, p. 130–193), Sartre argues that the future can never be reached because to 'reach' the future is to immediately render it past. Hence, he describes the future as a *future-past* and the past as a *past-future*.

Antoine is writing a biography of Adhémar, the Marquis de Rollebon, but eventually abandons the exercise deciding that he is merely trying to distract himself from his own futile existence by attempting to give Rollebon's existence a significance it did not possess. Rollebon is, or was, Antoine's only reason to be in Bouville.

> It is for his sake, for the sake of that little fellow, that I am here. When I returned from my travels, I could just as well have settled in Paris or in Marseille. But most of the documents concerning the Marquis's long stay in France are in the Municipal Library of Bouville. (*N*, p. 25)

Antoine sees the fact that he lives in Bouville because of an obscure French noble who died over a century before as yet another dimension of the contingency and absurdity of his existence.

When he is not writing, Antoine drifts about the town of Bouville – its cafés, streets and parks – anxiously contemplating the loss of all sense of meaning and purpose in his life. He is pursued by 'the nausea', which, to describe it simply for the time being, is an overwhelming and terrifying awareness of the utter contingency and absurdity of existence. When it catches up with him, as it does with increasing frequency and intensity, he experiences what can be described as a 'bad trip' during which he can no longer individuate objects by their function and all sense falls away from the world leaving nothing but infinite, naked, superfluous, nauseating existence. Though the novel makes no reference to mind altering drugs, and Antoine is not on drugs, the nausea undoubtedly echoes Sartre's disturbing, paranoiac experiences with the hallucinogenic drug mescaline with which he was injected under experimental conditions by his friend, Dr Daniel Lagache, in January 1935.[3] I shall return to the nausea in due course and examine it in more detail.

As a person who constantly recognizes that life has no meaning or purpose, Antoine is fascinated by the lies and bad faith by which bourgeois people – the *salauds* (swine or bastards) – seek to give their lives meaning and purpose. Sartre details the personal development of a typical *salaud* in his short story, *The Childhood of a Leader*, written around the same time as *Nausea*. Antoine feels nothing but contempt for the idiotic hat raising and idle chatter people indulge in to pass the time on a Sunday morning along the exclusive Rue Tournebride.

I see hats, a sea of hats. Most of them are black and hard. Now and then you see one fly off at the end of an arm, revealing the soft gleam of a skull; then, after a few moments of clumsy flight, it settles again...'Good morning, Monsieur. Good morning, my dear sir, how are you keeping? Do put your hat on again, Monsieur, you'll catch cold. Thank you, Madame, it isn't very warm, is it?' (*N*, pp. 67–68)

Of course, if life is the utterly meaningless and pointless cosmic accident that Antoine firmly believes it to be then hat raising rituals and idle chitchat are no more absurd than anything else that people do and are as good a way as any to pass the time between a pointless birth and a meaningless death.

Sartre acquired a somewhat prejudiced lifelong hatred of the middle classes during his very middle-class childhood. He consistently despises the bad faith that so characterizes the middle classes, but what, really, is so wrong with bad faith on a mundane level? Bad faith provides a coping strategy, it is a guard rail against the kind of anxiety that makes Antoine's life so wretched. Even Nietzsche, the great champion of authenticity, recognizes in *Beyond Good and Evil*, 'the *narrowing of perspective*, and thus in a certain sense stupidity, as a condition of life and growth' (Nietzsche 2003, 188, p. 112). Sartre would undoubtedly reply to the question, 'What is wrong with bad faith?', by saying that it is unthinking, lazy and life denying, that it oppresses the true, free human spirit, that it is a banal evil central to the hypocrisy and irresponsibility that causes so much trouble and suffering in the world. History, he would say, is characterized by injustice and violence, often the injustice and violence of people who acted in profound bad faith when they made those all too familiar excuses, 'I was only doing my job,' 'I was only following orders.'

Antoine's contempt for the *salauds* reaches its height when he visits Bouville Museum to look at the ostentatious portraits of the respectable, dutiful, now dead elders of the town. He realizes that these portraits are a vain, absurd lie. They portray the elders as taller, grander, wealthier, more significant, more substantial and infinitely less contingent than they were in real life. In having themselves portrayed in this fashion the elders were attempting to convince themselves and others of their necessity and indispensability; that they had a God given place in the universe and society, and above all that they had *rights*. 'Their faces,' writes Murdoch, 'are *éclatant de droit* – blazing with right. Their lives had a real *given* meaning, or so they imagined; and here they are, with all that added sense of necessity with which the painter's thought can endow them' (Murdoch 1968, p. 12). Though dead, there is a sense in which they are still trying to convince the world of their superiority and their entitlements. The portraits give the lie that these people have not really died but merely transcended to an even higher, even more respectable social class. The class of the super-bourgeoisie.

> But for this handsome, impeccable man, now dead, for Jean Pacôme, the son of the Pacôme of the Government of National Defence, it had been an entirely different matter: the beating of his heart and the dull rumblings of his organs reached him in the form of pure and instantaneous little rights. For sixty years, without a moments failing, he had made use of his right to live. These magnificent grey eyes had never been clouded by the slightest doubt. Nor had Pacôme ever made a mistake. (*N*, p. 124)

Roquentin avoids friendships but is nonetheless befriended in the library by Ogier P___ [*sic*], a man he nicknames the Autodidact.

'I for my part live alone, entirely alone. I never speak to anybody, I receive nothing, I give nothing. The Autodidact doesn't count' (*N*, p. 16). The Autodidact is attempting to educate himself in all knowledge autodidactically by working his way through the library catalogue from A to Z. 'It is a revelation; I have understood the Autodidact's method: he is teaching himself in alphabetical order. I contemplate him with a sort of admiration' (*N*, p. 48). The idea of the Autodidact came from a habit Sartre once had. He began recording his ideas alphabetically in an old notebook divided A–Z that he found in a subway. War under W, love under L and so on. This notebook was the start of his factum on contingency. The Autodidact stands for the absurdity of the notion that knowledge is finite and is something that can be acquired and mastered as a totality. His preoccupation with facts, with a reassuring, predictable, scientific view of the world, is a form of wilful ignorance and hence bad faith; a distraction from the harsh existential truths of the human condition that Antoine, for his part, is obsessed with: abandonment in a godless universe, freedom, responsibility, change, lack, indeterminacy, mortality, contingency and so on.[4]

The Autodidact is a humanist and a socialist, a lonely, unattractive, unloved man who rapturously declares his love for all mankind while politely seeking to label Antoine a misanthrope. His generalized love for all people is a desperate attempt to forge a link with them, a pathetic compensation for the fact that nobody cares about him, including Antoine. Antoine finds him physically and intellectually repulsive and flees a meal with him in disgust as he (Antoine) begins to suffer a serious attack of the nausea. 'I glance round the room and a feeling of violent disgust comes over me. What am I doing here? Why did I get mixed up in a discussion about humanism?' (*N*, p. 175). This attack is largely a reaction to the Autodidact's creepy theorizing about his humanism, which is both ridiculous and disturbing.

> One of the first times they locked us in that shed [two hundred prisoners of war] the crush was so great that at first I thought I was going to suffocate, then suddenly a tremendous feeling of joy came over me, and I almost fainted: at that moment I felt I loved those men like brothers, I would have liked to kiss them all. (*N*, p. 165)

Towards the end of the novel, in a powerful scene that is perhaps the dramatic highlight of the book, the Autodidact is exposed as a paedophile when he is caught stroking the hand of a schoolboy in the library.

A brown hairy object approached it [the child's hand] hesitantly. It was a thick finger yellowed by tobacco; beside that hand, it had all the grossness of a male organ. It stopped for a moment, rigid, pointing at the fragile palm, then, all of a sudden, it timidly started stroking it. (N, 234)

It emerges that he has touched little boys in the library before. The Corsican, a bad tempered library attendant whose job it is to keep order, throws him out after punching him in the nose. Antoine, who has watched the whole scene unfold with fascinated horror, unable to prevent its seemingly inevitable progress, takes rare pity on the Autodidact and follows him out of the library after challenging the Corsican for his unnecessary violence. Antoine awkwardly offers to take the Autodidact to a chemist but he begs to be left alone. Antoine allows him to walk away. Exposed and ashamed, the Autodidact's alienation is complete. His dreams of humanism and socialism and a completed education are dashed.

He must be walking about at random, filled with shame and horror, that poor humanist, whom men don't want any more... He was guilty in so small a degree: his humble, contemplative love for little boys is scarcely sensuality – rather a form of humanism. But it was inevitable that one day he should find himself alone again. (N, p. 228)

He is a ruined man who will be haunted for the rest of his life by a single event. 'He walks, he doesn't want to go home: the Corsican is still waiting for him in his room and the woman and the two boys: "Don't try and deny it, I saw you." And the scene would begin again' (N, p. 242).

Despite being a loner who strives to have no interest in the future, Antoine finds himself looking forward to visiting his former lover, Anny, in Paris. '*At the Rendez-vous des Cheminots.* My train leaves in twenty minutes. The gramophone. Strong feeling of adventure' (N, p. 194).

Anny always liked to play the game of 'perfect moments', to create 'privileged situations' (*N*, pp. 204–208). For her a privileged
situation was like the pictures in her childhood copy of Michelet's
History of France. These pictures were rare, only two or three in each
volume. She would anticipate them 50 pages in advance. The scenes
they pictured were privileged for being pictured – only three for the
entire sixteenth century. Beautiful, full of emotion and symbolism,
they froze a moment in history and perfected it. The pictures were
even more special for having a blank reverse side; a whole blank
page in a book of otherwise dense text. Antoine's clumsiness or
some other factor always made it impossible for Anny to turn life's
privileged situations into perfect moments and she often became
angry and frustrated. When she first kissed him on the banks of the
Thames, for example, she was sitting on nettles (*N*, p. 213).

In exploring the theme of perfect moments Sartre is again drawing a distinction between life and literature; life and art. Life is not
Michelet's *History* with its rare, perfect tableaux. A perfect photo-
graph of a sunset does not capture that sunset. The sunset itself was
in constant transition and the person who observed it and photo-
graphed it probably had some physical discomfort or something else
on his mind, if only the thought of what he had to do next. Sartre
argues in *Being and Nothingness* that being-for-itself is constituted
as a lack of being that it has to be and hence cannot be fulfilled. As
the negation of being it must surpass any particular obtained object
of desire towards a further unobtained object of desire. 'Hence the
constant disappointment which accompanies repletion, the famous: "Is it only this?" which is not directed at the concrete pleasure
which satisfaction gives but at the evanescence of the coincidence
with self' (*BN*, p. 126). Sartre concludes that complete satisfaction
is unachievable, that 'Man is a useless passion' (*BN*, p. 636), or, as
he puts it in *Nausea*, 'There are no adventures – there are no perfect
moments' (*N*, p. 213).

From the fact that the complete satisfaction of all desire is
unachievable, Sartre reasons pessimistically that everyone experiences constant disappointment. Is this a reasonable conclusion to
draw? Disappointment is certainly common, with events frequently
failing to live up to expectations, but there are also occasions when
events exceed expectations and satisfaction is achieved. It may be
that there are no perfect moments for people who have sunk to the
level of pessimism and self-absorption of Antoine Roquentin, but

many other less pessimistic and self-absorbed people claim to have experienced at least a few perfect moments in their lives; moments of pure excitement or delight when dissatisfaction was temporarily forgotten. Sartre argues that there are no perfect moments not least because time flies rendering coincidence with self impossible. He sometimes suggests, nonetheless, that the very transience of a moment can perfect it.

> So there, at one and the same time, you had that fence which smells so strongly of wet wood, that lantern, and that little blonde in the Negro's arms, under a fiery-coloured sky...the whole scene came alive for me with a significance which was strong and even fierce, but pure. Then it broke up, and nothing remained but the lantern, the fence, and the sky: it was still quite beautiful. An hour later, the lantern was lit, the wind was blowing, the sky was dark: nothing at all was left. (*N*, p. 18)

What does it mean to say that a person is satisfied? Does a person have to temporarily lose awareness of himself in order to achieve true satisfaction? Whatever the answers to these questions, it seems reasonable to claim that for many the experience of dissatisfaction is not as intense or as constant as Sartre, or at least Antoine, suggests. A person may discover on reflection that he is a 'useless passion' (*BN*, p. 636), but he does not always feel he is. Or is the opposite the case? A person feels he is a useless passion moment by moment, but on reflection he convinces himself he is not; that he was not. Sartre favours the latter view when he argues that common place events are transformed into adventures simply by recounting them. Perhaps the moment in the street described above was not perfect when it took place. It was not pure; recounting it purified it. Perhaps, despite his efforts to avoid it, Antoine is being nostalgic, forgetting that at the time he had cares that infected the moment with imperfection.

The scene in which Antoine and Anny meet is less manic than much of the rest of the novel. It is touching for its honesty and realism. Its very avoidance of cheap sentimentality gives it the sad, romantic quality of a *brief encounter*. Any intelligent person who has ever met with a former lover after a long absence would surely identify with this scene at some level. When they meet it is, at least in some respects, as though the four years since they last met had suddenly vanished. 'Yet in spite of everything it's her all right, it's Anny' (*N*, p. 195). Her mannerisms have not changed and she raises old grievances, as she always did, as though they had only arisen yesterday. She looks older, fatter, but she is still beautiful to him and he soon re-discovers his love for her. 'She has taken possession of me again, I have plunged back into her strange world, beyond absurdity, affectation, subtlety. I have even rediscovered that little fever which always took hold of me when I was with her, and that bitter taste at the back of my mouth' (*N*, p. 206).

It emerges that the reason she wrote asking to see Antoine is to tell him she has given up playing the game of perfect moments. 'I have a sort of – physical certainty. I can feel that there are no perfect moments' (*N*, p. 205). Antoine is astounded. In abandoning what was her fundamental project in life Anny claims she is outliving herself. 'She says only a single phrase: "I am outliving myself"' (*N*, p. 206). In no longer playing the game of perfect moments she has become more like Antoine, although, as he never played the game in the first place, except for her sake, he does not share her despair. 'I don't feel the same despair as she does, because I never expected very much. I am rather – astonished at this life which is given to me – given for *nothing*' (*N*, p. 216).

Antoine discovers that they have developed a similar attitude to life generally. '...we have lost the same illusions, we have followed the same paths' (*N*, pp. 213–214). Anny even suggests that she experiences something akin to the nausea.

'It isn't good for me either to stare at things too long. I look at them to find out what they are, then I have to turn my eyes quickly away.'
'But why?'
'They disgust me.'
I could swear – In any case there are certain similarities. (*N*, p. 207)

Anny repeats that she has outlived herself but Antoine can offer her no hope, no new reasons for living. Still in love they part company, perhaps for ever, realizing that nothing would be achieved by remaining together, that there is nothing they can do to help one another. The following day Antoine wonders around Paris in a 'highly nervous condition' (*N*, p. 220) thinking about Anny, thinking that their brief encounter will not slip into the past until her train leaves. He goes to the station and watches her depart for Dieppe and England with the wealthy man who keeps her. Just before her departure she sees him. They look at one another without expression but not without understanding that neither will ever attempt to cross the gulf of circumstances that separates them.

Back in Bouville, Antoine thinks:

> I am free: I haven't a single reason for living left, all the ones I have tried have given way and I can't imagine any more. I am still quite young, I still have enough strength to start again. But what must I start again? Only now do I realise how much, in the midst of my greatest terror and nauseas, I had counted on Anny to save me. My past is dead, Monsieur de Rollebon is dead, Anny came back only to take all hope away from me. I am alone in this white street lined with gardens. Alone and free. But this freedom is rather like death. (*N*, p. 223)

The existentialist playwright and novelist Samuel Beckett once wrote, 'I can't go on. I'll go on' (Beckett 2005, p. 418). Unless a person chooses to commit suicide he has no choice but to go on. To 'give up', whatever that means, is still a choice and however low a person sinks financially, socially, emotionally and philosophically, he still has to live with himself as a being perpetually obliged to choose his responses, a being unable to be anything in the mode of being it. This is the harsh existential truth at the heart of Sartre's conception of freedom, what he means when he says, 'I am condemned to be free' (*BN*, p. 462).

Antoine is in despair, but as much as he'd like to he cannot lose himself in despair so as to cease being a free consciousness of it. Antoine, like all people, is such a useless passion that he must despair even of becoming, as a last desperate means of escaping his free transcendence, a being in despair in the mode of being what he is. Sartre's position here echoes that of Søren Kierkegaard. In *The Sickness unto Death*, Kierkegaard considers a girl who despairs over the loss of her beloved: 'Just try now, just try saying to such a girl, "You are consuming yourself," and you will hear her answer, "O, but the torment is simply that I cannot do that"' (Kierkegaard 1989, p. 50). Like Antoine, the girl has to be herself as despairing rather than escape herself by having herself consumed by despair.

Both characters despair of being at one with their despair as a means of escaping their consciousness of despair.

Antoine cannot not move on in life and *Nausea* ends on a relatively optimistic note with him deciding to leave Bouville and write a novel. He does not think that writing a novel will distract him from his existence, as he hoped writing the biography of Rollebon would, but he hopes that once it is written he will be able to look back on writing it and that it will at least give some meaning and purpose to his past. Antoine's reasons for deciding to write – to give some shape, dignity and relative purpose to his life – are similar to Sartre's own reasons for deciding to write considered in Chapter 1.

> A book. Naturally, at first it would only be a tedious, tiring job, it wouldn't prevent me from existing or from feeling that I exist. But a time would have to come when the book would be written, would be behind me, and I think that a little of its light would fall over my past. Then, through it, I might be able to recall my life without repugnance. (*N*, p. 252)

The manuscript that the publishers Gallimard finally accepted on 30 April 1937 had the title *Melancholia*. The title was inspired by *Melencolia*, the famous sixteenth-century engraving by Albrecht Dürer picturing two inactive, dejected, winged figures and a sleeping dog surrounded by neglected tools and occupations. It was Gaston Gallimard himself, the founder of the publishing house, who rejected the title *Melancholia* in favour of *Nausea*. *Melancholia* was an apt title in many ways as melancholia – a mental state characterized by depression and irrational fears – is a pretty good description of Antoine Roquentin's psychological state. From the point of view of a psychiatrist, Antoine certainly exhibits some of the symptoms of psychosis, but to simply label him as psychotic or insane would be to dismiss the validity of his world-view as it is presented in the novel. It can be argued that far from being insane, Antoine is all too lucid. He is without the illusions and pretences, the vanities and pretensions, the dreams and false hopes that the vast majority of people require to make life tolerable. He has drunk the cup of truth to its last bitter dregs and from the alienated perspective he chooses he sees existence and the human condition for what they ultimately are: contingent, meaningless, pointless and absurd. Certainly, Antoine does not consider himself insane. When he reflects on how the world now strikes him compared with how it used to strike him before the days of the nausea, he is pretty sure it is the *world* revealing itself to him in a new way that is responsible for the change rather than any shift in his perception of it.

The odd thing is that I am not at all prepared to consider myself insane, and indeed I can see quite clearly that I am not: all these changes concern objects. At least, that is what I'd like to be sure about. (*N*, p. 10)

As the novel progresses, Antoine becomes increasingly suspicious of the distinction that is drawn between the world and ones perception of it. He realizes, and this is a feature of the nausea, that there is really no dualistic distinction between himself and the world. His body is an absurd, vegetable-like or crustacean-like object in that world and his consciousness is nothing but consciousness of a world that is utterly bizarre and surreal when seen for what it is apart from the human projects that give it a thin veneer of relative meanings. Later on, in *Being and Nothingness*, echoing the theory of intentionality of Brentano and Husserl, Sartre argues that consciousness *is* consciousness of___. 'All consciousness is consciousness of something' (*BN*, p. 16). He makes essentially the same point in *Nausea*, all be it in a far more dramatic way. He is concerned to show that the nausea, what was described earlier simply as Antoine's overwhelming and terrifying awareness of the utter contingency and absurdity of existence, is not simply a state of mind but the world itself.

His blue cotton shirt stands out cheerfully against a chocolate-coloured wall. That too brings on the Nausea. Or rather it *is* the Nausea. The Nausea isn't inside me: I can feel it *over there* on the wall, on the braces, everywhere around me. It is one with the café, it is I who am inside *it*. (*N*, p. 35)

It can be said that the nausea is Antoine's nauseated consciousness as a *relationship* to a world that is nauseating. The nausea is all pervasive. It seeps through all divisions imposed by human practices. It occurs when the apparent distinction between subject and object breaks down and consciousness loses itself in a world where objects cease to have the relative meanings ascribed to them by their label and/or their function. It is a suspension of the capacity, or at least the will, to recognize the relative purposes of human activities and artefacts. 'This huge belly turns upwards, bleeding, puffed up – bloated with all its dead paws, this belly floating in this box, in this grey sky, is not a seat... Things have broken free from their names. They are there, grotesque, stubborn, gigantic, and it seems ridiculous to call them seats or say anything at all about them' (*N*, p. 180).

The nausea is an awareness of contingency, or better, a sense of *absorption* in contingency. The notion of contingency is central to the philosophical vision of the novel; a novel that, as noted, began life as Sartre's factum on contingency. Contingency is a hugely significant theme in *Nausea* and in Sartre philosophy generally, a fact that is too often overlooked. What exactly is contingency as Sartre understands it?

Contingency is the state of being contingent, unnecessary and accidental. That which is contingent is not logically necessary, it need not be or be so. For Sartre, contingency is a fundamental ontological feature of existence. In *Being and Nothingness* Sartre argues that although being-in-itself is uncreated and not dependent on anything else for its being, its being is not necessary. As that which exists without reason for being, being-in-itself cannot be derived from a necessary law. As that which has no determinants or characteristics, being-in-itself cannot have the characteristic of being that which cannot not be. Being-in-itself *is*, but it is unnecessary, and in being unnecessary it is contingent. For Sartre, being-in-itself is contingent in the sense of being absurdly superfluous. Being-in-itself exists for no reason and for no purpose.

> ... being is superfluous (*de trop*)... consciousness absolutely can not derive being from anything, either from another being or from a possibility, or from a necessary law. Uncreated, without reason for being, without any connection with another being, being-in-itself is *de trop* for eternity. (*BN*, p. 22)

The terrifying apprehension of being submerged in an existence that is absurd, pointless, superfluous and contingent that Sartre labels 'the nausea', belongs to a consciousness that has no being of its own and exists only as a *relation* to this contingent existence – a relation by negation. For a person to suffer the nausea is for him to experience a state of naked, superfluous existence that not only surrounds him but with which he is continuous by virtue of his body. Human society, most human endeavour, aims to overcome contingency by imposing meanings and purposes on the world. This is achieved largely by naming and categorizing things. In naming something people believe they have made sense of it, ascribed meaning to it, grasped its essential essence, removed the contingency of its raw, nameless existence. But the truth, according to Sartre, is that things only have meaning and purpose relative to other things – words immediately link a thing to other things through language – and the whole only has the relative meaning and purpose that our ultimately pointless activities give it. Seen for what they are in themselves, apart from the system of instrumentality that defines them or the framework of meaning that explains and justifies them, objects are incomprehensible, peculiar, strange, even disturbing in their contingency. 'Words had disappeared, and with them the meaning of things, the method of using them, the feeble landmarks which men have traced on their surface' (*N*, p. 182).

Contingency for Sartre is mysterious and to be aware of contingency is to be aware of the unfathomable mystery of being. When the nausea hits divisions melt away and the unmysterious, functional particularity of things is lost. It is, therefore, the unfathomable existence of the world *as such* that is apprehended as mysterious by Antoine's nauseated consciousness rather than any particular phenomenon in it.

And then, all of a sudden, there it was, as clear as day: existence had suddenly unveiled itself. It had lost its harmless appearance as an abstract category: it was the very stuff of things, that root was steeped in existence. (*N*, p. 183)

In so far as any particular phenomenon, a tree for example, is identified by the nauseated consciousness it is grasped only as an indicator of the whole, as implying the whole, as continuous with the whole, as drowning in the whole and so on.

Or rather the root, the park gates, the bench, the sparse grass on the lawn, all that had vanished; the diversity of things, their individuality, was only an appearance, a veneer. This veneer had melted, leaving soft, monstrous masses, in disorder – naked, with a frightening, obscene nakedness. (*N*, p. 183)

The nausea is a grasping of the contingent existence of the world as an utterly mysterious whole; as mystical. Ultimately, it is not how things are that Antoine finds strange and mysterious; his awareness of the strangeness of objects is only a step towards a deeper revelation. It is the very being, the very *isness* of existence that he finds strange and mysterious. A concise line from Wittgenstein summarizes all this very well: 'It is not *how* things are in the world that is mystical, but *that* it exists' (Wittgenstein 2001, prop. 6.44, p. 73).

Sartre's challenge as a philosopher expounding an ontological theory of contingency is to use language to try to convey a sense of a world stripped of language and meaning. He clearly feels that literature, with its scope for description, its levels of irony, its capacity to convey ideas through action, atmosphere and streams of consciousness, is often more effective than straightforward philosophy at achieving this difficult feat. This is undoubtedly the main reason why his major work on contingency is presented as a novel, as a convincing descriptive narrative, rather than as a theory maintained in argument.

Sartre is not recommending that people should be like Antoine, dwelling obsessively on contingency and striving to live always under the aspect of eternity in a meaningless and absurd world. That way lies madness. Sartre himself, like most people most of the time, lived and acted very much in the world of relative meanings and purposes. Like most people most of the time, he kept his sanity and sense of perspective by directing his attentions to the task in hand, to the daily round and so on. Nonetheless, he clearly held that an occasional or background awareness of contingency is vital if a person is to achieve any degree of authenticity and to avoid living a lie. Sartre's philosophy is characterized by an abiding hatred and distrust of people (typically bourgeois) who seem totally unaware of life's contingency; people who, having once glimpsed life's contingency and been terrified by it, are fleeing from it. The fundamental project of such people is to evade their own contingency and that of the world by acting in bad faith. The world, they tell themselves, is not contingent but created with humankind as its centrepiece. They assume that they have an immortal essence, that their existence is inevitable and that they exist by divine decree rather than by accident. They believe that the moral and social values to which they subscribe are objective, absolute and unquestionable. Society as it is, as that which, in their view, is grounded in these absolute values, is seen by them to constitute the only possible reality. Like the *salauds* caricatured in the Bouville Museum, all they have to do to claim their absolute right to be respected by others and to have the respect of others sustain the illusion of their necessity is to dutifully fulfil the role prescribed to them by society or religion and identify themselves totally with that role. That is, identify themselves with the image of themselves they have fabricated in the minds of other people. By considering their being-for-itself as entirely a being-for-others they evade the anxiety of *having* to be themselves as free and indeterminate.

Great novels move a reader to empathize with their central character regardless of his or her personal and moral worth. Most readers of *Nausea* tend to admire Antoine Roquentin for having the honesty to recognize his limitlessly free and utterly superfluous existence in a meaningless and godless universe and, above all, for confronting the fact that there is nothing he was, is or will ever be in the mode of being it. It is widely held that Roquentin is a supremely authentic existentialist hero attempting to live his life free from bad faith in accordance with the existential truths of the human condition. However, it can be argued that Roquentin is not authentic but actually inauthentic and deluded. Arguably, he is attempting to *be* his own nothingness in a last desperate attempt to escape the indeterminacy of his being and as such has fallen into the most desperate project of bad faith – the faith of nihilism. In *The Ethics of Ambiguity*, Simone de Beauvoir compares the nihilist with the serious, *salaud*-type person who seeks to annihilate his subjectivity by treating himself as an object defined by social norms.

> The failure of the serious sometimes brings about a radical disorder. Conscious of being unable to be anything, man then decides to be nothing. We shall call this attitude nihilistic. The nihilist is close to the spirit of seriousness, for instead of realising his negativity as a living movement, he conceives his annihilation in a substantial way. He wants to *be* nothing, and this nothing that he dreams of is still another sort of being. (de Beauvoir 2000, p. 52)

Arguably, a genuinely authentic person realizes that although there is nothing that he is in the mode of being it, he must continually make himself be what he is by suspending disbelief in himself and playing a role to the best of his ability. Antoine is unable to play a role, to act upon the world in a concerted manner, because he has lost faith in his own performance of himself. Unable to make-believe he is anything at all he has come to the false belief that he is nothing at all, a non-being-in-itself. The striving to be a non-being-in-itself is at one with the impossible striving to be what Sartre refers to as a being-for-itself-in-itself. This, at least, seems to be true of Antoine as he is for most of the novel, during his deepest periods of melancholia and pessimism. By the end of the novel it seems he has undertaken to play some sort of coherent role, to undertake a creative project that will define him somewhat by seeing that pro-ject through to completion.

Rivalled only by Camus' *The Stranger,* which it inspired, *Nausea* has achieved cult status as the archetypal existentialist novel. Its central themes of contingency, absurdity, anxiety and alienation have become synonymous with existentialism in the popular con-sciousness, even if properly understood existentialism is a far more optimistic and constructive philosophy than *Nausea* suggests. As said, *Nausea* is a truly philosophical novel in its penetrating ques-tioning of the nature of existence, temporality and self-identity, but it is not, in the final analysis, a full-blow treatise on the philosophy of existentialism. Essentially, it is a witty, darkly comical, poetical, incisive, thought-provoking, poignant and unrelentingly disturbing exploration of extreme nihilism. '. . . its power resides in its charac-ter as a philosophical myth, which shows us in a memorable way the master-image of Sartre's thinking' (Murdoch 1968, p. 14). This book really will change the way you think and feel about your life, although possibly not for the better. A work of true genius.

ROADS TO FREEDOM TRILOGY

Roads to Freedom, published from 1945 to 1949, is a trilogy of novels set before and during World War II. The trilogy includes *The Age of Reason* (1945), *The Reprieve* (1945) and *Iron in the Soul* (1949). Sartre also wrote two chapters of a fourth volume titled *The Last Chance* before finally abandoning the project.

The period from 1938–39 saw Sartre immersed in the bohemian life of the Parisian avant-garde, flushed with the success of *Nausea* and *The Wall.* He had worked hard and waited a long time to reach this happy situation, but it was not to last. On 1 September

1939 Germany invaded Poland and Sartre was mobilized along with thousands of other reservists. He was assigned to a meteorological unit in charge of weather balloons and sent to Alsace, Northern France, near the German border. For the following eight months French and German troops faced each other from their entrenched positions along a frontier of several hundred kilometres. The Germans were busy elsewhere and except for the occasional exchange of artillery all was quiet. This stand-off came to be known as the 'phoney war'.

Sartre did not bemoan his fate but instead took advantage of the huge amount of free time he had to plunge into a creative frenzy. Apart from the vast outpouring of words that is his *War Diaries* and the countless letters to his mother and his lovers, he began simultaneously to draft *Being and Nothingness* and his second novel, *The Age of Reason*. The novel grew alongside *Being and Nothingness* for several years and echoes many of its central themes, particularly the themes of freedom, responsibility and being-for-others. Sartre considers his plans for the novel in his *War Diaries*, discussing his characters as though they are the Parisian friends they are certainly based on. Sartre continued drafting the novel after he was taken prisoner by the Germans in June 1940. In March 1941 he obtained his release with the aid of a false medical certificate declaring him unfit for military service. He returned to Paris and by the summer of 1941 the novel was finished and shelved until Paris was liberated and "such a scandalous thing" (de Beauvoir 2001, p. 410) could be published.

It was not to the war that Sartre turned for inspiration for the first volume of his trilogy, but to prewar Paris of the summer of 1938. His sudden departure from his Parisian life led him to evaluate it. Writing about prewar Paris in a wartime weather station in Northern France was not, however, an act of escapism or nostalgia. Unlike many novels of the period, *The Age of Reason* is not nostalgic about the years between the wars. Rather it casts a detached and objective eye on a group of largely pathetic, emotionally immature characters who are too self-absorbed to really notice or care about the gathering clouds of war that will soon change their narrow little lives beyond recognition. With the coming of war Sartre began to change from a thinker preoccupied with the personal into a very political animal. *The Age of Reason* reflects, indeed constitutes, the first stage of this transition; a transition that, over the length of the trilogy, takes its central character, Mathieu Delarue, from scrounging for the price of an abortion in Paris to shooting suicidally at advancing Germans from a church tower in rural France. Politics remains peripheral even by the close of *The Age of Reason*, but importantly by the close Mathieu has dispensed with the personal. He has narrowly avoided succumbing to marriage and fatherhood and has nothing left but his freedom. Although he does not yet know it, he is ready for the approaching war, for total commitment.

The Reprieve was written while the Germans occupied Paris. Started in 1942 it was completed in November 1944, three months after the city was liberated by Allied forces. Set in the autumn of 1938, about three months after the imaginary situation of *The Age of Reason* ends, it covers the eight days from 23 to 30 September leading up to the controversial Munich Agreement that gained Europe a temporary reprieve from war at the cost of appeasing Hitler and abandoning Czechoslovakia to Nazi tyranny. With *The Reprieve* politics and history enter the trilogy with a vengeance, although events are not unfolded in the form of an abstract historical account but via myriad personal perspectives. These personal perspectives are often those of characters first introduced in the previous volume.

The Age of Reason and *The Reprieve* were published together in September 1945, the month after the atomic bombing of Japan finally ended World War II. Sartre was by now France's leading intellectual voice, and the novels, not least because they defined a critical period in French history, were received with great enthusiasm by the French public.

It was four years before the third volume of the trilogy appeared, four years before readers could discover the fate of Mathieu Delarue, whose military service commenced at the end of the previous volume. *Iron in the Soul* (alternative title, *Troubled Sleep*) is set in June 1940, 21 months after the events of *The Reprieve*. The central historical theme of the novel is the defeat of France by the Germans, and certainly a major source of inspiration for the novel was Sartre's capture and imprisonment by German forces in June 1940. The capitulation of French forces, the POW camp and the all-too-human behaviour of the ordinary prisoners are described with the realistic detail of a first-hand account.

Of utmost importance as regards the political journey made by the trilogy, it is not the individualistic Mathieu who enters the POW camp – Mathieu has chosen his own dark destiny earlier in the story – but the communist Brunet. It is largely through Brunet's uncompromising Marxist gaze that we view the situation and the men caught up in it. Brunet sees the game of French captives and German captors as another symptom of the evils of capitalism and nationalism, evils that will continue when this particular war is over unless ordinary people of whatever nationality can win the class struggle. Brunet is admirable in seeing a POW camp as a good a place as any to foment a communist revolution. The first difficulty, however, is overcoming the weakness, cowardice and bad faith that most of the prisoners like to wallow in. Sartre is well aware of this difficulty and makes it Brunet's most constant source of frustration. *Roads to Freedom* as a whole nonetheless asserts Sartre's deeply held belief that there is no such thing as a fixed human nature, that with effort people can change for the better and fight to claim their personal and political freedom. As he writes in *Existentialism and Humanism*:

> One of the charges most often laid against the *Roads to Freedom* is something like this – 'But, after all, these people being so base, how can you make them into heroes?' The objection is really rather comic, for it implies that people are born heroes: and that is, at bottom, what such people would like to think. If you are born cowards, you can be quite content, you can do nothing about it and you will be cowards all your lives whatever you do; and if you are born heroes you can again be quite content; you will be heroes all your lives, eating and drinking heroically. Whereas the existentialist says that the coward makes himself cowardly, the hero makes himself heroic; and that there is always a possibility for the coward to give up cowardice and for the hero to stop being a hero. (*EAH*, p. 43)

Inspired to action by the momentous events of World War II Sartre dedicated his energies to the Marxist-existentialist[5] struggle for personal and political freedom for the rest of his career.

The Age of Reason

Set in Paris in June 1938, *The Age of Reason* tells the story of two days in the life of Mathieu Delarue, an unmarried philosophy professor in his mid-30s. Mathieu is somewhat based on Sartre: they were both born in Paris in 1905 and have the same profession. With few demands placed on him by his teaching job, especially now that term is over, Mathieu pursues a life free from serious commitment or responsibility, frequenting bars and cafés with his friends and students.

Although Mathieu repeatedly expresses a vague hankering to go and fight in the Spanish Civil War like his friend, Gomez, politics and the gathering clouds of war are as yet peripheral concerns. Mathieu has left-wing sympathies on an intellectual level, but he refuses to join the Communist Party when invited to do so by his one-time close friend, Brunet. Brunet warns ' "We shall be at war in September" ' (*AR*, p. 119) and declares that it is time for Mathieu to give up his empty notions of freedom and commit himself to a political cause. ' "...you are free. But what's the use of that same freedom, if not to join us?" ' (*AR*, p. 118). With the notable exceptions of Brunet and Gomez, Mathieu and his friends are primarily interested in themselves and each other and in their personal problems and anxieties.

Currently obsessed with Mathieu is a handsome young student, Boris Serguine, who, much to Boris' annoyance, is sarcastically referred to by Brunet and others as Mathieu's latest disciple. Boris is in the habit of saying and doing puerile things to try and impress Mathieu. He shows off a clasp-knife in a night club and shoplifts as 'a test of character' (*AR*, p. 140), though his main motive is to boast about the ordeal afterwards. Like many young men in Sartre's fiction, Boris lacks gravitas. He wants to be more substantial than he is and to command more respect than he does. He is in a stormy relationship with Lola Montero, an ageing but still attractive night club singer with a heroin addiction. Lola is besotted with Boris and very insecure about his feelings for her. She constantly asks Boris what he is thinking and demands assurances from him that never satisfy her. Boris desires her sexually when aroused but has no real affection or regard for her. In one rather farcical scene he is quite relieved, or at least quite resigned to the fact, when he mistakenly believes Lola has died of an overdose. Boris is not unpleasant company and Mathieu tolerates him, but his main motivation for associating with Boris is his infatuation with Boris' petulant, impulsive, self-obsessed sister, Ivich Serguine.[6]

Ivich is tantalizingly sensual yet frigid and often repeats that she does not like to be touched. Like Lulu Crispin in Sartre short story,

Intimacy, she has lesbian tendencies that she will not acknowledge with any real seriousness. Ivich does not reciprocate Mathieu's feelings. She does not, for example, miss him when he is absent as he misses her – he is not an *existential absence* for her – and she resents his attempts to win her affections and gratitude. Ivich is mentally unfocused and doomed to be 'ploughed' in her exams, a failure that will force her to return to a life of boredom at her parents' home in the provinces. Young, impractical and disorganized she is incapable of supporting herself in Paris. When she inevitably fails her exams, Mathieu, terrified that he will not see her again, frantically searches Paris until he finds her. He offers to keep her in the city by taking on extra work. 'She will accept, I shan't let her go before she accepts. I – I'll give private lessons, or correct proofs' (*AR*, p. 253). She grudgingly accepts his offer, at least temporarily, when Mathieu all but begs her to stay with the plea, ' "I can't endure the idea of not seeing you again" ' (*AR*, p. 254). His plan soon falls through when Ivich discovers what she describes as the 'sordid' (*AR*, p. 258) situation that Mathieu is currently involved in with his long-time girlfriend, Marcelle Duffet. Ivich departs, without 'a flicker of affection' (*AR*, p. 284) expressing the hope that she will be able to return to Paris next academic year.

Ivich is such a brilliantly drawn character that it is easy to share Mathieu's passion for her or at least to identify with it, while at the same time, like Mathieu, recognizing that she is sullen, self-centred, mean-spirited and lacking in any real virtues. We identify with Mathieu's infatuation with Ivich because infatuations with such people are so common. Mathieu's love for Ivich is essentially the desire to be loved by her. Sartre's view of romantic love generally is that it is always the desire to *be* loved. Mathieu wants Ivich to remain the absolute free spirit that she is – a free spirit that is revealed to him through her self-obsession, her lack of empathy, her cruelty – yet for that cruelly free spirit to *choose* to love him among all others. The love of such a cruel, evasive, difficult to possess creature is held to be of great value precisely because a person must be very special if they are chosen from among all others to receive it. Of course, if Ivich loved Mathieu he would possess her and she would thereby cease to be the evasive free spirit that so fascinates him. In a remarkable chapter of *Being and Nothingness* titled 'Concrete Relations with Others' (*BN*, pp. 383–452) Sartre explores in philosophical detail the complex phenomenon of romantic love and the reasons why the ideal of such love, unity with the other, is doomed to failure. Mathieu's unrequited love for Ivich serves as a concrete example for several of the dimensions of romantic love that Sartre explores in that chapter.

For seven years Mathieu has been involved in a relationship with Marcelle. Marcelle is intelligent and physically attractive, but passive, lazy and rather boring. She is quite the opposite of Ivich who is animated, restless and, at least as far as Mathieu is concerned, exciting. Marcelle tires easily and never goes out. She spends most of her time in a pink, stuffy, slightly smelly room at her mother's house. Mathieu is fond of Marcelle and is still sexually attracted to her, but he has no real passion for her. When she tells him she is pregnant he can think only of the threat to his profligate lifestyle, free from bourgeois expectations and constraints. They immediately agree, without any discussion, that she must have an abortion.

'There, now you know what's the matter,' said Marcelle. 'And what's to be done?'
'Well – I suppose one gets rid of it, eh?'
'Right. I've got an address,' said Marcelle. (*AR*, p. 15)

Inside, however, Marcelle is upset that Mathieu does not ask her how she feels about the situation. When she reflects later that the foetus inside her is to be killed she realizes that she wants to keep it after all, partly because if it is born there will be at least one person in the world who needs her. 'But she could not refrain from passing a hand over her belly, thinking: "It is there." Something living and unlucky, like herself. An absurd superfluous life, just like her own – Then she thought vehemently: "He would have been *mine*"' (*AR*, 70). She is strengthened in her resolve to keep the baby by her 'Archangel'; the suave homosexual, Daniel Sereno, another one-time close friend of Mathieu's who has for some time been paying regular visits to Marcelle without Mathieu knowing. Marcelle is only a distraction for Daniel, another one of his spiteful games. He is too filled with self-loathing to have any real affection for her, or for anyone save his cats – and he even tries to force himself to drown *them* at one point! In fact, he finds Marcelle and her pink room rather disgusting. 'Marcelle was just a solid, dreary smell, deposited on the bed; a huddle of flesh that would disintegrate at the slightest movement' (*AR*, pp 152–153). His only motivation for wanting Marcelle to keep the baby is to make Mathieu a husband and a father and thereby ruin his life.

It seems to be something of a prejudice on Sartre's part that having a baby is just about the worst thing that can happen to anyone. Nowhere in the novel are children spoken of with any positive regard. Marcelle's foetus is variously described as a tumour, a pustule, a blister, 'a little, vitreous tide within her... opening out among all the muck inside her belly' (*AR*, p. 20). Such are Sartre's thoughts, or at least those of his alter ego, Mathieu. When Mathieu meets a friend's little boy, far from being moved by the joys of an expectant father, he thinks:

> Pablo's expression was not yet human, and yet it was already more than alive: the little creature had not long emerged from a womb, as indeed was plain: there he was, hesitant, minute, still displaying the unwholesome sheen of vomit: but behind the flickering humours that filled his eye-sockets, lurked a greedy little consciousness... in a pink room, within a female body, there was a blister, growing slowly larger. (*AR*, pp. 43–44).

Interestingly, Sartre's general position appears to be that it is an act of bad faith to have children. To have children is to choose to be determined by the domestic circumstances child rearing demands rather than a choice to positively affirm one's own freedom. This seems an absurd view given that reproducing is so widespread and necessary, so natural, but there appears to be some truth in it when the motives for having children of at least some people are scrutinized. That mankind, including existentialists, would soon become extinct if nobody reproduced, does not mean that having children is never an act of bad faith. Certainly, some people have children in order to live for others rather than for themselves, in order to give themselves a ready made destiny, in order to avoid the effort required to pursue their own *genuine* creativity and so on. Children can be a convenient, guilt-free means by which people give up on themselves. All that can be expected of people with children, burdened as they are, is that they raise their children well, and often the self-thwarted ambitions of parents who have chosen to live vicariously are made to be the responsibility of their offspring. It seems fair to say that Sartre never really gives the role of children in the world the same kind of serious consideration he gives other human matters. Children, and the reasons or lack of reasons that people have for having them, belong too much to human biology, to the *natural self* that his most able contemporary critic, Maurice Merleau-Ponty, accuses him of ignoring in his quest to advance his theory of radical freedom.[7]

Now that Marcelle is pregnant Mathieu will no longer be able to maintain his liberty through a project of non-commitment and avoidance of serious choices. If he does not act decisively to preserve his independence, his usual avoidance of serious choices will see him conform to bourgeois norms as he drifts into parenthood and marriage with Marcelle. He doggedly sets about raising 4,000 francs for a safe abortion.

Though he loathes doing so, desperation drives Mathieu to ask his wealthy elder bother, Jacques, to lend him the money. Jacques is a lawyer and not the decent sort of person who will lend a brother money without asking too many questions. Instead, he is sanctimonious and judgemental. When he finds out what the money is for he cannot resist lecturing Mathieu about his responsibilities. There is some truth in what Jacques says about the way Mathieu lives his life, but he speaks with such assumed moral superiority in his advocacy of social conformity that he is detestable. Jacques is a typical bourgeois *salaud* (swine or bastard) reminiscent of those *salauds* described in *Nausea* and definitely the least sympathetic character in the novel. True to form, Sartre saves his strongest venom for his pet hate, the wealthy bourgeois, although it is out of his own mouth that Jacques reveals what a prejudiced, self-righteous, conservative coward he really is. He is a coward not least because he fears that lending money for an illegal abortion could involve him in a scandal. Speaking with the steady, deliberating tones of a lawyer he argues that Mathieu's relationship with Marcelle is like a marriage but without any of the responsibilities. He insists that now Mathieu is in his mid-30s he has reached, or should have reached, the age of reason, the age when a man must stop playing the bohemian and face up to his moral and social responsibilities, the age when it is his duty to marry, settle down, conform, sell out.

'…your youth has gone, and the bohemian life doesn't suit you at all. Besides, what is bohemianism, after all? It was amusing enough a hundred years ago, but today it is simply a name for a handful of eccentrics who are no danger to anybody, and have missed the train. You have attained the age of reason, Mathieu, you have attained the age of reason, or you ought to have done so,' he repeated with an abstracted air. (*AR*, p. 108)

Mathieu is literally invited to sell out by Jacques who refuses him the 4,000 francs he wants for the abortion but offers him 10,000 francs to marry Marcelle and keep the baby. Mathieu rejects Jacques' age of reason along with his cash offer, saying, ' "Your age of reason is the age of resignation, and I've no use for it" ' (*AR*, p. 108). Mathieu intends to define the age of reason differently, as the age when he asserts his freedom and refuses to conform. Mathieu leaves with his pride intact, regretting only that he forgot to say goodbye to Jacques' charming wife, Odette.

Mathieu is also refused the money by Daniel Sereno. Daniel can easily afford to give Mathieu the cash but refuses to do so because he secretly despises him and wants to destroy his freedom by obliging him to marry Marcelle. Daniel's hatred of Mathieu, although complex, is without any real basis. He resents the selfish way Mathieu treats Marcelle, even though he himself only patronizes her. He is envious of Mathieu for not being a homosexual and for being, as he imagines, so smug and secure in his sense of himself. He sees Mathieu as self-satisfied in his irresponsibility and his enjoyment of his freedom. Above all, Daniel is paranoid and in his homosexual self-loathing he misinterprets the attitude of others towards him. He imagines that Mathieu discusses him behind his back, not least with silly young students like Boris. When Boris declines to go for a drink with him, not because he dislikes him but because he is busy trying to steal a book, Daniel thinks:

Oh, I understand, I wasn't going to lay a hand on you, I am not worthy: and the look he flung at me when I told him I didn't understand philosophy, he wasn't even taking the trouble to be polite towards the end...I am sure he [Mathieu] puts them on their guard against me. 'Well, well' said Daniel, with a complacent laugh: 'It's an excellent lesson and a cheap one, too, I'm glad he packed me off: if I had been crazy enough to take a little interest in him, and talk to him confidentially, he would have promptly reported it all to Mathieu for both of them to gloat over.' ... 'He has discussed me with him!' That was an in-tol-er-able notion, enough to make a man sweat with fury... (*AR*, p. 148)

Like many of the characters in the novel – Lola with Boris, Boris with Mathieu, Mathieu with Marcelle and Ivich – Daniel suffers his being-for-others. He hates to think that there is a part of himself that Mathieu possess and passes judgement on without him being able to do much about it. In the philosophical terms of *Being and Nothingness*, Daniel hates to have his free transcendence transcended by the free transcendence of the Other; he cannot bear to be a transcendence-transcended. The judgement of others reduces him to a being-in-the-midst-of-the-world, to a mere object; it enslaves his freedom. 'In so far as I am the object of values which come to qualify me without my being able to act on this qualification or even to know it, I am enslaved' (*BN*, p. 291).

Most of the central characters in the novel suffer this sense of enslavement to the opinion of others to a lesser or greater extent. Mathieu, for example, feels enslaved by Marcelle when he leaves her house after she has told him she is pregnant.

> He stopped, transfixed: it wasn't true, he wasn't alone. Marcelle had not let him go: she was thinking of him, and this is what she thought: 'The dirty dog, he's let me down.' It was no use striding along the dark, deserted street, anonymous, enveloped in his garments – he could not escape her. (*AR*, p. 19)

Two notable exceptions, two characters who do not suffer their being-for-others, are Brunet at one extreme and Ivich at the other. Brunet has no interest in how others view him on a personal level. He cares only for the communist cause and views other people only in terms of their degree of usefulness to that cause. He sees people only as means to an end, as instruments. Like all fanatics, his error is that in fighting for a cause that is for the greater good of *people*, he has lost sight of people in the struggle. He is eventually led to confront this error, his lack of compassion for individuals, in the third volume of the trilogy. Ivich, for her part, is deeply self-absorbed and does not think of others when they are absent. On a deeper level, it can be argued that Ivich practises what Sartre refers to in *Being and Nothingness* as 'indifference' (*BN*, p. 401). She hides behind her hair, within her moods and her hypochondria, and simply refuses to exist for others. She is wilfully blind to the being of others as transcendences and thereby to her own being-for-others. She practises a sort of solipsism, acting as though she were alone in the world. Ivich appears to have discovered a way of no longer being threatened by the Other's transcendence, but in fact it is because she is so threatened by the Other's transcendence that she persists in her indifference. Indifference, then, is premised upon a deep insecurity and involves a profound isolation. Ivich is alienated by her alienation of the Other. In cutting herself off from the Other she is cut off from what she could be for the Other and from what the Other could make her be. It can be argued that Ivich and Brunet are not as far apart as they first appear, in that they are both indifferent to the being of others. On one level this is certainly true, but it appears that Brunet's indifference to people *as people* is very different from Ivich's. Ivich is indifferent to individuals because her world contains only herself, Brunet is indifferent to individuals because his world contains only mankind as a whole.

Repeatedly frustrated by his efforts to borrow the money he needs, Mathieu eventually steals it from Lola. Lola is relatively wealthy and careless with her cash and Mathieu is led to believe she will not notice the loss of a few bank notes. He is wrong in this assumption as, at the end of the novel, she arrives at Mathieu's flat looking for Boris believing that *he* has stolen her money. She is frantic with indignation, not at the loss of a few thousand francs but at the thought that Boris has taken her so utterly for granted, so utterly transcended her transcendence. '"I can hear him saying: 'The old girl is potty about me; she won't mind my pinching a little cash, she'll even thank me –' He doesn't know me! He doesn't know me!"' (*AR*, p. 285). It takes Mathieu considerable time and effort to convince Lola that he stole the money himself.

When Mathieu gives the money to Marcelle to pay for the abortion he has arranged it spells the end of their relationship. She had been led to hope, not least by Daniel's assurances, that Mathieu would marry her, that he loved her enough to want to do so. In producing the money, money he was even prepared to steal, Mathieu shows that he no longer loves her, that he values his freedom more. Faced with a situation that for once will not permit any compromise, with a straight, radical choice between doing his moral duty and maintaining his freedom, Mathieu chooses freedom. Marcelle flings the money in his face and at her insistence he leaves her for the last time.

The novel concludes with Daniel informing Mathieu that he plans to marry Marcelle. His reasons are complex; he hardly understands them himself. He is fond of Marcelle, so he claims, and wants to help her fulfil her wish of keeping her baby. 'I'm not marrying her as a sort of gesture. The fact is, what she wants above all is the baby' (*AR*, p. 296). Despite what he says, it seems clear he wants to conceal his homosexuality, which he is ashamed of, behind the respectable façade of marriage. He does not, however, conceal his homosexuality from Mathieu and with effort confesses to him that he is a homosexual. ' "Mathieu, I am a homosexual," he said' (*AR*, p. 294). Mathieu had no prior knowledge of Daniel's sexual preference but is 'not greatly astonished' (*AR*, p. 294). He wonders why Daniel has bothered to tell him. Daniel replies, ' "Well, I --- I wanted to see the effect it would produce on a fellow like you," ... "Also, now that there's someone who *knows*, I --- I shall perhaps succeed in believing it" ' (*AR*, p. 295).

In refusing to believe that he is a homosexual, in characterizing his conduct as a series of aberrations 'rather than the manifestations of a deeply rooted tendency' (*BN*, p. 63), Daniel is like the homosexual in *Being and Nothingness,* considered in Chapter 2 of this book, who acts in bad faith when he maintains that homosexuality is not the *meaning* of his conduct. In admitting his homosexuality to Mathieu he has made an important step towards overcoming his bad faith, although he is in danger of falling into the bad faith of labelling himself a homosexual-*thing*. Knowing that Daniel is a homosexual leads Mathieu to suggest that Daniel is marrying Marcelle as an act of martyrdom; a homosexual martyred to the institution of heterosexual marriage. Daniel does not deny it.

Though Mathieu suspects Daniel's motives for marrying Marcelle he nonetheless admires his ability to act decisively, to do something irrevocable. He begins to realize that true freedom consists in such decisive action and not in avoiding responsibility.

> He was intrigued by Daniel. 'Is that what freedom is?' he thought. 'He has *acted*: and now he can't go back: it must seem strange to feel behind him an unknown act, which he has already almost ceased to understand, and which will turn his life upside down. All I do, I do for *nothing*. It might be said that I am robbed of the consequences of my acts: everything happens as though I could always play my strokes again. I don't know what I would give to do something irrevocable.' (*AR*, p. 299)

Mathieu realizes he has always assumed the consequences of his actions were revocable. In coming to realize they are not always revocable, and in no longer wanting them to be so, he finishes with his youth and obtains his own personal age of reason. He has irrevocably lost Marcelle and Ivich and is alone with nothing. Though he has achieved his goal of maintaining his independence and escaping bourgeois conformity he recognizes that he is no more free without Marcelle than he was with her. He has, however, come to view freedom differently. Freedom, he has learnt, is not about avoiding responsibility but about choosing to commit oneself to a course of action, to a cause, without regret. Family life was not a course of action to which he wanted to commit himself and choosing it would have gone against his fundamental choice of himself, his lifelong fundamental project of asserting his freedom.

> He was sixteen... He had just thrashed a lad from Bordeaux, who had thrown stones at him... He had said to himself: 'I will be free,' or rather he hadn't said anything at all, but that was what he wanted to say and it was in the nature of a bet: he had made a bet with himself that his whole life should be cast in the semblance of that unique moment... 'I shall achieve my salvation!' Ten times, a hundred times, he had made that same bet... Mathieu was not, in his own eyes, a tall rather ungainly fellow who taught philosophy in a public school, nor Jacques Delarue the lawyer's brother, nor Marcelle's lover, nor Daniel and Brunet's friend: he was just that bet personified. (*AR*, p. 50)

It remains to be seen in what manner, through what committed actions, Mathieu will fulfil his fundamental project of asserting his freedom.

The Reprieve

The Reprieve covers the eight days from 23 to 30 September 1938 leading up to the controversial Munich Agreement. To understand *The Reprieve* it is vital to understand the historical events surrounding this agreement which many Czechs and Slovaks still refer to as a dictate or betrayal.

In March 1938 political scheming led to the bloodless annexation of Austria by Adolf Hitler's Nazi Germany. The annexation of Austria was an early step in the *Anschluss* or linkup of ethnic Germans. Hitler's sworn aim was to create a Third Reich by re-establishing the German empire.

> Ten millions of Germans situated outside the Reich in two great organised territories, wanted to re-enter the Reich. I should not have the right to appear at the bar of German history if I had been willing merely to ignore their claims. (*Re*, p. 270).

Following the unification of Germany and Austria, Hitler turned his attentions to the Sudetenland (named after the Sudeten Mountains), a large region of western Czechoslovakia bordering Germany and inhabited by a majority of ethnic Germans. These Germans wanted to unite with Germany and Austria but were prevented from doing so by agreements forged between Czechoslovakia and victorious Allied Forces at the end of World War I in 1918. Hitler made himself the advocate of the Sudeten Germans and demanded their liberation from Czechoslovakian oppression. In *The Reprieve* the tensions between the Sudeten Czechs and the Sudeten Germans are explored through the plight of Milan Hlinka and his family, Czechs who are victimized by their ethnic German neighbours.

War seemed inevitable if France and Britain were to stand by Czechoslovakia. France in particular had an alliance with Czechoslovakia and the Czechs expected France to come to their aid politically and militarily. France, however, under the leadership of Édouard Daladier, was politically and militarily unprepared and resolved to reach a solution that would, if at all possible, keep France out of hostilities. The political position of Britain under the leadership of Neville Chamberlain was more or less the same, although Britain resolved that they would declare war on Germany if France did. 'Milan Hlinka was no longer waiting. He had ceased to wait two days ago, on that awful day, lit by a flash of certainty: "They've let us down!"' (*Re*, p. 5).

Even if the obstinate political will displayed by the likes of Winston Churchill had prevailed, it is unlikely that France and Britain could have done much to help Czechoslovakia, at least in the short term. Jacques Delarue speaks with appeasing, cowardly, pro-Nazi motives but he has a point when he says to Mathieu and Odette:

> And where, I ask you, are we to come to their assistance? Because after all we should have to attack Germany just the same. Well,

then: where? In the east, there is the Siegfried Line, we should break our noses on that. In the north, Belgium. Are we to violate Belgium neutrality? Well then – where? Are we to go round by Turkey? That's just fantastic. (*Re*, p. 96)

In the early hours of 30 September 1938 Germany, France, Britain and Italy signed the Munich Agreement authorizing the German annexation of Czechoslovakia's Sudetenland, a move that effectively undermined Czechoslovakia's ability to function as a sovereign state. Czechoslovakia had not even been invited to a conference that saw Europe officially abandon it to Nazi tyranny. The reprieve won under the terms of the Munich Agreement represented the high point of *appeasement*, the ill-advised habit of attempting to appease and pacify Hitler by giving into his expansionist demands. Arriving back in Britain, Chamberlain famously waved his copy of the Munich Agreement declaring himself the bringer of 'peace for our time' (often misquoted as 'peace in our time'). However, the unhappy peace he and others secured by appeasing Hitler lasted just eleven months until Hitler broke the Munich Agreement by invading Poland. With the commencement of Word War II on 1 September 1939 'peace for our time' became nothing but a short-lived and unsatisfactory reprieve.

The fact that the above history lesson is required reveals the extent to which *The Reprieve* brings history and politics into the *Roads to Freedom* trilogy, although, as said, events leading up to the Munich Agreement are unfolded through a myriad personal perspectives rather than through an abstract historical account. Sartre's reasons for adopting this fragmented approach will be considered in due course.

The principal characters of *The Age of Reason*, Mathieu, Daniel, Marcelle, Brunet, Jacques, Odette, Ivich, Boris and Lola, reappear in *The Reprieve*, taking their place among a host of very widely dispersed subsidiary characters including children, political leaders, workers, peasants, shepherds, soldiers, prostitutes; anyone at all who is effected by the gathering clouds of war.

There is Gomez, now a General in the Spanish Republican Army, who meets with Mathieu briefly on his way back to Spain. Gomez declares 'I love war' (*Re*, p. 240) and hopes that the French will be drawn into one. He hates France for failing to intervene in the Spanish Civil War on the side of the Republicans. France abandoned the left-wing Republicans to the extreme right-wing Nationalist forces of General Franco, just as it will abandon Czechoslovakia to the extreme right-wing forces of Adolf Hitler.

In contrast to Gomez there is Philippe, the son of a French General. Declaring himself a pacifist he runs away from home planning to go to Switzerland using false papers. He flatters himself that he is a deserter but he is not actually old enough to be called-up. He is soft and effeminate and constantly struggles to convince himself that his pacifism does not conceal cowardice. He is comparable to the pacifist, Garcin, in Sartre's play, *In Camera*, written about the same time as *The Reprieve*. Garcin is doomed to struggle for all eternity to convince himself that his pacifism was not cowardice. Philippe eventually hands himself into the police and is reclaimed by his bullying father. Phillipe is not the only character in *The Reprieve* plagued by the suspicion that he is a coward.

Pierre is called-up. As he returns to France from Morocco by ship he is sick with fear at the thought of mutilation and death, or, at least, he allows himself to succumb to seasickness as a temporary distraction from his fear. He cannot bear his girlfriend, Maud, whom he considers his social inferior, knowing he is a coward. 'It's certainly the first time I've worried about what a tart might think of me...But she's got me, he thought, as he slipped on his jacket: she *knows*' (*Re*, p. 138).[8]

Three other characters of note in *The Reprieve* are Charles, who is severely disabled, Birnenschatz the rich Jew and Gros-Louis the shepherd.

Charles is bedridden and has no active part to play in the war of able-bodied people, the 'stand-ups' as he calls them.

> Five and a half feet or so above his head, it was war, tempest, outraged honour, patriotic duty: but on the floor, there was neither war nor peace: nothing but the misery and shame of the sub-men, stricken and laid upon their backs. (*Re*, p. 260).

Reduced to an object Charles is evacuated in a goods train from one side of France to the other away from the life he knows and the nurse who loves him.

Birnenschatz wants to think of himself as a Frenchman rather than a Jew and does not want to identify himself with other Jews who are suffering under Nazi tyranny. ' "What's all this? Us Jews?" he asked. "Don't know 'em. I'm French myself. Do you feel like a Jew?" ' (*Re*, p. 83). Birnenschatz is what Sartre describes in *Anti-Semite and Jew*,[9] written soon after *The Reprieve*, as an inauthentic Jew. The inauthentic Jew seeks to escape anti-Semitism by escaping his own Jewishness. He assimilates himself into the culture around him through religious conversion, intermarriage and so on. He often adopts, like Birnenschatz, and like the assimilated Jews Sartre knew personally, a rationalist, cosmopolitan stance. When Czechoslovakia is eventually abandoned to the Nazis, and with it its population of Jews, Birnenschatz feels ashamed. ' "I feel ashamed," he said darkly' (*Re*, p. 372). In shame he recognizes his inauthenticity and identifies himself with the Jewish people. He becomes an authentic Jew.

Gros-Louis, one of the few genuinely endearing characters in the novel, is an illiterate shepherd who has drifted into Marseilles looking for work. He discovers there is a war brewing but does not know who with or why. Unable to read his army book he does not realize he has been called-up and that he is officially a deserter. Lost and lonely he gets drunk with two sailors who mug him. He eventually discovers that he is required to make his way to the barracks at Montpellier. He travels there still confused about the nature of the wider circumstances that have taken over his life.

There is even at least one character who is totally unaffected. Armand Viguier had fought in Word War I, believing it to be, as was commonly thought, the war to end all wars. He dies secure in that belief.

> Armand Viguier was dead, and no one could now declare him right, nor wrong. No one could change the indestructible future of his dead life. One day more, one single day, and all his hopes might well have collapsed; he would discover that his life had been crushed between two wars, between the hammer and the anvil. But he had died on the 23 September 1938, at four o'clock in the morning, after seven days in a coma, and had taken peace away with him. (*Re*, p. 56).

As to the central character of the trilogy, Mathieu waits to be called-up as he relaxes on the Mediterranean coast with Jacques and Odette. Although largely apolitical he determines to take responsibility for his being-in-situation – his *historical* being-in-situation – and to fight in the war when it comes. Out for a morning walk he reads a notice informing him that all reservists of his category are mobilized with immediate effect. He is moved but not shocked or afraid. What started as just another rather boring day by the sea suddenly becomes 'arrowlike' (*Re*, p. 73); it points to the north, to Paris, to sleepless nights and war. 'He was not upset by this, nor anything else; nor amused any longer: it was, in any case, an interesting and rather picturesque turn in his life' (*Re*, p. 74). He believes war will usher in a new, more vital and committed phase of his existence, it will make him a man of action and consign his irresponsible and profligate youth to the past. Mathieu is bored with life. Like Anny in *Nausea* he feels he has out-lived himself.

> Mathieu had opened his eyes, which felt limp and clammy in their sockets, the eyes of a newborn baby, still sightless, and he thought: 'What's the good of it all?' as he did every morning...There was nothing to look forward to any more, nothing whatsoever to undertake. And yet he would have to get up, join in the ceremony, find his way through the enveloping heat, and perform all the gestures of the cult, like a priest who has lost his faith. (*Re*, pp. 66–67)

Given that he must die one day anyway, perhaps of old age, after a certain number of dull, pointless days, Mathieu decides to *seize* his death, or at least to seize war and the very real possibility of death. It seems to him he can only fulfil his fundamental project of asserting his freedom and achieve the salvation he has dreamed of since childhood by *choosing* death. A straightforward suicide would suffice and when he gets back to Paris from the South he toys with the idea of throwing himself from a bridge. 'A plunge, and the water would engulf him, his freedom would be transmuted into water. Rest at last – and why not? This obscure suicide would *also* be an absolute, a law, a choice, and a morality, all of them complete' (*Re*, p. 309). It seems, however, that he would prefer to die in a less obscure way, asserting his personal freedom in face of the world and the efforts of other people to determine, control and oppress him. Mathieu seeks what might be called a noble death, but not martyrdom. A martyr sacrifices himself for others, for some political or religious cause, Mathieu seeks death for his own entirely individualistic reasons.

His wealthy elder brother Jacques, who in *The Age of Reason* challenges Mathieu's irresponsible lifestyle and his decision to obtain money for an abortion, now challenges Mathieu's resigned and uncomplaining attitude towards conscription and the approaching war. ' "Look here," said Jacques. "You're not asking me to believe that you are resigned to going off, like a sheep to the slaughterhouse?" ' (*Re*, p. 92). Jacques has clear sympathies with Nazism and is in favour of the appeasement of Hitler. ' "I know you don't like the Hitler régime. But after all, it is quite possible not to share your prejudices against it" ' (*Re*, p. 94). Though he does not really believe it, he hopes, like Chamberlain, that the Munich Conference will bring lasting peace. Mathieu is uninterested in Jacques predictable, right-wing intellectualizing about the complex political situation and can only think, ' "*What is he afraid of?*" ' (*Re*, p. 96), as his mind repeatedly drifts back to his growing, unspoken love for Jacques' wife, Odette. Mathieu delays his departure briefly in order to rendezvous with Gomez then leaves for Paris, Odette having given him a secret goodbye kiss on the lips.

Boris' stormy relationship with Lola has calmed somewhat, but only because he sees it as a finite exercise and is therefore prepared to indulge her and give her the attention she craves. He fantasizes, rather comically, that he has been raised for war, that a heroic death will round his life off nicely. Not least, going off to war will allow him to escape Lola's clutches with impunity.

'I can't even imagine what I should be like if it hadn't broken out.' He thought of his life, and it no longer seemed to him too short. Lives are neither short nor long. It was a life, that's all: war at the end of it. He felt as though he had been suddenly invested with a new dignity, because he had a function in Society, and also because he was going to die a violent death, and his modesty was hurt. It was surely time to go and fetch Lola. (*Re*, p. 286).

Unlike Mathieu, Boris has a young man's romantic notion of his own death. He views it as though it were the death of another, something impressive he will be able to boast about afterwards, a grand gesture, like stealing books or carrying a clasp-knife. Unwilling to wait a year until he is old enough to be conscripted, he joins up for three years. This foolish yet admirable act of bravado puts to rest his concerns about being a coward.

Marcelle is now married to Daniel who has grown thoroughly bored with her pregnancy and her company. Relaxing at the seaside with Marcelle, while reassuring her without much conviction that there will be no war, Daniel gazes at a bare backed youth digging a grave for a dead dog and is overcome by the homosexual desires he is so ashamed of. He tries to ignore his desires and shrug them off. He wonders if the shock of war with its 'visions of tainted, wrecked and bleeding bodies' (*Re*, p. 112) will snap him out of his desires and finally put an end to them, but he realizes that his desires will endure the horrors of war and that war will probably afford him opportunities to indulge himself. He imagines himself in a lull in the fighting, sitting and eyeing the bare back of a young soldier.

Bored, dissatisfied, ashamed, desperate, he has a kind of religious experience, a revelation that he is not alone. '*I am not alone*, said Daniel aloud' (*Re*, p. 117). He writes about it in a long, rambling letter to Mathieu. 'God sees me, Mathieu: I feel it and know it' (*Re*, p. 344). The suggestion is that he has found a religious means of escaping the guilt and self-loathing he feels in response to his homosexuality. Suddenly, he is no longer a homosexual because homosexuality is the transcendent meaning of conduct he chooses to indulge in to satisfy his desires, he is a homosexual because God's look fixes him in his being and makes him a homosexual-*thing*. As a being-for-itself rather than a being-in-itself, Daniel is only ever the transcendence of his facticity, a homosexual in the mode of perpetually being what he is not, but through religion he attempts to *be* what he is, he attempts to be a homosexual facticity before God. 'I am seen, therefore I am. I need no longer bear the responsibility of my turbid and disintegrating self: he who sees me causes me to be: I am as he sees me' (*Re*, p. 345). At the end of *The Age of Reason* when Daniel confessed his homosexuality to Mathieu he was in danger of falling into the bad faith of labelling himself a homosexual-*thing*, *The Reprieve* sees him fall into that particular project of bad faith.

Towards the end of the novel Mathieu is ready to leave Paris for Nancy to commence his military service. Having spent the night with Iréne, a straight-talking young woman he met the evening before, Mathieu returns to his apartment to collect his suitcase. He discovers an unexpected visitor, Ivich. He is not particularly surprised to see her or moved by her presence as he once was. He still cares for her but his old infatuation has gone. She is disconcerted by his new found air of indifference. Fulfilling the promise to support her in Paris that he made in *The Age of Reason* he gives her all his worldly possession including his salary and departs. She shows him slightly more gratitude than she has shown him on previous occasions but he is no longer interested in what she thinks. As his train pulls out of Paris he feels a thrill of joy. He is glad to leave behind him his job, his apartment, Paris, Ivich, glad that the life he has known is dead. He reads Daniel's long, rambling letter about his religious experience just to get it out of the way. 'Stale trash' (*Re*, p. 346) he thinks as he crumples it up and throws it out of the window. He looks forward to a future that will bring 'war, fear, death perhaps, and freedom' (*Re*, p. 340). Before he reaches Nancy it becomes clear that Hitler is to be appeased and that there will be peace, at least for a while. Nonetheless, he has no intention of going back to the life he has abandoned. ' "I'm free, and shall remain so," he thought' (*Re*, p. 376).

Whereas *The Age of Reason* is a masterpiece of miniaturization that takes place in central Paris over just two days, *The Reprieve* deliberately and radically dispenses with continuity of place and action – though not continuity of time, which it cleverly maintains – to produce a panoramic, multifaceted view of a Europe teetering on the brink of total war. *The Age of Reason* could be adapted into a play, *The Reprieve* could only be adapted into a movie. On the one hand, Sartre was influenced by the non-linear fiction and 'stream of consciousness' method of the American writer, John Dos Passos, and, on the other hand, by the work of film directors such as Eisenstein and Pudovkin. *The Reprieve* reflects these influences as it exploits to the full the cinematic possibilities of the novel form. Like a movie, a novel has the capacity to shift location in an instant and to weave a meaningful stream of consciousness from a medley of many people's words and thoughts. *The Reprieve* has an overtly cinematic quality, relentlessly cutting from one scene to another, from one character to another, sometimes in mid-sentence. The novel's fragmented structure can be confusing at first, but the writing is expertly managed and soon serves to produce a coherent and almost omnipresent overview that forges profound connections between separate events.

Mathieu ate, Marcelle ate, Daniel ate, Boris ate, Brunet ate, their instantaneous souls were brimming with clammy little joys, in that one moment – war – war that Pierre dreaded, Boris accepted, and Daniel welcomed, would enter clad in steel, the great stand-up war, the white men's crazy war. In that moment: it had exploded in Milan's room, it was pouring out of all the windows, it surged into the Jägerschmitts' abode, it prowled round the ramparts of Marrakesh, it breathed upon the sea, it crushed the buildings in the rue Royale, it filled Maurice's nostrils with the smell of dog and sour milk; in the fields and cowsheds and farmyards it *did not exist*; but it played heads or tails between two pier-glasses in the wainscoted salons of the Hotel Dreesen. (*Re*, p. 62).

The very structure of the novel indicates that only the novelist, film-maker or historian can have this overview, and then only after events have taken place. Great political events such as wars, invasions and reprieves are identified as a single unified phenomenon only with the benefit of hindsight; at the time there is nothing beyond the series of individual lives, thoughts, decisions, triumphs and tragedies. Mathieu thinks that war is nowhere in particular. One cannot touch it or point to it, yet it is everywhere at the same time, it is every action that comprises it. Hence, the housewife tying up a food parcel or the pacifist collecting a petition make war as much as the soldier firing a gun.

And yet, each of those consciousnesses, by imperceptible contacts and insensible changes, realizes its existence as a cell in a gigantic and invisible coral. War: everyone is free, and yet the stakes are set. It is there, it is everywhere, it is the totality of all my thoughts, of all Hitler's words, of all Gomez's acts: but no one is there to make that total. It exists solely for God. But God does not exist. And yet the war exists. (*Re*, p. 277)

With the exception of Hitler, with his fanatical visions of world domination, the statesmen and political leaders that feature in *The Reprieve* are placed on a par with all the novel's other characters in that they too, and rather disturbingly, are seen to be without an overview or a clear sense of the nature and direction of events. Sartre repeatedly refers to British Prime Minister, Neville Chamberlain, for example, as the 'old gentleman' (Chamberlain was 69 at the time) as a means of disengaging him from his broader historical context and exposing him as no more effectual than any other old man swept along by circumstances. 'The old gentleman turned to Hitler, he looked at that evil, infantile face, the face of a human fly, and he was stricken to his very soul' (*Re*, p. 61). The decisions of Chamberlain and the other politicians mentioned in the novel shape world history, but like the decisions of the 'ordinary' characters in the novel, their decisions are personal responses to the facticity of their immediate, concrete situation – a hot room, a meeting that has gone on too long, a feeling of frailty, a personal desire to avoid the blame of taking Europe to war.

Iron in the Soul

It is June 1940, 21 months after the events of *The Reprieve* and two years after those of *The Age of Reason*. The Germans have occupied Paris and France is defeated. The defeat of a nation is the central theme of *Iron in the Soul*, defeat as it is suffered, celebrated or refused by a variety of characters, many of whom have been introduced earlier in the trilogy.

The novel begins in New York the day after the fall of Paris on 14 June 1940. Gomez, now exiled following the defeat of the Republicans in the Spanish Civil war, sweats profusely in the humid New York heat as he seeks a job as an art critic – he was an artist before he became a General. A tough, proud man who loves war and is used to being obeyed, Gomez finds it humiliating to be reduced to a poor, unemployed Hispanic immigrant shunned by New Yorkers.

> A General! Gomez looked at his shabby trousers, at the dark sweat stains already showing on his shirt. He said bitterly: 'Don't worry: I'm not likely to boast. I know only too well what it costs a man here to have fought in Spain. For six months now I haven't had a smell of a job.' (*IS*, p. 10)

Preoccupied with their own concerns the Americans are unmoved by the plight of France and hardly give the war in Europe a thought. For his part, Gomez gloats over the fall of Paris on the grounds that the French did nothing when Franco entered Barcelona during the Spanish Civil War. ' "Well, now it's their turn, and I hope it chokes 'em! I'm *glad*!" ' (*IS*, p. 13). Gomez is vain and selfish and hardly gives a thought to his Jewish wife, Sarah, and their son, Pablo, left behind in France.

The novel cuts to Sarah and Pablo who are fleeing occupied Paris. Their taxi runs out of petrol and they are forced to continue on foot along with thousands of other refugees as Nazi planes roar overhead. As Jews, Sarah and Pablo's plight is more desperate than most. There is only a slim chance of escaping France to Portugal and even less of finding a ship to New York. Even if they get there, Gomez will not want them. 'A weariness that was neither generous nor willingly incurred set her heart thumping – the weariness of a mother, the weariness of a Jewess – *her* weariness, *her* destiny' (*IS*, p. 25).

We are not told what becomes of Sarah and Pablo, or Gomez for that matter. Until the novel comes to focus entirely on Mathieu, then finally Brunet, it makes relatively brief visits to various characters before abandoning them inconclusively to their war torn circumstances and the choices they must make. Real life seldom ties up lose ends and true to life *Iron in the Soul* does not do so either. Those characters that do not die are left as they were found earlier in the trilogy, struggling with their lifelong burden of ambiguity and freedom, most of them resorting to bad faith.

Boris is in a military hospital recovering from peritonitis. He remains the amusing, unrealistic dreamer we have come to know in the two previous novels. As he has failed to be 'decently and neatly killed' (*IS*, p. 57) in action he is wondering in a melancholic way what to do with a life that he did not anticipate still being in possession of. 'Besides, he thought, I am, in fact, dead. For all practical purposes he had died at Sedan in May 1940. The years of life remaining to him were a long vista of boredom' (*IS*, p. 57). Should he finally marry Lola and become a teacher or should he take the opportunity to escape to England in a plane to fight another day? He consults Lola as to what he should do, hoping for her permission to abandon her for war a second time. Boris, as we know, is self-obsessed and sees Lola only in relation to his own concerns. She, however, has serious concerns of her own – a life threatening tumour of the womb – and is no longer particularly interested in him. She was always trying to find out what he was thinking but she has finally realized there is nothing much inside his head. 'If he lost his gaiety of heart what would there be left?' (*IS*, p. 205). With his shallow thoughts and feelings he is incapable of providing Lola with emotional support. 'He speaks to me and kisses me, but when I come to die I shall be alone' (*IS*, p. 206).

Ivich has failed to take advantage of the independence bequeathed to her by Mathieu. Shortly after his departure she threw away her virginity thinking she was soon to die in a Paris air raid. She became pregnant and although she had a miscarriage she is now married to Georges, a boring, wealthy, 'lanky non-entity' (*IS*, p. 66). She longs for Georges to die in action so as to be free of him and her interfering in-laws. Always unrealistic, she begs her brother Boris to rescue her from a situation of her own making, proposing, even though she detests Lola, that the three of them live together on Lola's money.

> 'I've been thinking that you might let me join up with you. The three of us could live together on Lola's money.'
> Boris all but choked.
> 'So that's what you've been thinking!'
> 'Boris,' said Ivich with sudden passion: 'I just *can't go on* living with those people!' (*IS*, p. 72)

Boris no longer feels as close to Ivich as he once did and is tired of her selfish, capricious ways. He is not particularly interested in helping her and is more concerned about getting to England to rejoin the fight. 'He watched an aeroplane catch the morning light as it turned, and to himself he said: "The cliffs, the lovely white cliffs, the cliffs of Dover." ' (*IS*, p. 73).

Daniel walks the largely deserted streets of Paris as its German conquerors move in. He rejoices in an intoxicating sensation of power and freedom, triumphing in the defeat of a city and a people that he feels despised and alienated him for his homosexuality.

> They're running, running: they've never stopped running. He raised his head, laughing to high Heaven, and drew deep breaths. For twenty years he had been on trial. There had been spies even beneath his bed... And now, in a flash – stampede! They were running, the lot of them, witnesses, judges, all the respectable folk, running beneath the blazing sun, the blue sky, and a threat of aircraft over their heads. (*IS*, p. 93)

In the abandoned streets of Paris he finally feels unburdened of the being-for-others that has plagued him for so long in the form of shame and resentment. The occupation of his city has liberated him. All his judges have gone, he has transcended them. 'Marcelle's pupping at Dax; Mathieu's probably a prisoner: Brunet's almost certainly got himself bumped off. All the witnesses against me are dead or thinking of other things. It's I who am making a come-back' (*IS*, p. 93). He comes across the young pacifist coward, Philippe, who is contemplating committing suicide by throwing himself from a bridge. This time Philippe really has deserted from the army. Daniel finds Philippe soft and innocent and irresistibly attractive. At first his desires make him anxious. 'He thought: "Everything is going to begin again, everything – hope and wretchedness, shame and madness." Then, suddenly, he remembered that France was finished: "All things are permissible!"' (*IS*, p. 135). He proceeds to use all his charm and sophistication to seduce Philippe, enticing him back to his flat.

Jacques, Mathieu's bourgeois lawyer brother, is fleeing Paris with his wife, Odette. Jacques refuses the adventure of driving all night and they park in a lane to sleep. It emerges that it was Jacques idea to flee Paris – Odette had wanted to stay – but in a pathetic, bad faith ridden effort to conceal his cowardice from himself, Jacques craftily manipulates Odette into 'accepting' that *her* fears had been their motive for leaving.

> 'Are you trying to tell me' she said – and her voice was trembling – 'that you left Paris on my account?'
> 'It was a case of conscience,' he replied. He looked at her affectionately.
> 'You'd been so nervous all those last few days. I was frightened about you.'
> Amazement kept her silent. Why had he got to say that? Why did he feel obliged to say that? (*IS*, p. 189).

Dismissing Jacques as worthless and predictable, Odette dwells, as she does every night, on her love for Mathieu. While Jacques saturates himself in bad faith, elsewhere in France his brother is striving for authenticity, for salvation.

With the Nazis advancing rapidly, Mathieu's division is abandoned by its officers. Without leadership or hope the men languish in the misery of their defeat, blurring reality with drink or religion as they wait to be taken prisoner.

> No one likes us, no one: the civilians blame us for not defending them, our wives have got no pride in us, our officers have left us in the lurch, the villagers hate us, the Jerries are advancing through the darkness. (*IS*, p. 111)

A small unit determined to fight arrives on the scene and Mathieu joins them, following the example of a young soldier, Pinette, who dreads returning home defeated. Without reflecting too deeply, Mathieu makes a series of momentous choices: he picks up a discarded rifle, he takes up a position on a church tower with Pinette and a few other brave, stubborn men and engages the enemy.

Mathieu makes his choices not because he wants to be a hero, but to refuse the defeat that has undermined the dignity and mastered the destiny of the majority of his fellow soldiers. In *The Reprieve* Mathieu welcomed war as an opportunity to become committed and responsible, as an opportunity to assert his freedom. To accept defeat and capture would be to abandon his chosen path at the hour of reckoning and thus render all his previous actions meaningless. His brief fifteen minute stand against the Nazi's is all but futile in military terms, but for him it is an uncompromising and decisive act that is the ultimate affirmation of his freedom, the fulfilment of his lifelong fundamental project. With each shot he fires he dispenses with regret, vacillation, scruples, all his former bad faith, and finally takes absolute responsibility for his being-in-situation. Unlike most of the other characters in the novel, who remain submerged in bad faith, Mathieu achieves authenticity. 'He fired. He was cleansed. He was all-powerful. He was free' (*IS*, p. 225). We are not told what becomes of him, but given that the exit from the tower becomes blocked with fallen beams and Brunet sees the tower collapse, we are invited to assume Mathieu is killed.

The final 120 pages of the novel, which draw heavily on Sartre's own experiences as a prisoner of war, focus on the capture, imprisonment and eventual deportation to Germany of Brunet, the zealous, tough, self-disciplined and self-possessed communist who tried and failed to recruit Mathieu to the cause in *The Age of Reason*. Like Mathieu, Brunet has learnt to accept his being-in-situation without complaint or regret and strives to act positively and decisively in every circumstance. He is, or strives to be, authentic.

Brunet and thousands of other captured soldiers are marched to a prison camp where they are left to starve for several days. Believing rumours that food will soon arrive, the men lounge about grumbling and waiting to be fed. They fight like dogs over a few scraps of bread thrown mockingly by a German soldier. Brunet grinds a piece that falls at his feet into the dust. 'Brunet deliberately put his foot on the scrap of bread, and trod it into the ground. But ten hands laid hold of his leg, forced it away, and scraped up the muddy crumbs' (*IS*, p. 264). He commands his body to obey him and tries to fight his hunger by running around the camp, but he eventually collapses, remaining sick for several days until finally fed.

Brunet views his fellow prisoners with contempt. With a few exceptions they are slovenly, weak-minded dreamers, lacking self-discipline and in need of someone to obey. They are like children or monkeys with their idle chatter and false hopes. Brunet's analysis of them is correct but he is nonetheless harsh and judgmental. As a communist, Brunet wants to liberate mankind from oppression but he has no particular love or empathy for any individual. He thinks about making use of people, viewing them as instruments for achieving greater political ends. Schneider, a man with some communist sympathies who is Brunet's equal in composure and intelligence and his only real friend, accuses Brunet of acting like a surgeon at a post-mortem. With a level of detail that is somewhat tedious and improbable, Schneider and Brunet discuss the position of the French Communist Party (PCF) in relation to the USSR. Like Sartre himself for a long time, Brunet places too much faith in the honour and decency of the Soviet Union and naively pins many of his hopes upon it. He is unaware that the Soviet Union is in fact an utterly oppressive authoritarian state with a leader, Stalin, who is as brutal as Hitler.

As events unfold Brunet acquires some compassion for his fellow prisoners, but he is nonetheless irritated by their adherence to self-indulgence and idiocy. The few activists he recruits to the communist cause report that if the prisoners were released tomorrow there would be 'twenty thousand additional Nazis' (*IS*, p. 322). Their weak-mindedness and need for authority leads the prisoners to identify with their captors.[10] They need to believe in Nazi organization and decency, and above all that they will be released and not deported to Germany as forced labour. Brunet is resented by the majority for not sharing their delusions.

Their false belief that they are to be released is maintained even when they are packed onto a goods train. They act in bad faith, reassuring one another with unconvincing arguments and angrily dismissing all counter claims until it is beyond doubt that they are going to Germany.

A young man is shot for jumping from the train in a bid for freedom and at last the prisoners discover real anger towards the Nazis. 'The Frenchmen and the Germans glared at one another: *this was war*. For the first time since September '39, this was war' (*IS*, p. 348). Brunet believes that now the prisoners have learnt to hate oppression he can recruit them to the communist cause and influence the course of world history.

CHAPTER 5

SARTRE'S PLAYS

Sartre's interest in theatre began in the 1920s when he was a student at the École Normale Supérieure in Paris. He was part of an enthusiastic group of young wits who produced and performed satirical reviews poking fun at authority and the older generation. After graduation he focused on writing philosophy and prose fiction and may not have become a playwright had he not become a prisoner of war.

In 1940, as the best means of advocating freedom and promoting an anti-authoritarian agenda under the very nose of the Nazis, Sartre wrote, cast, directed and performed in the prison camp's Christmas play, *Bariona*. Set at the time of the birth of Christ, the play tells the story of the rebel Bariona, who, distrustful of news of the Messiah as told by the Magi, leads resistance against the forces of Herod, a puppet of Judea's Roman occupiers. The play's message of resistance was not lost on its huge, captive audience and Sartre and the rest of the cast received rapturous applause. Sartre, who played the role of the black magus, Balthazar, later wrote, 'As I addressed my comrades across the footlights, speaking to them of their state as prisoners, when I suddenly saw them so remarkably silent and attentive, I realised what theatre ought to be: a great, collective, religious phenomenon...a theatre of myths' (*ST*, p. 39). Sartre's love for the theatre was firmly established and over the next twenty-five years he was to turn repeatedly to drama as a means of conveying his philosophical and political ideas to audiences that otherwise may not have become familiar with them.

This chapter précis and analyses in chronological order the ten Sartre plays that were published and professionally produced after his early, amateur effort, *Bariona*.

THE FLIES

As the first Sartre play to be written and produced professionally, *The Flies* is generally described as Sartre's 'first play'. It returns to the theme of resistance to corrupt authority first explored three years earlier in *Bariona*. Just as the period drama of *Bariona* had proved the least personally risky means of advocating freedom and promoting an anti-authoritarian, anti-collaborationist agenda in a Nazi prison camp, so the period drama of *The Flies* proved the least personally risky means of doing the same in Nazi occupied Paris. As Sartre later said, alluding to an actual incident, 'The real drama, the drama I should have liked to write, was that of the terrorist who, by ambushing Germans, becomes the instrument for the execution of fifty hostages' (*ST*, p. 188).

Based on the Ancient Greek legend of Orestes, *The Flies* is an implicit commentary on the tense political situation that Sartre encountered in Paris on his return from captivity in Germany in 1941. Interestingly, Sartre came full circle with his final play, *The Trojan Women*. It makes use of an Ancient Greek legend to pass comment on the Algerian War of Independence. Sartre obtained his release from Stalag 11D, Mount Kemmel, Germany in March 1941 with a forged medical certificate declaring him unfit for military service. By his own admission he enjoyed the hard but generally convivial atmosphere of the prison camp but felt he could only truly use his talent and fame against the Nazi tyranny, and those among his fellow countrymen who sympathized or even collaborated with it, by returning to the centre of his web of influence. Back in Paris he wasted no time. He founded the resistance movement 'Socialism and Freedom' and wrote his major philosophical masterpiece, *Being and Nothingness*, a work in which he argues that freedom, choice and personal responsibility for one's actions are fundamental and inalienable features of the human condition. *The Flies* and *Being and Nothingness* appeared not only in the same year, but in the same month – June 1943. They belonged to the same engaged, wartime, project of consciousness-raising, subtle in approach yet nonetheless powerful and daring, that by 1945 had established Sartre as a world-renowned thinker, moral authority and champion of liberty – as the writer who had resisted.

The Flies is set in the Ancient Greek city of Argos in North East Peloponnesus. Calling himself Philebus, Orestes returns as a young man to Argos, the town of his birth. Orestes was sent away as a child 15 years earlier when Aegistheus murdered Orestes' father, King Agamemnon, and married Orestes' mother, Clytemnestra. Argos has become a dismal place plagued by flies. The flies epitomize the sin and corruption of the people of Argos and the collective remorse they continue to suffer for failing to defend Agamemnon or avenge his murder. The god Zeus says, 'They are only bluebottles, a trifle larger than usual. Fifteen years ago a mighty stench of carrion drew them to this city, and since then they've been getting fatter and fatter' (*F*, Act 1, p. 237). Orestes has only recently become aware of his personal history and his links with Argos so initially he is not inclined to take revenge on Aegistheus. Orestes plans to leave Argos without interfering and is encouraged to do so by the god Zeus who enjoys the misery and repentance of the people of Argos and wants the situation to remain as it is.

Orestes, as Philebus, meets his sister Electra. She tells him how Clytemnestra treats her as a slave in her own home for refusing to honour Aegistheus. Orestes, still as Philebus, then meets Clytemnestra. She says she has no remorse for her part in the murder of Agamemnon but confesses that she has been racked with guilt for 15 years for sending her child Orestes away. She says that confession is the national pastime of Argos and that the endless guilt and repentance of its people is like a pestilence. 'Most travellers give our city a wide berth...The people of the Plain have put us in quarantine; they see our repentance as a sort of pestilence, and are afraid of being infected' (*F*, Act 1, p. 256). This pestilence reaches its height once a year on the Day of the Dead when the ghosts of the dead are believed to rise up from the underworld to torment the people of Argos.

Inspired by the arrival of Orestes, though she still does not know who he is, Electra dances with joy on the Day of the Dead defying the ghosts to attack her. She tells the people that ghosts are just shadows of remorse imagined by the living. 'But what is it you're so frightened of? I can see all round you and there's nothing but your own shadows' (*F*, Act 2, Scene 1, p. 269). The people start to believe her until Zeus frightens them back into their state of remorse by moving a large boulder.

Orestes offers to help Electra escape Argos but she refuses to run away. He realizes that he too must stay, he must avenge his father's death and rid Argos of its pestilence of remorse. Though he is an intellectual who has never killed a man he realizes he must become a warrior and take decisive action. He reveals his true identity to Electra. Acting against the will of Zeus, Orestes kills Aegistheus and Clytemnestra refusing to feel any remorse for his deed yet taking full responsibility for it.

> I have done *my* deed, Electra, and that deed was good. I shall bear it on my shoulders as a carrier at a ferry carries the traveller to the farther bank. And when I have brought it to the farther bank I shall take stock of it. The heavier it is to carry, the better pleased I shall be; for that burden is my freedom. (*F*, Act 2, Scene 2, p. 296)

Electra is not so strong willed as her brother. She succumbs to guilt and is reduced to begging Zeus for forgiveness for her part in the killings. Orestes reveals himself to the people as the son of Agamemnon and the rightful king of Argos but he refuses to take the throne. He leaves the town taking the pestilence of flies with him.

The play explores the key existentialist themes of freedom and responsibility through the radical conversion of Philebus the peace loving intellectual into Orestes the warrior. A person may not be prepared for present crises by his past experiences, but it is nonetheless bad faith for him to declare, 'I was not meant for this' or 'This should not be happening to me.' Orestes resists bad faith and achieves authenticity by rising to the demands of his circumstances and fully realizing his being-in-situation. Orestes is free to choose not to choose in the situation in which he finds himself and to walk away from Argos and its troubles, but instead he chooses to act positively, to avenge his father's death and to live with the consequences of killing his mother. Unlike his unfortunate sister Electra who falls into the bad faith of regretting her past deeds and praying for absolution, Orestes triumphs over both God (Zeus) and guilt becoming a true existentialist hero. He asserts his free will against the will of God revealing the limitlessness of human freedom. He takes full responsibility for his past deeds accepting that he is the sum total of all his actions and in so doing overcomes regret: the desire to repent and the desire to be forgiven.

The Flies is a call to arms, not only to those oppressed by Nazism but to people in every time and place. It seeks to illustrate the inadequacy of pacifism in face of extreme situations that require decisive action. To be authentic a person must rise to the occasion in which he finds himself. He must fight violence with violence if necessary and take full responsibility for his actions without remorse.

IN CAMERA (NO EXIT OR BEHIND CLOSED DOORS)

Alternatively titled *No Exit* or *Behind Closed Doors*, *In Camera* is Sartre's best-known and most iconic play. Simple in structure (one act, once scene) and intellectually accessible, it epitomizes the absurdity, anxiety and hopelessness that are synonymous with existentialism in the popular consciousness. With its assertion that, 'Hell is other people' (*IC*, p. 223), it certainly contains the best-known maxim in all of Sartre's plays, if not his entire writings.

In Camera appeared within a year of *The Flies*, opening at the Théâtre du Vieux-Colombier, Paris, on 27 May 1944. Unlike *The Flies*, *In Camera* falls short of being an implicit commentary on the political situation of the time, but in focusing on captivity and conflict generally it certainly explores themes that had a particular relevance to Parisian audiences living under Nazi occupation. Sartre had recently experienced a very obvious captivity as a German prisoner of war (though he appears to have rather enjoyed it), and the French underground press had several times visited the subject of prisoner psychology. As for conflict, *In Camera* revisits in a very concrete way themes that were explored somewhat more abstractly the previous year in *Being and Nothingness*. Sartre's analysis of the phenomenon of being-for-others led him to the damning conclusion that 'The essence of the relations between consciousnesses is not the *Mitsein* [being-with]; it is conflict' (*BN*, p. 451). It is this damning conclusion that Sartre seeks to reinforce and further publicize with his play *In Camera*.

In Camera begins with a valet showing Joseph Garcin into a Second Empire style drawing room with three sofas. On the mantelpiece are large bronze ornaments and a paper knife. The room has no windows or mirrors. The room surprises Garcin, he had expected to find something different. He asks where the instruments of torture are. It soon emerges that Garcin is dead and that the room is in hell. The valet says there is nothing beyond the room but passages and more rooms, that there is no outside. Garcin learns that sleep is impossible in the room, it is never dark and he cannot blink let alone shut his eyes. Without windows, mirrors, darkness, sleep, dreams, books or anywhere to escape to, there is no respite, none of the distractions that made Garcin's life on earth bearable, distractions that made Garcin bearable to himself. 'I shall never sleep again. But then – how shall I endure my own company?' (*IC*, p. 184).

The valet exits, closing the only door behind him. Garcin explores the room before trying to ring a bell by the door that does not work. He tries the door without success. He beats it with his fists and calls the valet. Nothing happens. He gives up and sits down just as the valet enters with Inez Serrano. Inez has no questions for the valet who exits once again. Inez briefly inspects the room then asks abruptly where Florence is. Garcin doesn't know where or who Florence is. He introduces himself politely to an unfriendly Inez who asks, 'Must you be here all the time, or do you take a stroll outside now and then?' (*IC*, p. 187). Garcin would like to be alone too, to ponder his life and set it in order, but the door is locked, trapping them in each other's company. As he sits in silence Garcin's mouth twitches with fear, which soon irritates Inez. Garcin asks, 'How about you? Aren't you afraid?' (*IC*, p. 187). Inez argues that as she has no hope she has no fear. They wait for something to happen, Garcin hiding his twitching mouth behind his hands.

The valet enters with Estelle Rigault, an attractive young woman who immediately mistakes Garcin for someone she knows whose face has been shot away. She realizes her mistake when Garcin removes his hands. Revealing herself as vain and superficial, Estelle laughingly complains that the unoccupied sofa will clash with her blue dress. Garcin politely offers his sofa. Estelle introduces herself to Inez and Garcin who vie for her attention. The valet exits for the last time. No one else is coming, ever.

Each tells how they died. Estelle died of pneumonia the day before; she can picture her funeral, her sister trying to cry. Inez died of gas inhalation last week. Garcin took 12 bullets in the chest a month ago. He can picture his wife waiting outside the barracks where he was shot, not knowing he is dead. He says that she got on his nerves.

They consider their lives, how quickly time passes on earth now they are dead, all the while irritating each other. Though it is hot Estelle forbids Garcin to remove his coat as she loathes men in shirtsleeves. Inez admits to not caring much for men at all. They wonder why they have been put together as they have nothing in common.

Estelle had expected to meet old friends and relatives. She wonders if she knew Inez in life, but rejects this possibility snobbishly when Inez tells her she was only a postal-clerk. Garcin puts their being together down to chance; Inez thinks there is method in it. They wonder, if they have been put together deliberately, if anything is expected of them. They grow increasingly suspicious of the situation and of each other.

The question of why they are in hell inevitably arises. Estelle claims not to know, snobbishly accusing 'understrappers' (*IC*, p. 193) of making a mistake. Garcin is equally evasive. He claims he was a man of principle shot for being a pacifist. Inez tells them they are play-acting. People are not sent to hell by mistake. 'Yes, we are criminals – murderers – all three of us. We're in hell, my pets, they never make mistakes, and people aren't damned for nothing' (*IC*, p. 194). In confronting the other two Inez realizes why there is no torturer in *their* hell: they will torture each other. Attempting to avoid this they agree to ignore each other, to work out their own salvation in silence, but the silence is brief.

Inez begins to sing about beheadings while Estelle tries to put on make-up without a mirror. It makes her feel queer. She feels non-existent when she cannot see herself. Inez offers to be her mirror. The tiny reflection Estelle sees in Inez' eyes is not useful. Inez guides Estelle's hand as she applies her lipstick, telling her she looks lovely. Estelle is embarrassed by this intimacy and distrustful of Inez words. How can she know, without a real mirror, that Inez is telling the truth? Inez realises she can torture Estelle by being a false mirror and lying to her about how she looks. Estelle wants Garcin to notice her looks. A man, she thinks, will confirm her beauty with his desire. Inez is annoyed that Estelle is more interested in Garcin who is trying to ignore her than in Inez who is attentive.

Garcin insists it is better if they try to forget each other's presence. Inez retorts that it is impossible to do so. 'To forget about the others? How utterly absurd! I *feel* you there, down to my marrow. Your silence clamours in my ears' (*IC*, p. 200). She says she would prefer to fight it out with them, so they return to the question of why they are in hell.

Garcin admits that he treated his wife badly. 'Night after night I came home blind drunk; stinking of wine and women' (*IC*, p. 202). He took a live-in lover and allowed his wife to serve them.

Inez broke up a relationship between her cousin and Florence by turning Florence against him. The women began an affair, giving him hell until he was run over by a tram. Inez cruelly teased Florence that they had killed him until one night Florence crept out of bed, turned on the gas and killed them both.[1]

Estelle is less forthcoming but eventually her story is prised from her. She had an affair with Roger, a poor man of a lower social class. A baby was born in Switzerland, in secret. Roger was delighted, Estelle was not. She drowned the baby in a lake and returned to her rich husband in Paris. Roger shot himself. Estelle tries to cry but the distraction of tears is not available in hell.

As each pictures life on earth moving rapidly on, as they are dismissed or forgotten by the living, they turn increasingly to each other for attention and confirmation. Inez wants Estelle to turn to her, Estelle, who wants to exist only as an attractive object, turns to Garcin to be loved. She hopes to see herself as a lover sees her, as an object of value, even though in truth she is a worthless murderer. Garcin is not interested in Estelle for her own sake. Neither is he sorry about his treatment of his wife. His main concern in hell is for his reputation. Did he refuse to fight because he was a pacifist or a coward?[2] In constantly asking himself this question he is similar to Philippe, a character that appears in *The Reprieve* and *Iron in the Soul*. Like Philippe, Garcin is plagued by the suspicion that he is a coward. He meant to die well at his execution but failed to do so. He pictures friends on earth dismissing him as a coward and is tortured by the fact that he can no longer act to change their opinion. He turns to Estelle for confirmation that he is not a coward but she is so superficial he cannot take her opinion seriously. To her a coward is only someone who looks cowardly. She does not care if Garcin is a coward or not, she just wants a man, any man, to love her and confirm her existence as a desirable object. Estelle is grateful for any attention she gets from Garcin, whatever his motive.

Garcin is so disgusted that Estelle would have him even as a coward, and moreover that she can do nothing to confirm that he is not a coward, that he says he would rather endure physical torture. 'Open the door! Open, blast you! I'll endure anything, your red-hot tongs and molten lead... Anything, anything would be better than this agony of mind' (*IC*, p. 219). The door flies open but Garcin will not exit. Estelle tries to push Inez out. Inez begs to stay; she is a coward and fears going. Estelle releases Inez in surprise when

Garcin announces that he has decided to stay because of Inez. Inez is surprised too. Garcin shuts the door. He has recognized that, unlike Estelle, Inez knows what it is to be a coward. It is *her* he must convince that he is not a coward. 'She – she doesn't count. It's you who matter; you who hate me. If you'll have faith in me I'm saved' (*IC*, p. 220). Garcin offers Inez arguments: Had he lived longer he would have done brave deeds, etc., but she is not impressed. She tells him, 'One always dies too soon – or too late' (*IC*, p. 221). She is able to make Garcin a coward simply by thinking him one, by wishing it. Garcin is at her mercy, but she is also at his because he can exclude her by giving Estelle his attention, attention that Estelle is keen to receive and return, not least because it upsets Inez. However, in turning to Estelle to spite Inez, Garcin is plagued by the thought that Inez sees him as a coward. He turns back to Inez to convince her he is not a coward. In realizing that Inez will always see him and judge him and that he cannot control her opinion of him Garcin understands he is in hell. 'There's no need for red-hot pokers. Hell is – other people!' (*IC*, p. 223). Garcin tells Estelle that he cannot love her while Inez is between them, watching. Estelle stabs Inez with the paper knife. Inez just laughs and stabs herself to show Estelle the futility of it. They all laugh at their eternal damnation to this intolerable situation before slumping dejectedly on their respective sofas.

What Sartre really wants to examine in *In Camera* is not some impossible, supernatural, nightmare scenario, but a key aspect of our being on earth. Namely, the existence of other people and the profound and often disturbing impact that their existence has on the nature and value of our own personal existence. In short, he wants to examine the phenomenon of *being-for-others*. In Chapter 2 of this book, in the section on being-for-others, it was argued that every person exists for others as well as for himself. A person is his being-for-others, but he is it over there for the Other. The Other only has to look at him to take possession of at least a part of what he is. Under the gaze of the Other he is made to be responsible for what the Other sees. He is subject to the Other's judgment of him, and although he can try to influence this judgement he can never gain complete control over it or even know for sure what it is. Consider the scene in which Inez offers to be Estelle's mirror (*IC*, pp. 197–199). As there are no real mirrors in the room Inez offers to tell Estelle what she looks like, but Estelle cannot trust this pseudo-mirror. If Estelle wants to know how she looks, how others see her, then it would help her to look in a mirror, but it is not at all helpful for her to take feedback from Inez on how she looks. Nobody can be just a mirror. A real mirror can distort, but it cannot lie as Inez does when she tells Estelle she has a pimple on her cheek. Even when Inez tells the truth, Estelle cannot know it is the truth, and whatever honest view Inez expresses is subject to change, subject to her freedom. Inez makes an unreliable and uncomfortable mirror for Estelle. Estelle wants to see herself as a familiar object, as a face in a mirror, she does not want to see the Other seeing her and forming unknowable evaluations of her. Inez suggests that she is nicer than Estelle's mirror, to which Estelle replies,

> Oh, I don't know. You scare me rather. My reflection in the glass never did that; of course I knew it so well. Like something I had tamed --- I'm going to smile and my smile will sink down into your pupils, and heaven knows what it will become. (*IC*, p. 198)

In being subject to the judgement of the Other, a person is at the mercy of the freedom of the Other, he is, as Sartre puts it, 'enslaved' (*BN*, p. 291) by the freedom of the Other. The freedom of the Other transcends his freedom, transcends his transcendence, reducing him to what he is for the Other. This situation is clearly illustrated in the relationship – as it is by the end of the play – between Garcin and Inez. Garcin cannot convince himself that he is not a coward, hence he desperately needs Inez to assure him he is not a coward. But Inez is a free being and he cannot determine her opinion. Even if he could determine her opinion he would not be satisfied because he needs her opinion to be freely given for it to have any power to persuade him. Garcin suffers the agony of being subject to Inez' freedom, she can make him the coward he loathes to be simply by thinking him a coward. Being dead, he cannot *act* as a hero in order to influence her opinion, but even if he could act the hero there is no guarantee she would adopt the view of him he wants her to adopt. She might simply dismiss him as rash or foolish, as a coward nonetheless. Even if Inez were not cruel and inclined to think the worst of him, there would still be no guarantee.

Garcin is obliged to exist, to suffer, Inez' negative opinion of him. He cannot stop thinking about it, it prevents him from making love to Estelle. If he were alive he could act to try and convince himself, or others besides Inez, that he is not a coward. He could flee Inez' presence and in time dismiss her as an insignificant Other, as people tend to do with those who have formed very low opinions of them. But in Sartre's nightmare scenario Garcin can no longer act, he can no longer transcend himself towards the heroic being he would like to be. He can no longer flee his present, unsatisfactory being towards the future, or flee the one who judges him. Estelle is too superficial to count as a genuine Other and all other beings have faded, so Garcin is stuck, pinned down as the vile, cowardly thing Inez' cruel freedom wishes him to be. As the only remaining Other, Inez is to him all others. She is his supreme and only judge on an everlasting judgement day.

Philosophically, Sartre rejects the possibility of any form of after-life, arguing that death is not a possibility one can experience for oneself. Death is the end of all possibility; it is complete annihilation. *In Camera*, therefore, is not a prediction of a possible afterlife. The play is simply claiming that *if* there were an eternal afterlife, it would be hell to spend it in the company of other people. Indeed, it would be so bad that annihilation is infinitely preferable. The play progresses inexorably through mounting conflict towards Sartre's damning conclusion, his famous sweeping statement, 'Hell is other people' (*IC*, p. 223). But is it really true that hell is other people? Does the play actually allow this damning conclusion to be drawn? There is so much else in that miserable room besides the people present that makes it hellish. In that place hell is not only other people, hell is no windows, no mirrors, no darkness, no sleep, no books, no tears, no exit. An eternity in one miserable room with a handful of people and no distractions would be hell, but would it not be the circumstances rather than the company that made it so? It depends on the company. The characters in the play are particu-larly unpleasant, selfish and pathetic (the reason why they are in hell), but what about an eternity with Buddha or Mandela or other decent people of your own choice? Presumably not so bad as an eternity with Garcin the drunken, cowardly adulterer, Inez the self confessed 'damned bitch' (*IC*, p. 202) and Estelle the infanticide. Arguably, the play does not allow the universal conclusion to be drawn that hell is other people, but simply the conclusion that an eternity trapped in a single miserable room with Garcin, Inez and Estelle, or people like them, would be hell. Either that, or under the aspect of eternity everything becomes hell: other people whoever they may be, solitude, oneself, pleasure, consciousness – anything. It would all become unbearable, yet a person would have to bear it, wouldn't they.

MEN WITHOUT SHADOWS
(DEATH WITHOUT BURIAL OR THE VICTORS)[3]

Allied Forces liberated Paris on 25 August 1944. World War II ended the following May. Some French intellectuals who had backed the wrong side, approved the Third Reich and written for the collaborationist press emerged from the occupation as villains. Sartre emerged as a hero and a formidable voice in postwar France. He had more than done his bit, as a conscript, a prisoner of war, an escapee and an insurgent. With subtlety and discretion, avoiding futile recklessness but not genuine personal risk, he had resisted. From *Bariona,* through *Being and Nothingness* to *The Flies* he had proclaimed the centrality of human freedom. He had contributed to the underground press, criticizing the Germans and the pro-German Vichy regime of General Pétain. Most notably, he had founded 'Socialism and Freedom', a resistance group that sought a third political way between the resistance of the capitalist Gaullists on the right and the Communists on the left. Always with one eye on the bigger picture Sartre wanted the politics of 'Socialism and Freedom' to shape a liberated, postwar France, but squeezed between two much larger resistance movements Sartre's group eventually folded.

It is not surprising, then, that *Men without Shadows,* Sartre's first postwar play, is about the French Resistance. It is, in a subtle, realistic way, a play dedicated to the memory of the ordinary men and women who fought and died for the Resistance, lest their bravery and their suffering be forgotten. As in *In Camera,* we find a group of people imprisoned in awful circumstances. There is the same claustrophobia and sense of hopelessness, but it is an atmosphere rooted in history and politics and the banal brutality of men, rather than in an improbable, nightmarish metaphysics. From their different perspectives, worldly and other-worldly, the two plays explore many of the same heavyweight Sartrean themes: being-for-others, conflict, the banality of evil, fear, bravery, cowardice, death and oblivion.

Men without Shadows, completed in 1946, is set in 1944 in World War II France. Forces loyal to the pro-German Vichy regime have captured a group of Resistance fighters. Locked in an upstairs room, handcuffed, the prisoners await their fate: to be tortured then killed. The youngest of them, François, shows his fear and frustration by complaining that he did not expect such dire consequences when he joined the Resistance. 'Did you warn me when I came to you in the first place? You told me, the Resistance has need of men, you didn't tell me it needed heroes. I'm no hero – I tell you!' (*MWS*, Act 1, Scene 1, p. 178). The others, François' sister, Lucie, and three older men, Sorbier, Canoris and Henri, are more resigned. They fear pain and death but their primary concern is to avoid exposing themselves as the cowards they suspect themselves to be. If the prisoners scream and beg for mercy their torturers will triumph. If they keep silent they will win a moral victory. They view the situation more as a battle of wills on a personal level than as anything to do with the cause for which they are fighting. As they initially have no useful information to give their interrogators, they are more concerned with trying not to disgrace themselves than with betraying others.

Sorbier is taken out and tortured. His screams are heard in the distance. The leader of the group, Jean, is brought into the room. The enemy do not know who he is. In their view he is simply a man they are detaining temporarily while they check his story. Jean's arrival gives the others information they must now try to withhold. They prefer this as it gives their suffering meaning and purpose and will provide a mental distraction when they are tortured.

> 'Listen,' says Henri, 'if you hadn't come, we'd have suffered like animals, without knowing why. But you have come, and now everything has got a meaning. We can fight. Not for you alone, but for all the boys. I thought I was finished, but I see I might still be useful. With a bit of luck, I might even feel I'm not dying for nothing.' (*MWS*, Act 1, Scene 1, p. 190)

Sorbier returns to the room supported by militiamen. He collapses in pain against a trunk, ashamed of his screams, his limited courage. Seeing Jean he says he would have betrayed him had he known he was there. 'I tell you I'd have betrayed my own mother. It's all wrong that one moment can destroy your whole life' (*MWS*, Act 1, Scene 1, p. 187). Canoris and Henri are tortured. Henri cries out in pain but neither man betrays Jean. Sorbier is tortured again.

Unable to stand the pain he tells his torturers he will give them information if they untie him. Untied he runs to the window and jumps to his death. Lucie is tortured and raped but does not crack. She returns to the room feeling emotionally dead, unable to love Jean as she had at the start of the play. 'I think I ought to love you. But I can't feel my love anymore. I can't feel anything' (*MWS*, Act 2, p. 206).

Jean has been growing increasingly guilty that the others are suffering for him. He feels excluded and wants to share their suffering in order to feel he is one of them. He wants François to denounce him so that he can be tortured along with the others. He hopes Lucie will love him again if this happens. He even attempts to torture himself by beating his hand with a log. Lucie is not impressed. She argues that it does not compare with the torture she and the others have suffered because it is not a violation. A person cannot violate himself. 'You can break your bones, you can tear out your eyes. It's you, you who have chosen to inflict the pain. Each of our wounds is a violation because they were inflicted by other people' (*MWS*, Act 2, p. 214).

Fearing that François will talk under interrogation, Henri strangles him to death. Lucie does nothing to defend her brother. Still unaware of Jean's identity the torturers release him and the following morning the three surviving prisoners are sent for. Suspecting that the remaining prisoners will not crack under torture and having no real appetite for brutality anyway, Landrieu, the enemy leader, says he will spare their lives if they talk. Unable to crack them with torture, Landrieu is now trying to bribe them. He is no longer particularly interested in any information they have to give, he simply wants to win the battle of wills with them by any means available. Lucie feels they have won a moral victory; that their torturers have gained nothing but a sense of shame. 'We've won! We've won! This moment makes everything worthwhile... You raped me and you are ashamed. I am clean again. Where are your pincers and your thumbscrews? Where are your whips? This morning you beg us to live. The answer is no. No! You must finish what you've begun' (*MWS*, Act 3, pp. 222–223).

Canoris wants to talk and give false information agreed with Jean before his release. The other two do not even want to give false information if it looks as though they cracked. Henri wants to die to be rid of the guilt of killing François. Lucie wants to die to disgrace her killers and to be rid of the shame of being raped. Canoris convinces Henri that he must live in order that his future actions justify his killing François. Together they persuade Lucie that life is still worth living if she can stop dwelling on her suffering and enjoy the simple pleasures that life offers. They give Landrieu their false story and he is prepared to spare them. Unfortunately, Clochet, a sadist who enjoys torture for its own sake – a man who sold cream cakes before the war – acts against Landrieu's orders and has the prisoners shot.

Comparable to Sartre's 1939 short story, *The Wall*, which is also about prisoners of war facing death, *Men without Shadows* explores the complex psychology of torturers and tortured, executioners and condemned, and the struggle for transcendence that exists between them. It is not enough for the torturer to inflict pain or even death, he gains ascendancy over his victim only if his victim cracks by crying out, pleading for mercy and ultimately disclosing information. If the tortured person endures his suffering and remains silent he has refused to be a victim, he has won the power struggle with his torturer and gained ascendancy over him. Sartre suggests that the fear of losing this power struggle, the fear of being exposed as a coward and having to live with that knowledge, can become greater than the fear of pain and death. The subject of cowardice fascinates Sartre; it is a recurrent theme in his work.[4]

Of the utmost importance to many of Sartre's characters is the question of whether or not they are a coward and the question of whether or not others think they are a coward. War permeated Sartre's life, and undoubtedly such questions become highly pertinent during times of war, but do most people, even in times of war, attach quite as much importance to being or not being a coward as Sartre suggests? Surely, some people are genuinely untroubled and unashamed that they have always chosen to respond to situations in a cowardly way. Sartre's reply to this might well be that only the lowest scoundrel could feel untroubled and unashamed if his cowardice prevented him, for example, from defending his family against violence. Extreme situations force people to confront themselves, to discover through their responses what they are capable of. Can they muster the courage to be of some worth when the chips are down or are they worthless cowards? Only the most subhuman person could be completely indifferent to what he finds – completely indifferent towards himself. Given that to be a person is to have projects and to care about outcomes, to evaluate and to care about findings, such an indifferent person seems an impossibility. Fortunately perhaps, as Sorbier notes (*MWS*, Act 1, Scene 1, p. 188), many people are lucky enough – have the moral luck – to live their entire life without encountering circumstances that force them into absolute self-confrontation. 'Lots of people,' says Sorbier, 'die in their beds, with a clear conscience. Good sons, good husbands, good citizens, good fathers – ha! They are cowards like me and they'll never know it. They're just lucky' (*MWS*, Act 1, Scene 1, p. 188).

People who are tortured are often tortured for information about others. They may endure torture and remain silent to protect others, or they may endure only for the sake of their own pride. Whatever their motives, their silence benefits others, leaving others feeling uncomfortably indebted. Through the character of Jean, Sartre explores the situation of a person for whom others suffer torture. Jean's lack of suffering excludes him from the group and makes him feel inferior. He experiences such intense guilt over his lack of suffering that he desires to be tortured himself. His own torture would remove his guilt and sense of inferiority and reunite him with those who have suffered for him. Jean's guilt is an instance of what has come to be known in modern clinical psychology as *survivor guilt* or *survivor syndrome*: a mental condition suffered by some people when they recognize that they have avoided, escaped or survived a situation that others have fallen victim to. Sartre identifies, at least in the kind of survivor guilt that Jean experiences, an element of victim envy. Jean is envious in so far as he feels excluded from and inferior to a group united and elevated by a terrible collective experience.

A recurrent theme in the play is the fear people have of dying without a witness and being utterly forgotten. Lamenting the fact that after he dies he will not be an existential absence, Henri says,

> I shan't be missed anywhere, I leave no gap. The underground is crammed, the restaurants crowded. I shall slip out of this world and still leave it full. Like an egg. I've got to realise that I'm not indispensable. I wish I could be indispensable. To something, or to someone. (*MWS*, Act 1, Scene 1, p. 183)

And as he says more pointedly later on, 'To die without witnesses is real annihilation' (*MWS*, Act 1, Scene 1, pp. 189–190). Before she is raped and loses her love for Jean, Lucie consoles herself with the thought that she will live on in his memory. Though dead, she will continue to have a being-for-others. 'We've all got Jean. He is our leader, and he is thinking of us' (*MWS*, Act 1, Scene 1, p. 183). After she is raped she ceases to care about Jean, to care that he cares for her and thinks of her. She cares only what her abusers think of her, as though her being-for-others existed exclusively for the men who attacked her pride and transcended her transcendence. Her only desire is to be tortured again, to regain her transcendence by shaming her torturers with her silence and dignity. 'All I want is for them to come for me again, and beat me, so I can keep silent again, and fool them and frighten them' (*MWS*, Act 2, p. 214). Jean accuses her of pride. 'Is it my fault?' she replies. 'It was my pride they attacked. I hate them, but they still hold me; and I hold them. I feel nearer to them than I do to you' (*MWS*, Act 2, p. 214).

The fear the prisoners have that they will not be missed after they have died, their fear of oblivion, gives the play its English title. They fear being men without shadows, anonymous corpses that died for nothing with only their killers knowing how or when they died. Sartre gives the last words of the play to the sadistic killer, Clochet, who speaks just before the last prisoner is shot. 'In a moment, no one will think of this any more. No one but us' (*MWS*, Act 3, p. 229).

THE RESPECTABLE PROSTITUTE

The Respectable Prostitute is Sartre's American play; the only play he set in the USA. The year before the publication of the play Sartre spent five months in the USA, from January to May 1945, as the guest of the US State Department. The play was undoubtedly inspired to a significant extent by this visit. Sartre was among a small group of French journalists who undertook the uncomfortable two-day flight from Paris to New York in an unpressurized DC-8. He was representing Albert Camus' Resistance newspaper, *Combat*, and the leading French daily, *Le Figaro*. He enjoyed neither the journey nor the company of the other journalists but he was excited to be visiting a country that had always loomed so large in his imagination. In many respects Sartre had a romantic view of the USA inspired by the American comic books, detective stories, novels and movies he had devoured as he grew up. For Sartre, the USA was a land of freedom and adventure where anything might happen. Its architecture, art and music represented the future. It had always provided the perfect antidote to the middle-class stuffiness of his early years; it would now provide five months of welcome relief from the dull austerity of war torn France.

First-hand experience of skyscrapers and bright lights only served to fuel Sartre's love for this vast, complex country that had liberated his own from Nazi tyranny, and for the rest of his life he never ceased to appreciate the boldness and optimism of the USA, and of New York in particular. Like many left-wing European intellectuals, however, he became increasingly critical of certain aspects of the USA, not least its interventionist postwar foreign policy, but above all the shameful and undemocratic way in which black Americans were treated by the white majority.

As his notes on the USA made during the long flight reflect, Sartre had already given the country a lot of serious thought, particularly the contemporary American literature of John Dos Passos and William Faulkner. In the 1930s he had recommended these writers to his students, lectured on their themes and techniques and praised them in articles of literary criticism published in *La Nouvelle Revue Française*. In *Being and Nothingness* (*BN*, pp. 427–428), during his analysis of sadism, Sartre quotes at length from Faulkner's *Light in August*, a novel in which an Afro-American, Joe Christmas, is hunted down and castrated by the 'good citizens' of Jefferson, Mississippi. Faulkner's novel, with its focus on the theme of racial hatred in the USA, greatly influenced Sartre in his writing of *The Respectable Prostitute*. Through his reading Sartre was well aware of the evils of racial segregation and inequality in the USA prior to encountering it for himself. Encountering it – witnessing two black soldiers refused a table in a dinning car, for example – motivated him to become one of the first intellectuals outside of the USA to join the struggle against it. On 16 June 1945, *Le Figaro* published Sartre's article, 'What I Learned About the Black Problem', in which he writes, 'In this country, so justly proud of its democratic institutions, one man out of ten is deprived of his political rights; in this land of freedom and equality there live thirteen million untouchables'. For Sartre, it was particularly galling that widespread, institutionalized racism should fester at the heart of a country that in other respects had so much to commend it and had done so much to further the ideals of human liberty and opportunity. With his play *The Respectable Prostitute* he continued to add his voice to the voices of those who recognized that the existence of officially sanctioned racial oppression in the so-called 'land of the free' was an indefensible, intolerable and ultimately unsustainable contradiction.

Like the Faulkner novel that helped to inspire it, *The Respectable Prostitute*, completed in 1946, is set in the Deep South of the USA. Sartre visited the Deep South, including New Orleans, during his aforementioned trip. The background to the play is an unprovoked attack by four white men on two black men that took place on a train the previous day. During the attack one of the black men was shot dead. The white men have lied that they acted to stop the black men from raping a white girl. Accused of rape, the surviving black man has become a fugitive. The play begins with him calling at the door of the central character, Lizzie MacKay, asking her to hide him and testify to his innocence. Lizzie refuses on the grounds that she has 'enough troubles of my own, without getting mixed up in other people's' (*RP*, Scene 1, p. 11). He pleads that he will be killed by the white folk if she does not help him but she slams the door in his face. Lizzie witnessed the attack and is the white girl who is supposed to have been raped. She arrived by train from New York the previous day with the intention of making a living as a prostitute. Fred, her first client, a man she has spent the night with, enters from the bathroom unaware of who was at the door. Fred has enjoyed his night with Lizzie but his motive in picking her up was not primarily sexual. He is the cousin of Tom, the murderer, and is part of a plot to persuade Lizzie to testify against the black man.

The police arrive, friends of Fred, and threaten to charge Lizzie with prostitution unless she signs a statement accusing the black man of rape. She refuses. Senator Clarke arrives, Fred's father, and adopts a more subtle approach to persuade Lizzie to sign. He implores her to spare the life of Tom's poor mother who will die of shock if her son is convicted. He implores her to be a good American and to save a young, white, Harvard educated man of respectable family; a man who is an employer, a leader and 'a solid rampart against communism, trade unionism, and the Jews' (*RP*, Scene 1, p. 28). He asks her what Uncle Sam would do if he had to choose between such a man and a useless Negro who does nothing but loaf, sing and buy fancy clothes. He tells her the whole town will be grateful if she signs the statement. 'The Negro? Bah! If you sign, the whole town will adopt you. The whole town. All the mothers of the town' (*RP*, Scene 1, p. 29). He insists that a whole town cannot be wrong if it thinks someone has done the right thing. Bewildered, flattered and moved to patriotism by his emotive words Lizzie signs the statement.

Twelve hours later the black man climbs in through Lizzie's window and hides behind a curtain as the noise of a mob grows outside. The senator returns to tell Lizzie that his sister is grateful, that in signing the statement and saving her son Lizzie 'did the right thing' (*RP*, Scene 2, p. 30). He gives her a hundred dollars, supposedly a gift from his sister. Lizzie is scornful of the gift. Although part of her still wants to believe the senator's fancy words, she realizes he has bamboozled her into betraying an innocent man and that the money is just a sordid pay-off. The senator leaves, promising to return. The black man appears from behind the curtain and again pleads with Lizzie to help him. She asks what will happen if he is caught. 'They'll have no mercy; they'll whip me over the eyes, they'll pour cans of gasoline over me' (*RP*, Scene 2, p. 33). As the manhunt nears her door, Lizzie, to her credit, says she will tell them he is innocent.

> For twenty-five years they've fooled me. White-haired mothers! Heroes! Uncle Sam and the American Nation! Now I understand. They won't catch me out again! I'll open the door, and I'll say: 'He's here. He's here, but he has done nothing. I was forced to sign a false statement. I swear by Almighty God that he didn't do anything.' (*RP*, Scene 2, p. 34)

The black man insists that they will not believe her. She tells him to hide in her bathroom just before a group of armed men arrive at her door. She astonishes, horrifies and arouses the men by telling them that she was the girl the black man raped. 'Come and fetch me when you've got him' (*RP*, Scene 2, p. 35). The ruse works and they go away.

The black man reappears but has to hide yet again as Fred arrives saying that he has taken part in a lynching. 'They caught a nigger. It wasn't the right one. They lynched him all the same' (*RP*, Scene 2, p. 36). He all but admits to having been sexually aroused by the violence as he declares his desire for Lizzie. He hears a noise in the bathroom and investigates. As the black man flees he fires and misses then throws his gun down on the table. Protesting the black man's innocence, angry that Fred and his father have duped her, Lizzie aims her revolver at Fred. He defends himself with arguments similar to those used by his father, the senator, to defend Tom. He claims that as the only male heir of an old and powerful American family he has a right to live.

> My father is a senator; I shall be a senator after him; I am his only male heir and the last of my name. We have made this country and its story is our story. There have been Clarkes in Alaska, in the Philippines, in New Mexico. Dare you shoot the whole of America? (*RP*, Scene 2, p. 38)

Lizzie surrenders the gun. Fred promises to buy her a fine house and visit her regularly. 'You'll have coloured servants and more money than you ever dreamed of, but you must do everything I want' (*RP*, Scene 2, p. 38). She acquiesces and becomes his mistress, his respectable prostitute.

The play clearly highlights the violence and injustice of racism in the Southern USA prior to the emergence of the Civil Rights Movement. It shows how this racism is rooted in an ideology of white supremacy that appeals to patriotism and a distorted version of history, and how it is promoted by corruption and nepotism at the highest levels of authority. Politically radicalized by the events of Word War II, Sartre sought to expose what he saw as a great hypocrisy. The USA had helped to defeat Nazism abroad in the name of liberty and democracy, yet it tolerated racial prejudice, inequality and violence on its own streets.

Lizzie represents the ordinary person caught up in this or any other unfavourable political situation. She is well-meaning with an initially clear sense of justice but she is too easily influenced by the rhetoric of those with power and wealth. She ultimately fails to stand up for justice by eventually yielding to the demands and expectations of those she has sought to resist. She falls into bad faith, aspiring to relinquish responsibility for herself in order to become a plaything of the ruling class. In Sartre's view, her acquiescence makes her a collaborator, as responsible in her own banal way for the racial injustices that surround her as those who actually commit the crimes. Sartre's message is revolutionary: injustice will continue until ordinary people like Lizzie find the intelligence and courage to positively affirm their freedom by resisting corrupt authority.

In the same year that he published *The Respectable Prostitute*, 1946, Sartre also published *Anti-Semite and Jew*, a book in which he explores the nature and causes of anti-Semitism in Europe. Both works explore the bigotry and racial hatred directed by a white, Christian majority towards a significant minority perceived to lack any real individual identity or value. A minority perceived as socially, morally and culturally inferior, who nonetheless supposedly represent a serious threat to what someone like Senator Clarke would refer to as 'decent white folk'. In Europe, particularly the Europe of the 1930s and 1940s, the myth of white supremacy largely manifested itself as anti-Semitism. In the USA it largely manifested itself as racial hatred of a black underclass. Sartre's general point is that racial supremacists and bigots the world over share similar characteristics. Like Fred and his father they all appeal to their precious *rights*, the sanctity of their good name and their family ties, their history and their membership of a proud nation. They believe that their existence is necessary if not God given, and certainly of greater value than the lives of members of those ethnic groups they despise. Fred and his father are *salauds* (swine or bastards) comparable to the smug *salauds* of Bouville in Sartre's novel, *Nausea*, or to the desperately racist *salaud* that Lucien Fleurier becomes by the end of Sartre's short story, *The Childhood of a Leader*. Lucien Fleurier's view of the 'dagos' that frequent café La Source is analogous to Senator Clarke's view of the 'niggers' in his town. 'They could dress in clothes from tailors on the Boulevard Saint-Michel in vain; they were hardly more than jellyfish, Lucien thought, he was not a jellyfish, he did not belong to that humiliated race.' (*CL*, p. 141). 'Lizzie,' says Senator Clarke,

> this Negro you are protecting, what use is he? He was born God knows where. I have fed him and what does he do for me in return? Nothing at all. He doesn't work, he loafs and sings all day; he buys zoot suits and fancy ties...I wouldn't even notice his death. (*RP*, Scene 1, p. 28)

Fred and his father hail from a different continent but in their hauteur, narrow-mindedness and bad faith they would find much in common with the *salauds* of Bouville or with Lucien Fleurier and his fascist friends.

DIRTY HANDS (CRIME PASSIONNEL)

Dirty Hands or *Crime Passionnel* was completed in 1948. Like *The Respectable Prostitute* of two years earlier, it examines personal ethics within a fevered political situation. Whereas *The Respectable Prostitute* focuses on how the political intrudes into the personal, *Dirty Hands* focuses on how the personal intrudes into the political. Lizzie, the central character of *The Respectable Prostitute*, is trying to mind her own business when politics comes knocking at her door. Hugo Barine, the central character of *Dirty Hands,* places himself at the centre of a political crisis intending that his actions in that crisis will allow him to overcome perceived personal inadequacies.

Increasingly, Sartre was coming to recognize that the personal life of the individual and the political life of the collective are never separate. Each individual is shaped by the historical and political context in which he exists, just as that context is woven out of a myriad personal desires, ambitions, dislikes, prejudices and neuroses. At the heart of *Dirty Hands* is a psychoanalytical study of an individual in a given sociological context. This kind of study became Sartre's philosophical obsession, a key feature of his overall philosophical project from the late 1940s until blindness forced him to stop writing in the early 1970s. His aim was to *totalize* the individual, to reveal him as both a product of, and a reaction to, the immediate social circumstances of his family life and the broader social and political circumstances of his age and culture.

With this aim in mind he published several increasingly exhaustive psychoanalytical biographies of writers; exercises in existential psychoanalysis. Around the same time as *Dirty Hands* he published a biography of Baudelaire, in 1952 an acclaimed biography of Genet, and finally in 1971–72 a vast 2,800 page biography of Flaubert titled *The Family Idiot*, his last major work. He also abandoned after a considerable amount of work a biography of the poet Stéphane Mallarmé. 'The Flaubert', as Sartre nicknamed *The Family Idiot*, employs the 'regressive-progressive' method first formulated in his 1960 work, *Search for a Method*. The method involves synthesizing the results of a regressive psychoanalysis of personality with the results of a progressive sociological investigation into an individual's economic, political, historical and cultural milieu. Only by this method, argues Sartre, can an individual be comprehended as a unified whole, as a totality. *Dirty Hands* exhibits in embryonic form what later became the regressive-progressive method, all be it as applied to a fictional, though not untypical, character.

The most philosophically significant aspect of *Dirty Hands* is the psychological study of Hugo Barine that it offers. It is, however, best known as an expression of Sartre's disillusionment with communism and has often been used by anti-communists to attack communism. As a play written by a world-famous left-wing intellectual its criticisms of communism seem to have more force than do criticisms of communism made by right-wingers. In short, *Dirty Hands* appears to carry the polemical force of self-criticism. In actual fact, Sartre did not 'see the light' and reject communism with *Dirty Hands*. The play merely satirizes a fictional communist party of a fictional country for making a U-turn and adopting policies that it has previously dogmatically and violently rejected. It is *all* political dogmatism that refuses to engage in reality or to compromise, or that is very slow to do so, that Sartre wishes to censure, rather than communist ideals and aspirations as such. Sartre wrote the play partly as a reaction to what he saw as the dogmatism and arrogance of the French Communist Party (PCF) of the late 1940s. More specifically, he was attacking the dogmatism and arrogance of certain personalities within the PCF that he had personally clashed with over issues relating to the political direction of postwar France. We see here an instance of that inevitable entangling of the personal and political with which Sartre became so philosophically preoccupied. Although he was never a member of any communist party, Sartre remained, broadly speaking, a communist long after he wrote *Dirty Hands*. He remained a committed Marxist until a few years before he died and he never ceased to support a range of left-wing causes.

In 1952, as the Cold War intensified and a right-wing French government sought to silence the PCF, Sartre moved back towards it and gave it his strongest support. He was now defending, in an emergency, the very right of the PCF to exist and to have a voice, rather than its specific policies. It was during the Cold War period that *Dirty Hands* was most often used as an instrument of anti-communist propaganda. Sartre grew so tired of this exploitation of his play by the political right that, uncharacteristically, he paid heavy damages to have performances of it in Vienna stopped while he was attending a Marxist conference there in December 1952. As he wrote in the newspaper *Le Monde* sometime later, on

25 September 1954, 'I do not disavow *Dirty Hands*, I only regret the way it was used. My play became a political battlefield, an instrument of political propoganda.' Largely because it has been exploited in a way that Sartre should have foreseen when he wrote it, *Dirty Hands* has proved to be his most enduringly controversial play, perhaps the reason why in France it has out sold all his other plays.

Hugo Barine is a young man sent to assassinate Hoederer, a leading figure of the radical, left-wing political party to which they both belong. A faction within the party wants Hoederer assassinated because of his plans to form a national coalition government with liberals and conservatives. Such a compromise, any compromise, is considered an intolerable deviation from official party policy. Hugo's own motives in wishing to carry out the assassination are highly questionable. 'Am I playing? Am I serious? Mystery–' (*DH*, Scene 2, p. 33). Does he genuinely want to further a political cause in which he believes or are his motives really personal? Hugo is in bad faith in so far as he seeks to convince himself that his motives are entirely political. As the play reveals, he is not so much driven by political idealism as by a desire to change himself and thereby the way others view him. Hugo is deeply dissatisfied with his being-for-others. Other party members dismiss him as a young, bourgeois intellectual, the ordinary people laugh at his political views and his campaigning, his wife Jessica treats him like a child and his father sees him as a failure. He is so desperate to be taken seriously that he is prepared to kill. He hopes and believes that by killing he will become a mature man of substance, a decisive man of action who will be feared and respected for his ruthlessness and admired for the apparent firmness of his convictions. Like Paul Hilbert, the central character of Sartre's short story *Erostratus* who also becomes a killer, Hugo wants to take final and complete control of his being-for-others through a decisive act that will define him beyond question. As he says at the end of the play, 'I thought I was much too young; I wanted to hang a crime round my neck, like a stone' (*DH*, Epilogue, p. 113). Hugo wants to exchange the insubstantiality and indeterminacy he feels so strongly as a being-for-itself, for the solidity and substantiality, not of a being-in-itself, but of a being-for-itself-in-itself – a being that is founded upon itself rather than upon the world of which it is conscious.

Not unlike Lucien Fleurier, the central character of Sartre's short story, *The Childhood of a Leader*, and many other characters in Sartre's stories, novels and plays, Hugo is struggling with issues of self-identity. Sartre recognizes that this is true of all people to some extent. As he says of himself in *Words*, the autobiography of his childhood, until he decided to become a writer he felt as though he was travelling on a train without a ticket; travelling through life without justification for his absurd existence. Sartre also recognizes that every person, every being-for-itself, is striving in vein to become a being-for-itself-in-itself. Fortunately, unlike Paul Hilbert, Lucien Fleurier and Hugo Barine, most people do not seek to obtain this goal through violence, although many do. Hugo wants to feel significant, necessary and indispensable, and he sees winning positive regard from others as a way of achieving this. Unfortunately, he is incapable of winning positive regard from others by reasonable, constructive means because he is self-obsessed and shows others too much resentment for them to warm to him. In desperation he decides to *demand* positive regard from others, or at least grudging respect, by becoming a killer.

Ironically, the only character in the play who shows Hugo respect and is prepared to take him seriously is Hoederer. Hugo finds himself drawn to Hoederer who is strong, intelligent and respected and seems to possess the mature, heroic substantiality Hugo lacks. Above all, Hoederer is decisive. He is prepared to get *dirty hands* acting with expediency against the endlessly theorizing idealists and political purists in his party to secure a genuine practical advantage. 'My hands are filthy. I've dipped them up to the elbows in blood and slime. So what? Do you think you can govern and keep your spirit white?' (*DH*, Scene 4, p. 95). By acting alongside Hoederer, Hugo has the opportunity to change the person he is and become a true revolutionary, but he does not have the imagination or will to commit himself to such a project. As Hoederer is finally obliged to point out, Hugo will never become a true revolutionary because he has no love for people. Hoederer's words are particularly powerful and resonant, not least because they apply so accurately to contemporary terrorists and suicide bombers who seek to promote political and religious ideologies of human improvement through mass indiscriminate slaughter. 'You don't love your fellow men, Hugo. You only love your principles' (*DH*, Scene 4, p. 96). Indeed, Hugo hates people as he hates himself. 'I know you, my boy, you're a destroyer. You hate men because you hate yourself; your purity is the purity of death and the revolution you dream of isn't ours; you don't want to change the world, you want to blow it apart' (*DH*, Scene 4, p. 96). Hoederer concludes that Hugo is too much of an intellectual ever to be revolutionary. 'An intellectual is never a true revolutionary; he's only just good enough to be an assassin' (*DH*, Scene 4, p. 97).

Hoederer's words are proved right when Hugo eventually shoots him in a fit of jealously after Jessica develops an infatuation for him. Hugo's killing of Hoederer is not the cold-blooded political assassination Hugo wanted it to be, but neither is it truly a crime of passion. Hugo is motivated by a sense of his own inadequacy and insubstantiality far more than by any passion he has for Jessica.

Two years later Hugo is released from prison. The party has U-turned and adopted Hoederer's policy of collaboration, the policy for which they condemned Hoederer to death. Hoederer's reputation has been rehabilitated. The party want to cover up the fact that they sent Hugo to kill him. They want Hugo to take on a new identity and to forget that he ever knew Hoederer or killed him. They want him to deny his past and Hoederer's. During his time in prison Hugo has become increasingly ashamed that he killed Hoederer in a fit of jealousy. He wishes he had killed him for being a collaborator, that his motives had been moral and political. That way he would feel less ashamed. He decides he would feel most ashamed if he denied killing Hoederer altogether. To deny that he killed Hoederer would make it appear Hoederer died by accident and for nothing. 'If I deny my act, he becomes an anonymous corpse, a wreckage of the Party. Killed by chance' (*DH*, Epilogue, p. 119). Hugo decides he owes it to Hoederer to assert that he was sent by the party to kill him, thus emphasizing that Hoederer did not die by chance and for nothing.

> A man like Hoederer doesn't die by accident. He dies for his ideals, for his policy, he is responsible for his own death. If I recognize my crime before you all, if I reclaim my name of Raskolnikov, if I agree to pay the necessary price, then he will have had the death he deserved. (*DH*, Epilogue, pp. 119–120)[5]

In a sense, the party give Hugo the opportunity to finally kill Hoederer for the political reasons for which he was sent to kill him in the first place. The party enable Hugo to redeem his past and to achieve authenticity like his hero Hoederer. At the end of the play, like Hoederer, Hugo stands up for his beliefs and asserts his freedom in face of the execution he will suffer because of his refusal to follow party orders. Hugo is one of several characters in Sartre's fiction that achieve authenticity in face of death. The most notable example is Mathieu Delarue in the novel, *Iron in the Soul*, but there is also Pablo Ibbieta in the short story, *The Wall* – although Ibbieta narrowly avoids his execution in the end.

THE DEVIL AND THE GOOD LORD
(LUCIFER AND THE LORD)

Three years separate *Dirty Hands* and Sartre's next and reputedly favourite play, *The Devil and the Good Lord*, also called *Lucifer and the Lord*,[6] completed in 1951. In the meantime he had completed his epic war trilogy, *Roads to Freedom*. Like *Dirty Hands*, the play opened at the Théâtre Antoine, Paris, under the direction of Simone Berriau. It proved to be as successful as it was controversial and ran without interruption from 7 June 1951 until March of the following year. This lavish production had a star-studded cast including the legendary Maria Casarès, most famous as Death in Jean Cocteau's 1950 film, *Orphée*.

The Devil and the Good Lord is long and structurally complex, seeking to explore all the existentialist and Marxist themes that had accumulated in Sartre's philosophy up to that point. As in *Dirty Hands*, there is the intricate interplay of the personal, social and political that increasingly fascinated Sartre; an interplay brilliantly analysed in his biography of Jean Genet published the following year. Like Hugo Barine and Genet, Goetz, the central character of the play, wants to assert his personal identity in face of the Other. Whereas, for Hugo, the Other is other people, for Goetz, at least until he ceases to believe in him, the Other is primarily God. In this and certain other respects Goetz resembles Genet.

The play and the biography were written concurrently and it is not surprising that some of the character traits the biography identifies are sampled in the play. For instance, Sartre tells us how the young Genet, an orphaned charity case, had no right to the things he was given. '...they were quite free not to give him what he was not free not to accept' (*SG*, p. 9). Everything was a gift for which Genet had to be grateful. Nothing was really his own. Hence, he stole to have a 'possessive relationship with things' (*SG*, p. 12). Ironically, only stolen things felt as though they belonged to him, they were genuine appropriations rather than charitable gifts and he enjoyed his power of ownership over them. Goetz reveals the same key character trait as Genet when he argues that he hates to be granted anything. Goetz prefers to take what he wants, to steal it, from land to sexual intercourse. 'Nothing belongs to me except what I take' (*DG*, Act 1, Scene 3, p. 74). When his 'lover' Catherine tells him his caresses make her shudder, he replies, 'Good. If you ever get the idea of wanting to come to my arms, I shall drive you away immediately' (*DG*, Act 1, Scene 3, p. 75).

Although admirable for the many psychological, philosophical, theological and political themes it weaves together, the play is arguably overloaded with them; too busy, too multifaceted, too much of a convoluted rant, for any one theme to emerge with great clarity. In her autobiography, *Force of Circumstance*, Simone de Beauvoir tells how the director of the play took to wandering about the theatre during rehearsals imitating a pair of scissors with her hands (de Beauvoir 1987, p. 240). Further trimming by the director would surely have benefited the play. Although the play has some pointed and pithy one-liners, as a whole it lacks the crispness and minimalism of Sartre's earlier dramatic works. As Cohen-Solal notes, critics at the time 'reproached the play for not knowing whether to be intellectual, philosophical, metaphysical, boring, chatty, or verbose' (Cohen-Solal 2005, p. 318).

What the critics focused on above all else, however, was the plays sustained attack on religion and its strident atheism. Some critics who believed that there is a God to insult described the play as blasphemous, and it certainly is blasphemous if blasphemy is at all possible. One character who is belligerently opposed to the clergy, the socialist revolutionary Nasti the Baker, tells the Archbishop, 'Your Holy Church is a whore; she sells her favours to the rich' (*DG*, Act 1, Scene 1, p. 56). And later on, to take another example, Goetz charges God with non-existence: 'You see this emptiness over our heads? That is God...The silence is God. The absence is God. God is the loneliness of man. There was no one but myself; I alone decided on Evil; and I alone invented God' (*DG*, Act 3, Scene 10, p. 168). The atheism and irreverence of the play is reminiscent of the popular lecture, *Existentialism and Humanism*, which had caused such a stir five years earlier. 'Thus, there is no human nature, because there is no God to have a conception of it' (*EAH*, p. 28).

Evidently, Sartre found writing the play and assisting with its extravagant production very demanding. As his friend Jean Pouillon recounts, Sartre, now in his mid-40s, nearly collapsed at a rehearsal, the glass he was attempting to put down at the time slipping from his grasp. Up to this point Sartre had always been so tough and energetic, so invincible. His entourage, including Simone de Beauvoir, expected no less and were deeply shocked by the incident. Sartre's lifestyle – the drink, the drugs, the relentless work schedule – was beginning to catch up with him.

The Devil and the Good Lord is set in Medieval Germany. It begins at the siege of Worms. Stirred up by Nasti the Baker, the men of Worms have decided to kill 200 priests who are shut up in the monastery. Heinrich, a priest of Worms, is given a key by his bishop as the bishop dies. The key unlocks a secret tunnel from the town. Heinrich can save the priests if he betrays the town to the besieging army. He is confronted with the difficult choice, the unavoidable radical choice, of saving 200 priests or 20,000 men. 'The poor will massacre the priests, or Goetz will massacre the poor. Two hundred priests or twenty thousand men, you leave me a fair choice. The question is to know how many men equal a priest' (*DG*, Act 1, Scene 1, p. 60). Heinrich decides he should save the priests, not least because his bishop has commanded it. He escapes the town through the secret tunnel and meets with Goetz the leader of the besieging army. By the time he meets Goetz, Heinrich is unsure about what he should do and strives in bad faith to relinquish responsibility for his being-in-situation. He views *choice* as though it were a power that is granted, a power that he can refuse, and he seeks to fool himself that choosing not to choose is not itself a choice. When Goetz tells him he holds the lives of twenty thousand men in his power, he replies, 'I refuse to accept that power. It comes from the Devil' (*DG*, Act 1, Scene 2, p. 66). Goetz insists that he possesses it despite his refusal.

Goetz is an evil, violent man who has betrayed his half-brother Conrad and caused his death. It emerges that Goetz chooses to be evil in order to exercise his freedom and assert his will over the will of God. He believes that if he is sufficiently evil he will *force* God to damn him thus revealing a limit to God's power. Goetz offers various arguments to persuade Heinrich to tell him where the secret tunnel is. He tells Heinrich that it would be wrong to spare the lives of the people of Worms. Killing them will prevent them from killing the priests and so save them from eternal damnation and so on. 'Do you know what they'll gain by it? If they die tonight before they kill the priests, they will keep their hands clean; everyone will meet again in heaven' (*DG*, Act 1, Scene 2, p. 67). The play is full of such theological arguments and dilemmas. They are characteristic of the medieval period and were taken very seriously at that time. Sartre clearly enjoys exploring them, both for their own sake and for the purpose of opposing a medieval Christian world-view with an atheistic, existentialist world-view.

The play takes an unexpected turn when Heinrich convinces Goetz that there is nothing special about doing evil because everyone is doing it, whereas nobody has ever done only good. Goetz likes the idea of being the only person to do only good. He undergoes a radical conversion from evil, undertaking to live righteously. He lifts the siege of Worms without bloodshed and returns to his own lands. To the consternation of the neighbouring barons, and even to the socialist, Nasti, who forsees the dire consequences of such a sudden unilateral move, Goetz gives his lands away to his peasants. Peasants on the neighbouring lands revolt demanding the same and a war begins that costs more lives than a massacre at Worms would have done.

One of the main aims of the play is to argue that good and evil are in fact indistinguishable. As Goetz says, 'I wanted to do Good: foolishness: on this earth and at this time, Good and Evil are inseparable' (*DG*, Act 3, Scene 11, p. 172). Any action can produce positive or negative consequences that were not or could not be foreseen. As for intentions, they are no clearer than the consequences of actions. A person can be in bad faith with regard to his motives and intentions. Goetz initially believes that in giving his lands away he is motivated by kindness and a desire for social justice, but he later questions his motives recognizing that his desire to do good stems from a selfish desire to be better than everyone else. He wonders if perhaps he has given his lands away as a final betrayal of his despised family. He even wonders if everything he does, including good, is done only to satisfy an appetite for betrayal: 'Listen priest; I had betrayed everyone, including my own brother, but my appetite for betrayal was not yet fulfilled; so, one night, before the ramparts of Worms, I invented a way to betray Evil' (*DG*, Act 3, Scene 10, p. 166).

Some of the arguments and claims regarding himself that Goetz makes as he relentlessly scrutinizes good and evil and his motives for doing them seem rather far-fetched and contrived. Also, much of what he says is further confused in the relentless onrush of his self-obsessed raving. All that emerges with any real clarity, all that needs to emerge perhaps, is that he is deeply confused about who he is and why he acts. Sartre wants to present Goetz as authentic, as a kind of Nietzschean *overman* who is prepared to continually question and confront God, the Devil, other people and himself, but instead he comes across as little more than an irate philosophical talking head; an implausible caricature with no real human substance.

At the end of the play Goetz undergoes a second radical conversion – his capacity for radical conversions seems more a mark of mental instability and capriciousness than any real greatness of spirit. Unable to decide throughout the play whether Lucifer or the Lord guides his actions, he finally decides that neither exists. He becomes the leader of what remains of a peasant army, striving to be a man of action rather than a man who desires to be good or evil. He repeatedly and triumphantly declares that God is dead. 'Hilda! Hilda! God is dead' (*DG*, Act 3, Scene 10, p. 170). And again, 'There was no trial: I tell you God is dead' (*DG*, Act 3, Scene 10, p. 170). He even declares, 'I killed God because He divided me from other men...I shall not allow this huge carcass to poison my human friendships' (*DG*, Act 3, Scene 11, p. 174). Sartre's use of the phrase, 'God is dead,' echoes the atheistic philosophies of Arthur Schopenhauer and his successor Friedrich Nietzsche, who can be broadly described as existentialist in their outlook.

Schopenhauer argues that the enlightenment destroyed the very idea of God as an explanation for existence and a justification for morality. Nietzsche later summarized this view in the maxim, 'God is dead'. For Schopenhauer, the so-called 'death of God' implies that people are doomed to pointless suffering and despair in a meaningless universe. Nietzsche agrees with Schopenhauer's dismissal of God, but he attempts to push Schopenhauer's nihilism to its ultimate conclusion, to demolish faith in religious-based values to such an extent that it becomes possible to re-evaluate all values, including moral values. For Nietzsche, nihilism carried to its conclusion annihilates itself as a value and becomes anti-nihilism. To overcome nihilism people must overcome the guilt and despair of having, like Goetz, 'killed God'. To achieve this people must become what Nietzsche calls *Übermenschen* (overmen), people who have overcome themselves, their personal failings and their inauthenticity. *Übermenschen* create their own values and take full responsibility for themselves and their actions without regret. The process of personal and philosophical enlightenment that Goetz goes through during *The Devil and the Good Lord* is essentially that advocated by Nietzsche, and in that respect Goetz is, or is intended to be, a Nietzschean style *Übermensch*. By the end of the play Goetz might well declare, as Nietzsche declares in *The Gay Science*:

> Indeed, we philosophers and "free spirits" feel, when we hear the news that "the old god is dead," as if a new dawn shone on us; our heart overflows with gratitude, amazement, premonitions, expectation. At long last the horizon appears free to us again, even if it should not be bright. (Nietzsche 1974, 343, p. 280)

Darkly comical, the play generates an atmosphere of fear and hysteria as it traverses a broad range of existential and theological issues, raising questions and dilemmas about morality, love, hate, reason, superstition, salvation, damnation and the silence of God. There are also various Marxist themes running throughout the play with Sartre, like Marx, attributing the greater part of human suffering to religious superstition and social inequality. Sartre was to explore these Marxist themes in far greater depth a few years later in his *Critique of Dialectical Reason*. Above all, the play explores the nature of human freedom, motivation and morality in light of the existence or non-existence of God.

KEAN, OR DISORDER AND GENIUS

In the early 1950s Sartre was embroiled in Cold War politics. He attacked Western governments and defended Soviet communism at a time when many of his contemporaries were becoming disillusioned with it.[7] With one notable exception his activities and his writings were directly motivated by his political concerns. That notable exception was his lively 1954 adaptation of Alexandre Dumas' 1836 play, *Kean*, not only Sartre's least political work during the Cold War period, but the least political of all his plays. 'To the devil with politics!' (*K*, Act 2, p. 34). The obvious question, 'Why did

Sartre write *Kean* at this time?', has no obvious answer, but there is scope for informed conjecture.

Sartre liked to be unpredictable; to defy expectations, and it is not absurd to suggest that part of his motivation for writing *Kean* was that nobody expected him to write such a play when he did. The very occurrence of the play in the Cold War years seems to be Sartre stressing that he is not simply the political animal his critics now take him to be. He is reminding them that he has other strings to his bow, that he remains the author of *Nausea, Being and Nothingness* and *The Age of Reason*, masterpieces that focus on the individual abandoned in the world rather than upon contemporary political themes. *Kean* is a work that stands with those great works, those treatises on the fundamental truths of the human condition, rather than a work that comments on the grubby political realities of the day. It is a play out of the blue by a predictably unpredictable writer about a famously unpredictable character actor who spent his tumultuous life playing many parts.

Since childhood Sartre had enjoyed playing several parts at once, working on various projects simultaneously, so perhaps he wrote *Kean* not so much as a respite from the politics of the day – although writing it must have provided such a respite – but rather for the sake of diversity, to tax his brain and test his skills in another direction. It is certainly true of Sartre that he was often seized by new ideas on the spur of the moment that led him to embark on grand schemes when he was already overloaded with existing projects and commitments. *Kean* appears to have been such a scheme. Clearly, he must have been hugely inspired by the Dumas original at some point; inspired to draw out and emphasize its intriguing psychological themes in order to produce what stands as a major work of existential psychoanalysis.

Kean revisits the purely existentialist, pre-Marxist concerns of the early Sartre, exploring once again issues of personal identity, bad faith and authenticity as it highlights the relentless, free, angst-ridden transcendence of being-for-itself. But it is more than a mere recapitulation, a harking-back. It significantly advances Sartre's grand biographical project, his sustained attempt to provide a comprehensive answer to his most abiding philosophical question: 'What is it to be a person?' This grand project began with his psychoanalysis of Baudelaire in the mid-1940s and culminated in the early 1970s with *The Family Idiot*, his vast biography of Flaubert – arguably the most ambitious attempt ever made by one person to systematically understand another. Along the way Sartre explored the personalities of Genet, Mallarmé and Sartre, seeking to comprehend each of these people as a unified whole. He also explored the personality of Edmund Kean, and Edmund Kean should not be forgotten, as he often is, when recalling Sartre's various real-life character studies.

The great English Shakespearian actor Edmund Kean (1789–1833) was a womanizing alcoholic whose intense and turbulent personality spilled over into his brilliant performances of Shakespeare's tragic heroes. Kean was highly paid and hugely popular but his lifestyle gradually took its toll on his finances, health and reputation. He collapsed on stage in 1833 playing Othello to his son's Iago and died a few weeks later.

Sartre's play largely preserves the farcical plot and witty, comical, melodramatic tones of Dumas' original. Repeatedly drunk, pursued by creditors and increasingly broke, Kean is having, or attempting to have, a love affair with Elena, Countess de Koefeld, wife of the Danish Ambassador. Kean is jealous of the attentions shown to Elena by his friend and patron, The Prince of Wales. Under the guise of making a wager, The Prince offers to pay Kean's debts if he ends his affair with Elena, claiming that it is damaging diplomatic relations between England and Denmark. Meanwhile, Kean is pursued by a beautiful young heiress, Anna Danby, who desires to be his lover and protégé. She and Kean are both pursued by her fiancée, Lord Neville. The play climaxes with Kean playing Othello to Anna's Desdemona at Drury Lane Theatre while Elena and The Prince watch from a box close to the stage. Elena is jealous of Kean's attentions to Anna while Kean is jealous of The Prince's attentions to Elena. Anna cannot remember her lines and the prince starts to discuss the failing performance with Elena. Motivated by jealously, Kean orders the prince to be quiet and to let him do his job.

> Where do you think you are? At court? In a boudoir? Everywhere else you are a prince, but here I am king, and I ask you to be quiet, or we will stop the performance. We are working, sir, and if there is one thing the idle should respect, it is the labour of others. (*K*, Act 4, Scene 2, p. 99)

In a performance that The Prince describes as 'magnificent' (*K*, Act 4, Scene 2, p. 102), Kean goes on to harangue his audience before leaving the stage.

But who were you applauding? Eh? Othello? Impossible – he was a sanguinary villain. It must have been Kean...Well, here he is – your beloved Kean. [*He drags his hands over his face, smearing the make-up.*] Behold the man! Look at him. Why don't you applaud? Isn't it strange! You only care for illusion. (*K*, Act 4, Scene 2, p. 101)

It appears that Kean is ruined but the play contrives a happy ending in which The Prince forgives Kean, Elena returns to her husband and Kean departs for America with Anna.

For Sartre, as for Dumas, the play is primary a study of the character of Edmund Kean. Kean does not know who he really is, just as the young Sartre considered in Chapter 1 of this book did not know who he really was until his decision to write defined him as a writer. Kean suspects that he is nothing more than the parts he plays, that even when he is not acting on stage he is playing the part of Edmund Kean the great actor. 'I am nothing, my child. I play at being what I am' (*K*, Act 2, p. 51). Kean plays the part of Hamlet or Kean just as the Prince of Wales plays the part of the Prince of Wales. Sartre's view that people can only ever play at being what they are, a view emphasized repeatedly in *Kean*, was first put forward in *Being and Nothingness*. In that work, as noted in Chapter 2, Sartre describes a waiter who plays at being a waiter because it is impossible for him, or for anyone, to be a waiter in the mode of *being* one (*BN*, pp. 82–83). As a negation of being-in-itself that must perpetually negate being in order to be, being-for-itself is never a fixed entity. A person is never what they are, they have to constantly aim at being what they are without ever being able to become it.

But if I represent myself as him [whoever or whatever it is I aim at being], I am not he; I am separated from him as the object from the subject, separated by *nothing*, but this nothing isolates me from him. I can not be he, I can only play at *being* him; that is, imagine to myself that I am he. And thereby I affect him with nothingness...I can be he only in the neutralized mode, as the actor is Hamlet, by mechanically making the *typical gestures* of my state and by aiming at myself... (*BN*, p. 83)

Kean is not even an *actor* in the mode of being one. He only ever strives to be an actor through acting. An actor is not what he is, acting is simply what he does. A person who supposes that he is a fixed entity is in bad faith. In so far as Kean is always acutely aware that he is not a fixed entity he is an authentic being who has overcome bad faith. At times, however, when the endless change of masks threatens to overwhelm his sanity, when he feels he is respected only as an actor and not as a person, that nobody takes him seriously, Kean expresses the desire to give up acting and *become* a cheesemonger or a jeweller. At one point, still acting of course, he tells his factotum, Solomon, that he is no longer an actor. 'Cry from the housetops that a shopkeeper called Edmund has recovered his senses' (*K*, Act 5, p. 104). Though he strives to convince Solomon – 'Oh well – it will have to happen by degrees. I will imitate the natural until it becomes second nature' (*K*, Act 5, p. 106) – Kean fails to convince himself. He recognizes that he would still have to play the part of a shopkeeper; that he would be unable simply to be one. His desire to give up acting is just another act, as are his infatuations, his bouts of apparent insanity and his attempts at sincerity. 'Under a sham sun, the sham Kean cried the tale of his sham sufferings to his sham heart' (*K*, Act 5, p. 105).

Kean is able to convince others, at least for the duration of his performance, that he is Hamlet or Othello, but he is unable to convince himself that he is Kean. His life would be less turbulent and disorganized, though perhaps less exciting and attractive to others, if he could achieve the bad faith required to impose some coherence upon his personality. His personality is so incoherent that he even objects to having to accept the consequences of his past actions. He is utterly irresponsible and does not, for example, see why he should pay for jewellery ordered six months before for a woman he no longer loves. 'Are you mad? You choose the moment I love Elena to make me pay for a necklace I gave Fanny? It would be the worst of betrayals' (*K*, Act 2, p. 36). He has played many parts since then and loved several women and is certainly no longer the person he was. The law, of course, insists that he is the person he was and holds him accountable for his actions.

Sartre's exploration of Kean's character is an exploration of the indeterminacy of being-for-itself. His exploration of Kean's relations with others is an exploration of being-for-others and those modes of being, such as love, that are aspects of being-for-others. Kean's love for Elena is an act. Elena loves Kean the actor and as such her love is conditional. It is evident that if Kean ceased to be a stage actor Elena would cease to love him. As Kean is the parts he plays, Elena's love for him is love of the parts he plays. Moreover, as the parts he plays are subject to Elena's interpretation, she is in love with her own idea of Kean rather than Kean himself. After all, she cannot be in love with Kean *himself* when Kean has no self. They discuss running away together. Elena says she would go anywhere with the man she loves, 'to the galleys, to the very scaffold' (*K*, Act 5, p. 114), but when Kean says he will give up acting and become a jeweller in Amsterdam she is suddenly far less enthusiastic about fleeing England with him. Imitating her, Kean exclaims, 'To the galleys! To the scaffold! To the ends of the earth! You see, you were only acting' (*K*, Act 5, p. 116).

Sartre also makes the point that people often exist more clearly and distinctly for others than they do for themselves. This is because a person is able to believe more easily that the being of another person is fixed and substantial than he is able to believe that his own being is fixed and substantial. Kean is more real to an audience as Lear or Hamlet than he is to himself as Kean. For others, Kean is the Great Kean, the great performer, and he must constantly command their love and attention in order to be reassured that he exists. Similarly, Elena is the beautiful Elena for others and the Prince of Wales is the noble prince for others. Nobody can be great, beautiful or noble alone.

> The result is you enjoy your beauty through the eyes of others, and I discover my genius through their applause. As for him, he is a flower. For him to feel he is a prince, he has to be admired. Beauty, royalty, genius; a single and same mirage. We live all three on the love of others, and we are all three incapable of loving ourselves. (*K*, Act 5, p. 117)

Not least, the play is a commentary on the corrupting and destructive influences of fame. Flattered and over-indulged, famous people often become like Kean, spoilt and irresponsible. Furthermore, the adoration they crave ultimately disappoints them because it is not directed towards them but towards their public persona. The more closely they identify themselves with their public persona the more intensely they suffer the capriciousness and spitefulness of their audience. If they distance themselves from their public persona they grow to resent it as a grotesque caricature that distorts and obscures them, a being-for-others that others hold them responsible for even though it is not them.

> I must be a fool, for I cannot understand why all England places me at once so high and so low. [*Crying out*] You are tearing me apart! Between your admiration and your scorn, you are destroying me. Am I king or buffoon? Tell me! (*K*, Act 2, p. 47)

NEKRASSOV, A FARCE IN EIGHT SCENES

Whereas *Kean* turns its back on the Cold War politics of the time in which it was written, *Nekrassov*, completed in 1955, casts a satirical and cynical eye on that political situation. *Nekrassov* is essentially a scathing attack on the methods and machinations of the French, pro-capitalist, right-wing press during the Cold War. Various factors inspired Sartre to launch this attack. In 1954 he returned from his first trip to the USSR and was inclined to say favourable things about his communist hosts, things which he later admitted he did not entirely believe (*Situations X*, p. 220). Furthermore, having reacted against the dogmatism and arrogance of the French Communist Party (PCF) in the late 1940s in his play *Dirty Hands*, the first half of the 1950s saw Sartre defending the very right to exist of the PCF against a hostile French government and the popular press that helped prop it up. Not least, Sartre was outraged by the McCarthy anti-communist witch-hunts that had recently taken place in the USA.[8] He saw France as suffering from the same atmosphere of national, anti-communist paranoia as the USA, an atmosphere in no small part whipped up by the media. The play is to some extent a comment on McCarthyism, although McCarthy is mentioned only once. 'Here, read this telegram. It's from McCarthy, offering me an engagement as a permanent witness' (*Ne*, Scene 5, p. 222).

The play outraged the French press and was slated by all but the most left-wing newspapers. Many journalists felt betrayed by Sartre, a journalist himself. They felt the philosopher–playwright was talking down to them, questioning their competence and above all their integrity. They saw the play as a ridiculous caricature, which, in a sense, it is. Its very sub-title declares it to be farcical. The play is far-fetched, certainly in terms of its plot, because Sartre is deliberately lampooning the press. Nonetheless, as with all satire, the underlying moral and political message of the play is a serious and pertinent one. Some defenders of the play suggest that it was to avoid confronting its serious message that the press chose the convenient ruse of being offended. In *Combat* on 7 June 1955 Sartre wrote, 'What I have tried to do in *Nekrassov* is to write a satirical play…a certain sort of press is already crying out before it even knows what my play is about and before it has been hurt.'

Nekrassov is set in Paris in the early 1950s. Sibilot, a journalist who writes anti-communist propaganda for a right-wing newspaper, *Soir à Paris,*[9] faces dismissal by his editor, Jules Palotin, unless he can come up with a new idea. '…unless you can come into my office tomorrow morning at ten o'clock with a shattering idea, you can pack your bags' (*Ne*, Scene 2, p. 167). Sibilot's luck improves when he finds Georges de Valéra, an internationally renowned swindler, hiding in his house. Georges is on the run from the police and has just made an unsuccessful attempt to drown himself in the River Seine. To help Sibilot and to disguise himself, Georges decides to impersonate the Russian Interior Minister, Nikita Nekrassov, who, according to some news reports, has recently disappeared. Georges fools Palotin and the directors of *Soir à Paris* that he is Nekrassov and that he has defected to the West. They believe him, largely because it serves their interests to do so.

Georges offers *Soir à Paris* exclusive rights to publish a series of political revelations, including a list of names of those important enough to be shot by firing squad when Russia invades France. The directors want to know if they are on the list. Georges makes out that all of them save the chairman, Mouton, are listed. The directors are delighted. To be executed 'proves, sir, that I am a good Frenchman' (*Ne*, Scene 4, p. 205). Mouton is offended. 'And why, if you please, do they not deign to execute me?' (*Ne*, Scene 4, p. 206). Mouton demands to be listed. Georges says he will take his story to the *France-Soir* newspaper rather than list him. Out of favour, suspected of communism, Mouton declares Georges to be an impostor before making an angry departure.

Sartre succeeds here in ridiculing McCarthyism by turning it on its head. McCarthy fabricated lists of people he said were communist sympathizers. Georges, posing as Nekrassov, is fabricating a list of good Frenchmen he claims will be shot when the Russians invade. Whereas Americans feared being *on* McCarthy's list, Frenchmen will fear not being on Nekrassov's, as this will imply they are communist sympathizers. The end result is the same, a mood of hysteria and paranoia emerges in which everyone is potentially under suspicion. An atmosphere in which it becomes possible to destroy whoever one chooses by merely suggesting they are politically subversive.

> I shall raise the curtain a little at a time, and you will see the world as it is. When you mistrust your own son, your wife, you father; when you look in the mirror and ask yourself whether you aren't a communist without knowing it, then you are beginning to get a glimpse of the truth. (*Ne,* Scene 4, p. 213)

Thanks to the list, Sibilot saves his job and receives a pay rise. *Soir à Paris* achieves record circulation and the purposes of capitalism and anti-communism are served in a variety of ways: the directors and owners of the newspaper get even richer while the ordinary people who buy the paper are distracted by its revelations from thoughts of rebellion against their own government. Uniting the people against a common enemy in the form of communism strengthens their loyalty to their own non-communist political system. Returning briefly to McCarthyism, many historians note that the ultimate achievement of McCarthyism was to weaken opposition to the Cold War.

Although a genius at manipulating others, Georges begins to lose control of the situation when, not surprisingly, ordinary, decent people he does not even know are denounced as communists plotting with Russia to overthrow France. For example, Madame Castagnié, a typist at *Soir à Paris* with a sick daughter and no interest in politics, is dismissed for being a communist. Government agents, Baudouin and Chapuis, who have been acting as Georges' bodyguard soon discover that he is not Nekrassov. Nonetheless, they decide to preserve the illusion that he is Nekrassov in order that he can testify against two journalists, Duval and Maistre, that they wish to accuse of treason. '... if you give them over to us, you can be Nekrassov as much as you like' (*Ne*, Scene 6, p. 257).

They hold Georges prisoner but he escapes and makes arrangements with Veronique, Sibilot's daughter, to sell his story, 'How I became Nekrassov' (*Ne*, Scene 7, p. 270), to the socialist newspaper, *Libérateur*. The publication of the truth threatens to ruin *Soir à Paris*, exposing the editor and directors as either deceitful or hopelessly deceived. The former chairman, Mouton, returns to save the paper. He fires Palotin and replaces him with Sibilot who is given the task of writing the story that Georges de Valéra has sold out to the communists and Nekrassov has been kidnapped by the Russians. It is not expected that anyone will be convinced by this story but it will be enough to cast doubt on the truth of Georges' story in *Libérateur*. Charivet, a director, asks if *Soir à Paris* will be believed. 'No,' replies Mouton, 'but neither will they believe *Libérateur*. That's the main thing. By the way, my friend,' he adds, addressing Sibolot, 'the police found a further list among Nekrassov's papers –' (*Ne*, Scene 8, p. 282).

As said, the play satirizes the French right-wing press and the paranoid fear of communism that its propaganda helped to generate during the Cold War years. The serious message within the satire is clearly a Marxist one: the popular press throughout the Western world is owned and controlled by capitalists for the purpose of preserving and promoting capitalism. Inciting fear of communism or any other non-capitalist ideology helps to sell newspapers and to create a sense of collective identity and purpose in face of a common enemy. The masses are persuaded that they are better off and better protected under their system of government than are people who live under alternative systems. Veronique points out that to the workers of Billancourt who buy *Soir à Paris*, Georges' fabricated stories about the terrible conditions in Russia mean: 'Leave capitalism alone, or you will relapse into barbarism. The bourgeois world has its defects, but it is the best of all possible worlds. Whatever your poverty, try to make the best of it, for you can be sure you'll never see anything better, and thank heaven that you weren't born in the Soviet Union' (*Ne*, Scene 5, p. 232).

For Sartre, as for Marx, it is simply part of the ideology of the popular press that its primary function is to tell the truth. In reality, its primary function, apart from maximizing circulation, is to preserve the political and economic order that most benefits the kind of wealthy, powerful people who own newspapers. Exaggeration and lies further this end at least as much as telling the truth. Stripped of the ideology it perpetuates, that truth telling and reasoned argument are sacrosanct, the popular press is revealed as shaping the opinions of the masses through its relentless appeal to their fear, hatred, lust, envy and conceit. The popular press enables the ruling class to shape and define the social and political values of the masses to such an extent that the masses become incapable of distinguishing truth from lies, reality from appearance.

Nekrassov is often accused of being dated, as belonging very much to the Cold War period in which it was written. In a conversation recorded in 1960 Sartre himself described it as a 'flawed play'. It is certainly not among his most important works, partly because it does not explore the really big Sartrean philosophical themes and partly because it is a parody, a not particularly subtle satire peopled with amusing caricatures rather than rounded characters. Its value lies in the fact that it provides a coherent and accessible critique of the workings of capitalist propaganda, revealing key aspects of the relationship between capitalist society and the media machine that helps shape and maintain it. *Nekrassov* continues to offer much that is of interest, particularly to the disciplines of Sociology and Media Studies.

THE CONDEMNED OF ALTONA (THE SEQUESTERED OF ALTONA OR ALTONA OR LOSER WINS)

Four years passed before Sartre's next play appeared, *The Condemned of Altona*, alternatively titled *Altona* or *Loser Wins*. Though Sartre had written as much as ever, by his prolific standards the period 1955–59 had been a lean one for publications. This apparent quiet period, coupled with the fact that *Nekrassov* had been so badly received by many sections of the press in 1955, led some critics to describe *The Condemned of Altona*, first performed at the Théâtre de la Renaissance on 23 September 1959, as Sartre's 'comeback'; his return to form. Unlike *Nekrassov*, *The Condemned of Altona* was almost universally acclaimed and is generally recognized as a work that can take its place on the list of Sartre classics.

The Trojan Women which appeared six years after *The Condemned of Altona* is only a relatively short adaptation of a tragedy by Euripides, so, in a sense, *The Condemned of Altona* is Sartre's last play, the culmination of his career as a dramatist. He throws everything into *The Condemned of Altona*, a philosophically dense tragedy that explores both earlier and later Sartrean themes, both existentialism and Marxism, seeking to refine and amalgamate them. In this respect *The Condemned of Altona* is very much one of several satellite pieces to Sartre's vast *Critique of Dialectical Reason* which he was also labouring on at the time and which appeared the year after *The Condemned of Altona* in 1960. The *Critique* is the most ambitious and important work of the later Sartre in which he draws together the overall development of his philosophy since *Being and Nothingness*, the major publication of his early career, and responds to critics of the theory of existential phenomenology that he detailed in that work by attempting to synthesize it with Marxism.

Cohen-Solal nails it once again when she writes, '*The Condemned* is a sort of *No Exit*' (Cohen-Solal 2005, p. 382).[10] This brief remark reveals the bond between the older Sartre of the late 1950s and early 60s, and the younger Sartre of the first half of the 1940s. Written in 1944, *In Camera* (*No Exit*) is preoccupied with the idea that 'Hell is other people' (*IC*, p. 223), with notions of freedom, confinement, conflict, being-for-others, cowardice, guilt and justification. *The Condemned of Altona* incorporates these same themes into a Marxist critique of World War II and the postwar period that explores such historical and political issues as the role of capitalism in the Holocaust, German collective guilt and the verdict of future generations on the horrors of the twentieth century. In *The Condemned of Altona*, the 'Hell is other people' of *In Camera* is magnified through the lens of history and politics thereby becoming the issue of what the poet Robert Burns refers to as 'Man's inhumanity to man' ('Man was made to Mourn', st. 7, in Burns 1999). At the end of *The Condemned of Altona* its central character, Franz, says:

> The century might have been a good one had not man been watched from time immemorial by the cruel enemy who had sworn to destroy him, that hairless, evil, flesh-eating beast – man himself. (*CA*, Act 5, p. 165)

The Condemned of Altona is set in post-World War II Germany in the house of Gerlach, a wealthy shipping tycoon. Gerlach made a fortune building warships for the Nazis and another fortune helping to rebuild Germany after the War. Sartre uses the play to put forward the Marxist view that the wealthiest capitalists like Gerlach benefit regardless of who holds political power. Nazis or the USA, it is business as usual. When Franz charges his father with working for the Nazis, Gerlach replies, 'Because they work for me. They are the plebeian on the throne. But they are at war to find us markets, and I am not going to quarrel with them over a bit of land' (*CA*, Act 1, p. 41).

Gerlach is dying of throat cancer. His wealth cannot save him. His dying wish is to speak to his estranged eldest son, Franz, who has locked himself away for 14 years in the upper rooms of the house. Franz' needs are taken care of by his sister, Leni, with whom he is having an incestuous relationship. 'I, Leni, incestuous sister, love Franz, and I love him because he is my brother' (*CA*, Act 2, p. 72). As the play develops the backstory emerges of how Franz and his father became estranged and why Franz is a recluse.

Although he was not a member of the Nazi Party Gerlach senior collaborated with the Nazis, knowingly selling them land for a concentration camp, an act he dismissed by arguing that had he not sold them the land someone else would have. 'What is there to explain? Himmler wanted somewhere to house his prisoners. If I had refused my land, he would have bought some elsewhere' (CA, Act 1, p. 40). Disgusted by his father's weakness and lack of conscience Franz helped an escaped Rabbi and was arrested by the S.S. for harbouring a Jew. Using his influence with Goebbels, Gerlach senior secured Franz' release on condition that Franz enlist in the German Army. Franz returned traumatized and defeated from the Russian front and refused to leave the house. Soon after the war he took the blame for his sister's assault on an American soldier who tried to rape her. Gerlach senior persuaded the American authorities to overlook the matter and they agreed on condition that Franz emigrate to Argentina. Rather than leave Germany, however, Franz took to hiding in the upper rooms of his father's house. In time, his father travelled to Argentina and returned with a false death certificate for Franz, completing his son's isolation. Officially dead and suffering with acute mental health problems, Franz turned his back on the outside world and became a recluse. Afraid the authorities would discover he was alive and in Germany his family allowed him to remain in isolation.[11]

It is against this background that Gerlach senior persuades Johanna, the beautiful wife of his younger son Werner, to act as an intermediary between himself and Franz. Johanna gains access to Franz' rooms and in doing so disturbs a world where the insane but charismatic Franz strives to stop time while attempting to justify his war crimes to future generations. 'I ought to have known that she would upset everything. It took me five years to drive time out of this room, and you only needed a moment to bring it back' (*CA*, Act 4, p. 114). Franz wears chocolate medals and throws oyster shells at a portrait of Hitler. In his delusional, paranoid state he believes he is watched and judged by malignant crab-like creatures.[12] These creatures are man's worst enemy – the cruel, malevolent side of man's own nature. He raves at these creatures, recording his outpourings. At times he talks to the air imagining that crab-like representatives from the thirtieth century can hear him. He puts the horrors of the twentieth century and his own role in them on trial before these representatives of future generations.

> All unmasked, the balconies swarming with arthropods. You must know that the human race started off on the wrong foot, but I put the lid on its fabulous ill-fortune by handing over its mortal remains to the Court of the Crustaceans. (*CA*, Act 4, p. 126)

As a former actress, Johanna is intrigued by Franz' world of make-believe and soon establishes a close relationship with him that provokes the jealously of her husband Werner and his sister Leni. Johanna eventually persuades Franz to leave his room and meet with his dying father. During their first conversation since the war Franz admits to his father that he is the 'butcher of Smolensk'. He tortured Russian prisoners to death, not because he believed in the Nazi cause but because he was tired of feeling weak and powerless. The Nazi cause simply gave him an excuse to overcome his sense of powerlessness through a decisive act of evil.

> Hitler has changed me, made me, made me implacable and sacred, made me himself. I am Hitler, and I shall surpass myself... No! I shall never again fall into abject powerlessness... I'll display my power by the singularity of an unforgettable act; change *living* men into vermin. I alone will deal with the prisoners. I'll debase them into abject wretches. They'll talk. Power is an abyss, and I see its depths... I shall decide life or death with a penknife and a cigarette lighter. (*CA*, Act 5, p. 153)

Gerlach is not shocked by his son's confession and admits that he already knew about his war crimes as two Russians had attempted to blackmail him over the matter three years earlier. Father and son leave the house to commit suicide by driving a Porsche into the River Elba. The play ends with Leni locking herself away in her brother's rooms.

The philosophical focus of the play is German collective guilt, or the lack of it, in face of the Nazi atrocities. Divorced from the outside world in his private rooms, hiding from daylight and the passage of time, Franz sees himself as being on trial before all eternity for his war crimes and those of his nation. He identifies one of his crimes as a crime of omission, a failure to act against the Nazis. He resisted them when he helped the Rabbi but cooperated with them afterwards. Like his father, like the majority of the German people, he gave in to the Nazis. He could have resisted them regardless of the consequences, but in bad faith he acted as though he had no choice but to go along with them. Making an excuse of his weakness and his desire for self-preservation he simply despised the Nazis while acting on their behalf. When Franz' feelings of powerlessness and frustration became unbearable he overcame them by choosing to exercise the power of a torturer. For personal rather than ideological reasons he chose to identify himself with Nazi power, and in acting like a Nazi he became a Nazi. Franz serves to illustrate why ordinary people in adverse circumstances choose to commit atrocities. Franz' choice is understandable, but it is not excusable. He is unable to excuse himself despite 14 years of isolated soul-searching. Unlike most people who commit atrocities, Franz cannot forget or ignore that he is responsible for his actions. This much makes him a sympathetic character, unlike his father who shows no remorse.

Sartre's aim in *The Condemned of Altona* is not to attack the German people in particular. He sees the Nazi atrocities, chief among them the Holocaust, as being to the shame of all mankind, a product of mans' inhumanity towards man rather than, specifically, the inhumanity of Germans towards Jews. As a Marxist, Sartre identifies capitalism as the fundamental evil, characterizing Nazism as just one more manifestation of capitalism. Nazism required capitalism in order to arm itself. In return, Nazism provided capitalism with new markets and new opportunities for growth. The Nazis fell but the capitalists, whose interests the Nazis served, marched on with Germany soon recovering its economic prosperity to become the wealthiest country in Europe and the capitalist USA committing atrocities comparable to those of the Nazis. Sartre identifies the US nuclear bombing of Hiroshima as one such atrocity.

Fine victors! We know them. They were the same in 1918, with the same hypocritical virtues...It's the victors who take charge of history. They did so, and gave us Hitler. Judges? Have they never pillaged, massacred, and raped? Was it Goering who dropped the bomb on Hiroshima? (*CA*, Act 1, p. 37)

One reason that Franz gives for his isolation from the world is his desire to maintain the belief that Germany has been permanently destroyed by the war. He thinks the permanent destruction of Germany would be just and would to some extent atone for the war crimes of the German people. To discover that Germany has recovered, that its people have moved on, only adds to the acute sense of guilt that he continues to feel years after the war has ended. *Loser Wins*, the alternative title of the play, refers to the economic success that Germany enjoyed soon after losing World War II. Franz asks his father if Germany had to lose the war. His father replies, 'We had to play loser wins – as always' (*CA*, Act 5, p. 158).

THE TROJAN WOMEN

Of the ten Sartre plays that were published and professionally produced, *The Trojan Women,* completed in 1965, is the last. Appearing six long years after the ambitious *The Condemned of Altona*, a dramatic peak in which Sartre brilliantly ties together the various strands of his philosophy, *The Trojan Women*, a relatively short adaptation of a tragedy by Euripides, has been classed as something of an afterthought in Sartre's career as a playwright. In other respects, it neatly wraps up his dramatic career, allowing him to end as he had begun, utilizing an Ancient Greek legend to comment upon a contemporary political situation and upon war and oppression generally. Whereas his first professional play, *The Flies*, was a response to the Nazi occupation of Paris, *The Trojan Women* was a response to the Algerian War of Independence – Algeria's long and bitter struggle to escape French colonial occupation that finally succeeded in 1962. Sartre gave active, outspoken and sustained support to the Algerian independence movement, provoking various attacks on his reputation and person in the process.[13] He viewed the French occupation of Algeria as unjustifiable and hypocritical, controversially identifying it as being essentially the same as the German occupation of France during World War II.

The Trojan Women is set outside the walls of the city of Troy. The Greeks have finally defeated the Trojans after a siege lasting ten years. Reduced to mere spoils of war, the Trojan women and children await their fate at the hands of the Greeks. Some are killed, such as the child Astyanax, heir to the Trojan throne. Most are to be taken back to Greece as slaves. The women, particularly Hecuba the Queen of Troy, bemoan their fate and that of their dead menfolk, cursing the Greeks and the gods. 'You filthy Gods, you always hated me. And of all cities Troy was the one city you detested' (*TW*, Scene 5, pp. 343–344).

Hecuba's daughter, Cassandra, prophesies the death and destruction that will befall the Greeks on their journey home. She offers the Trojan women the consolation that ultimately the Trojan War will be as much a disaster for the Greeks as it has been for the Trojans. 'The vultures wait, and oblivion awaits them. Not a trace of these conquerors will remain; not even their shadow. Except for a handful who will crawl back to Greece only to find themselves unwanted and unwelcome' (*TW*, Scene 5, pp. 312–313).

Andromeda, the mother of Astyanax and the wife of Hector, Hecuba's slaughtered son, curses Hecuba, blaming her for the war. She reasons that had Hecuba smothered Paris at birth as the gods ordered, he could not have caused the war by taking Helen, the wife of the Greek king Menelaus, away to Troy.

> You are to blame. It was you who gave birth to Paris: that damned adventurer. Didn't the Gods themselves, foreseeing his future, order you to smother him? You refused: it is we who are punished for that: for your pride which you hawked around as a Mother's love. (*TW*, Scene 5, p. 320)

Menelaus reclaims Helen intending to take her back to Greece and execute her for adultery, but it is doubtful he will be able to resist her charms. It appears that Helen, the ultimate cause of the war, will escape punishment and even be rewarded. 'Look! Look at the coward,' says the Chorus. 'What a liar he is. There she goes now right onto his own ship, and he trailing behind her. Now the game's up. She'll bring him to heel and reign unpunished over Sparta. Nothing pays off like crime' (*TW*, Scene 5, pp. 338–339).

Helen's final triumph over Menelaus and her escape from justice reminds us of the maxim 'loser wins'; a maxim that is so central to Sartre's previous play, *The Condemned of Altona*, it forms its alternative title.

The play ends with the god Poseidon cursing mortals for making war and inflicting suffering on themselves. In bad faith men blame the gods for war, but war is the responsibility of men. War kills all in the end and brings only hollow victories. 'Idiots! We'll make you pay for this. You stupid, bestial mortals. Making war, burning cities, violating tombs and temples, torturing your enemies, bringing suffering on yourselves. Can't you see war will kill you: all of you?' (*TW*, Scene 5, p. 347).

Once it is known why Sartre adapted Euripides' *The Trojan Women* when he did, the meaning and significance of the play is largely self-explanatory and there is little requirement for further analysis. According to Sartre, Euripides wrote *The Trojan Women* to denounce Greek colonialism in Asia Minor. As Sartre said in *Bref: The Monthly Journal of the Théâtre National Populaire* in February 1965, in an article 'Why the Trojan Women?' by Bernard Pingaud: 'It was this colonialism of Greece into Asia Minor that Euripides denounced, and where I use the expression 'dirty war' in reference to these expeditions I was, in fact, taking no liberties with the original text.' For his part, Sartre adapted *The Trojan Women* to denounce contemporary European colonialism, particularly French colonialism in North Africa, and to condemn war and imperialism generally.

The play, for both Euripides and Sartre, seeks to emphasize the waste, futility, injustice and depravity of war and to call into question the distinction between victor and vanquished. In bringing death and destruction to both sides war is a means by which mankind defeats himself. This point echoes one of the pivotal claims of Sartre's previous play, *The Condemned of Altona*: man is his own worst enemy. The age old point that war is man's defeat of himself has particular resonance in the Nuclear Age where all-out war between super-powers would assure mutual destruction.

CONCLUSION

Sartre's drafts of *The Age of Reason* were typed-up by Simone de Beauvoir's sister, Hélène, whose nickname was Poupette. He posted them to her in Paris at regular intervals from his various military posts in Northern France during the Phoney War of 1939–40. As he tells us in his *War Diaries*, Hélène wrote to her sister commenting on her experience of being immersed in Sartre's work:

> Typing Sartre's works always makes me gloomy. Talking to him is a tonic. Reading his works, then thinking about something else – that might still be all right. But living up to one's neck in them is dreadful. I hope that, within himself, he isn't like the people he portrays in his books, for his life would be scarcely endurable. (*WD*, p. 338)

It is highly unlikely that anyone who has immersed themselves in Sartre's fictional works for any length of time could entirely reject Hélène's sentiments. The quote leaps out of the *War Diaries* and is memorable precisely because it has such a strong ring of truth to it. Having immersed myself in Sartre's fictional works for the writing of this book I can certainly identify on an emotional level with what Hélène is saying, although I think (as she probably did also) that there is far more to the experience of reading Sartre than simply finding it dreadful. I recall rereading *In Camera* in the garden on a pleasant summer afternoon and sneakily counting the pages to gauge when I would finally be released from that depressing, claustrophobic room and the company of those awful people, Inez, Estelle and Garcin. At the same time I was forced to acknowledge the intellectual brilliance of the work and Sartre's superb craftsmanship as a writer, not least in creating such a hellishly oppressive atmosphere.

There is more wit, irony and dry humour in Sartre than he is often given credit for – not least in *In Camera* – but the fact remains that he is not exactly a laugh a minute and nobody in their right mind reads him for the fun of it. *Kean* is his only cheerful work, but its joviality probably derives from the Dumas original from which it was adapted rather than from Sartre himself. Sartre does not undertake, as some writers do, Dickens for example, to give his readers a warm glow during or after the experience of reading him, unless such a glow can be derived from the satisfaction of having learnt something, of having gained some profound insight into human existence. Of course, in this respect Sartre is not unlike many or most great authors. Nobody reads Kafka, Dostoevsky or Conrad for the fun of it either, although in the end it depends on what is meant by 'fun'. I can only speak for myself, but I certainly find reading Sartre more enjoyable and certainly more rewarding than watching Australian soap operas or daytime TV. Living up to my neck in countless episodes of *Neighbours* or *Oprah* really would be dreadful. I'm sure I'm not alone in thinking that there is nothing more dreadful than that which is mindless and inane. Sartre, to give him his due, is the very antithesis of mindless and inane.

Sartre is personally committed to considering weighty subject matter – insanity, guilt, hatred, war, death, etc. – in order to deliver hard, uncompromising lessons on the human condition, the human predicament. He pushes his reader out of any comfort zone that he might be hiding in, forcing him to confront unpleasant truths, not least about himself. The reader is obliged to recognize his own flaws in Sartre's all too human characters; he is obliged to ask himself, 'How would I cope in that terrible situation, what choices would I make?' When I read Sartre's fiction I often find myself thinking, 'Thank goodness I'm not in that situation, that I'm not a conscript forced to choose between violent resistance and miserable defeat, or a prisoner of war facing torture, humiliation and death.' But then I'm obliged to think that it is only a matter of luck, a matter of circumstance and facticity, that I am not Mathieu or Ibbieta. It is quite possible that in future I or anyone could be in their shoes and even if I am lucky enough not to be, life will still inevitably confront me with awful situations and terrible choices.

So, Sartre does not write simply to tell stories and to entertain. As he argues in his 1948 work *What is Literature?*, considered in Chapter 1, the purpose of literature is not to entertain but to challenge and provoke. If a work does not shake a reader up and goad him into new attitudes and actions by asking pertinent questions then it is failing to do its job, it is simply not literature but some other lesser art form; a mere diversion.

Interestingly, Sartre was intrigued rather than offended by Hélène's remarks and spent most of his diary entry for 14 March 1940 reflecting on them. Indeed, he continued to ponder the whole issue of so-called 'gloomy literature' for many years, finally stating in *What is Literature?*, that 'there is no gloomy literature' (*WL*, p. 47). True literature is never gloomy, he argues, for it always aims to liberate people by making them aware of their freedom.

In his diary entry he identifies himself closely with his two most significant character creations, his alter-egos, Antoine Roquentin and Mathieu Delarue, acknowledging the undeniable fact that they are both, as we have seen, extremely gloomy. They are him, he insists, but he adds that he is never so gloomy and that life for him is not all that bad. He writes: 'In reality, they are *me, stripped of the living principle*' (*WD*, p. 338). What has been stripped from them, or denied them in the first place in order that they may better serve Sartre's philosophical and literary purposes is, Sartre insists, his own passion, pride, faith and optimism. 'I stripped my characters of my obsessive passion for writing, my pride, my faith in my destiny, my metaphysical optimism – and thereby provoked in them a gloomy pullulation' (*WD*, p. 339). Sartre appears to consider 'the living principle', the hope, pride, passion and faith that springs eternal in the hearts of men despite the stark, inescapable truths of the human condition, to be philosophically unjustifiable if not inexplicable – the reason why he refers to his optimism as 'metaphysical'. Nonetheless, he recognizes that as a living man rather than a fictional character he too possesses an abundance of 'the living principle'. He is not his characters and it is far easier to create a character that serves certain literary objectives by being consistently negative than it is to be so consistently negative oneself. 'The essential difference between Antoine Roquentin and me is that, for my part, I write the story of Antoine Roquentin' (*WD*, p. 338).

Sartre seems to have found it far easier to create gloomy angst-ridden characters than positive, happy ones. Characters who are full of the joys of life are, it seems fair to say, totally lacking from his pantheon. Was he unable to create them, or would such characters fail to serve his literary and philosophical purposes? Considering his books, his characters and what he expects the overall effect of the *ensemble* of his works to be, he writes:

> My novels are experiments, and they're possible only through disintegration. It seems to me that the ensemble of my books will be optimistic, because through that ensemble the *whole* will be reconstituted. But each of my characters is a cripple. To tell the truth, Mathieu is to become a totality in my last volume – but he'll die immediately afterwards. That's the reason, I think, why I write gloomy books without myself being either sad or a charlatan, and believe in what I write' (*WD*, p. 339).

It is perhaps the greatest irony of Sartre's fiction that, as a whole, it conveys an ultimately optimistic and uplifting vision or message via a parade of troubled, angst-ridden, gloomy characters saturated with personal defects and weaknesses. Arguably, the overall message of the ensemble – the stories, the novels, the plays – succeeds in being optimistic precisely because Sartre's characters are so generally flawed and pathetic. With discomfort Sartre's reader recognizes his worst traits writ-large in Sartre's characters, yet pathetic and flawed though Sartre's characters are, at least some of them manage to overcome themselves, transcending their bad faith to achieve dignity and authenticity and a certain kind of salvation. If Sartre's characters can become heroes when they are so defective and ordinary then so can anyone.

Sartre's fiction holds a mirror up to people that does nothing whatsoever to flatter them. They are shown to be weak-minded, evasive, petty, spiteful, cowardly, irresponsible and wilfully deluded about themselves, each other, their situation and life in general. Sartre's harshness, however, aims not at condemning mankind but at identifying the real starting point for personal transformation and overcoming. It is because he has this positive agenda, because he believes in the possibility of transformation and overcoming, that his outlook is far from hopeless and nihilistic. His writing, his philosophy, is far better described as honest and uncompromising than gloomy and depressing. Certainly many people who would admit to finding Sartre gloomy and depressing at times would also admit to finding him hugely inspiring and motivating at others. I for one.

Sartre is inspiring not least because he is a brilliant psychologist with a remarkable capacity to understand and appreciate why people behave as they do. This is an important aspect of his humanity though not its core. Ironically, his humanity, at least as a writer, consists most essentially in his *limited* sympathy! He is not in the business of making excuses for people and he spares them the dishonour of pitying them. As a writer he refuses to be sentimental about human weakness, preferring to pay people the respect of insisting that they are always capable of improvement, of reaching their full potential. From out of his dark world comes the clear message that it is possible with effort for anyone to give up making excuses and to cease being a slave to fear, anxiety and other people. What is Sartre ultimately doing in his fiction, in his writing as a whole, if it is not delivering this inspiring message.

Sartre writes to inform us, show us, advise us, warn us, in very broad terms that do not seek to stifle our individuality and freedom, how we ought and ought not to live. He is at heart a true moralist in the grand tradition of the great moral philosophers from Socrates onwards. He is even something of a moral preacher, though like all the best moral preachers, his pronouncements are given in the form of persuasive stories and fables rather than as direct commandments. Like all true philosophers he is ultimately interested in ethics, in answering the question, 'How should one live given what one knows about what there is and the way things are?' And his answer, basically, is face up to reality with dignity by taking full ownership of your inalienable freedom without regret.

Sartre's dour assertion that mankind is 'condemned for ever to be free' (*AR*, p. 243) is well know. What is far less well known is his far more upbeat contention that with the right kind of attitude to life a person can *choose* his freedom in such a way that it is no longer something to which he is condemned – a burden, an affliction, an irksome metaphysical punishment – but what he values most in life and lives to affirm.

NOTES

CHAPTER 1: SARTRE'S WRITING

1. In declining the 1964 Nobel Prize for Literature Sartre insisted that it was his policy to refuse official distinctions – he had refused the Legion of Honour after World War II – and that 'The writer must refuse to let himself be transformed by institutions, even if these are of the most honourable kind, as is the case here' (Sartre press statement, taken by Carl-Gustav Bjurström, 22 October 1964.) As Annie Cohen-Solal puts it, 'Sartre had refused to be embalmed alive, to be made into a living statue and prematurely canonized' (Cohen-Solal 2005, p. 449). Unintentionally, Sartre enjoyed both the prestige of having been offered the prize and the notoriety of having rejected it.

2. Contrary to popular belief, Sartre was not a major drug user, or at least he was not in the habit of indulging in hard drugs for purely recreational purposes. He enjoyed alcohol and tobacco but did not use other recreational drugs to any significant degree. He took a hallucinogenic drug only once, under experimental conditions. The experiment, in which Sartre was injected with mescaline, took place in 1935. Though he achieved his philosophical aim of experiencing a genuine hallucination, Sartre had a bad trip, the reason why he never repeated the experience. For several months he suffered disturbing flashbacks in which he imagined crabs and lobsters were pursuing him in the streets.

   The mescaline experience and the crustaceous flashbacks that followed are echoed in his surrealistic 1938 novel, *Nausea*. To dispel another common misconception, however, mind altering substances are not referred to in the novel and its central character, Antoine Roquentin, although arguably psychotic, is not a drug addict.

   Sartre mainly used drugs in a semi-medicinal way, to help him work rather than for recreation. As he grew older he permanently damaged his health with the various stimulants he took to maintain his enormous literary output. Most notably, he took Corydrane tablets, a one-time legal and widely available mixture of aspirin and racemic amphetamine.

3. Sartre's first novel, he tells us in *Words*, was called *For a Butterfly* (*W*, p. 90). He wrote it in violet ink in his 'Exercise-book for novels' (*W*, p. 90). It told the story of a professor, his daughter and a young explorer

searching the Amazon for a precious butterfly. Everything was borrowed from a comic book Sartre had recently read.

> Did I see myself as a plagiarist? No. As an original writer: I touched up and renovated...New and complete sentences formed in my head with the unwavering certainty attributed to inspiration...I knew inspiration at the ages of seven and eight. (*W*, p. 91)

4. 'I had always found the word genius suspect: I even came to loathe it altogether. Where would be the anguish, the ordeal, the temptation resisted, even the merit, if I had gifts?' (*Wo*, p. 117). Sartre never viewed his achievements as the product of a gift, an inherent capacity, but as the product of a supreme conjuring trick, a lifelong mission to make himself out of nothing. He did not write because he was special, he was special because he wrote. 'I have never seen myself as the happy owner of a "talent": my one concern was to save myself – nothing in my hands, nothing in my pockets – through work and faith' (*Wo*, p. 158). Incidentally, this passage from the final paragraph of his autobiography, *Words*, echoes a passage from his 1954 play, *Kean*. Kean, who is nothing but the parts he plays and whose genius lies in acting, says: 'I live from day to day in a fabulous imposture. Not a farthing, nothing in my hands, nothing in my pockets, but I need only snap my fingers to summon spirits of the air' (*K*, Act 2, p. 31).

CHAPTER 2: SARTRE'S EXISTENTIALISM

1. Sartre's conclusion that the upsurge of being-for-itself is an unfathomable mystery, that any attempt to account for it produces only hypotheses that cannot be validated or invalidated (*BN*, p. 641), does not have to be readily accepted. As being-for-itself expresses the way of being of every conscious human organism, and does not express the way of being of organisms lower down the evolutionary scale, it might be possible to develop an evolutionary theory of the emergence of consciousness that explains the evolutionary development of consciousness and identifies the point at which fully developed consciousness was reached. The major stages along the path from primitive, non-conscious life-forms to a life-form possessing fully developed consciousness might have been as follows: Successful environment seeking required increased sensitivity – perception. Sophisticated environment seeking required recollection of situations absent from present experience – thought. Communication of such recollections to other members of the species – basic language. Cooperation between members of the species to shape the environment, and regulation of relations between members of the species involved in this enterprise – highly evolved language, self-concept, conscience.
2. Past, present and future are not three distinct and substantial elements, but three unified dimensions, each of which, being nothing in itself, is outside of itself in the other two and has meaning only in terms of the other two. Sartre refers to this structure as 'ekstatic' and to each of

the three dimensions of time as an 'ekstasis' (*BN*, p. 160). 'Ekstatic' is derived from the Greek 'ekstasis' meaning 'standing out from'.

3. God is essentially a for-itself, a conscious, knowing being, yet his consciousness is held to exist fundamentally rather than as a relation or a negation. In short, God's existence and essence are assumed to be one. The ontological argument for the existence of God – first formulated by the medieval philosopher, Anselm – assumes this unity of existence and essence. For Anselm, the most perfect conceivable entity must have the attribute of existence. So, for Anselm, God's essence implies his existence. God is the ultimate for-itself-in-itself.

4. In *The Imaginary*, an exploration of the imagination and mental images, Sartre argues that understanding a perceived object is like serving an 'apprenticeship' (*Im*, p. 9). We learn more about the object the longer we perceive it and the more aspects we explore. A mental image, on the other hand, has no hidden appearances, no transphenomenal aspects. It discloses nothing because it has only the appearances a person's intentions give it as he gives them. A mental image is known all at once, there is no apprenticeship to be served. Sartre writes:

> In perception, knowledge is formed slowly; in the image, knowledge is immediate... An image is not learned: it is organised exactly as the objects that are learned, but, in fact, it is given whole, for what it is, in its appearance... I can keep an image in view as long as I want: I will never find anything there but what I put there. (*Im*, p. 9)

5. Sartre was struck at an early age by what he later termed *existential absence*. In *Words* he tells of a gathering of the Institute of Modern Languages where his grandfather pronounced, ' "Someone's lacking here: it's Simonnot" ' (*Wo*, p. 58). This pronouncement caused Sartre to almost see Simonnot's absence like a pillar in the centre of the crowd. He also recounts his thoughts when he read about the huge anticipation generated in New York by Charles Dickens' imminent arrival. New York was 'lonely, widowed, orphaned, and depopulated simply by the absence of the man it was expecting. I murmured: "There's someone lacking: it's Dickens!" ' (*Wo*, p. 106).

6. It can be argued that 'Hell is other people' (*IC*, p. 223) is an unjustifiable generalization and that Sartre's insistence on the universality of human conflict is largely motivated by personal considerations. Arguably, he speaks too much from his own experience and overemphasizes one aspect of human behaviour for dramatic effect. As Gregory McCulloch writes: 'It is hard not to see here plain autobiography, and/or Sartre the novelist, intent on embodying a powerful though partial view of the human condition' (McCulloch 1994, p. 139). When Sartre suggests that the gaze or look of another person is always threatening he ignores the evidence of certain concrete situations, such as, for example, the protective-protected look between parent and child. In Sartre's defence it is important to note that he shows some appreciation of the capacity people have for being together without conflict in his account of Heidegger's notion of *Mitsein*, the 'we' subject (*BN*, pp. 434–452). He

acknowledges that rather than always seeking to transcend each other, people are capable on certain occasions of submerging themselves in an *us*. This submergence in an *us*, however, is often maintained through conflict with a *them* as opponent and/or hate object – Sartrean conflict at the group level.

7. On this subject and others Sartre holds remarkably similar views to the Austrian philosopher, Ludwig Wittgenstein. Wittgenstein argues in his masterful early work, *Tractatus Logico-Philosophicus*, published twenty-two years before *Being and Nothingness* in 1921, that 'Nothing *in the visual field* allows us to infer that it is seen by an eye' (Wittgenstein 2001, prop. 5.633, p. 57). This remains the case even when what is 'in the visual field' is a reflection of the eye that is seeing.

Although Wittgenstein died only a few years after Sartre became well known outside of France, it is likely he was aware of Sartre, but there appears to be no evidence that he ever read Sartre in any detail, if at all. Sartre, on the other hand, admits to reading Wittgenstein, or at least to knowing of him, when he writes in *Words*, 'I would rather read "thrillers" than Wittgenstein' (*Wo*, p. 49).

8. World War II politicized and radicalized Sartre. He strove against Nazi tyranny as a conscript in the French Army, as a prisoner of war and as a member of the Resistance. Immediately after the war he spoke out against anti-Semitism in Europe and the oppression of black people in the USA.

In 1954 Sartre made the first of several trips to the Soviet Union. He was a supporter of the communist ideal, although he grew increasingly disillusioned with the existing Soviet system and condemned the Soviet invasions of Hungary and Czechoslovakia in 1956 and 1968 respectively. Often accompanied by Simone de Beauvoir, he travelled the world during the 1950s and 60s as an unofficial ambassador of the French left, giving his blessing to various Marxist regimes, most notably in China and Cuba. He spent a month in Cuba in 1960 where he met his heroes Fidel Castro and Che Guevara.

The campaign with which Sartre became most involved on a personal level during the postwar years was the long and bitter struggle for Algerian independence that almost tore the French nation apart. In 1960 Sartre's became the most famous signature on the 'Manifesto of the 121' calling for 'insubordination' by French troops in Algeria. Some in high office considered the document treasonable and Sartre would have faced trial and possible imprisonment had President De Gaulle not shown the political savvy to avoid a damaging confrontation with France's leading left-wing intellectual with his famous declaration, 'You do not imprison Voltaire.' Sartre was such an outspoken critic of the French colonial policy in Algeria that in both 1961 and 1962 his Paris apartment was bombed by the O.A.S., a terrorist organization opposed to Algerian Independence.

Sartre's factual and fictional writing was inspired, perhaps above all else, by the universal philosophical concerns that his various political campaigns raised.

9. In being translucent, in being consciousness through and through, consciousness is conscious of itself as conscious. That is, the translucency of consciousness allows for what Sartre calls *non-thetic consciousness (of) consciousness*. If it were not conscious of itself as conscious, consciousness would not be conscious, it would not be. The non-thetic consciousness that consciousness has of itself as conscious should not be confused with self-consciousness or self-reflection proper – what Sartre calls *thetic self-consciousness* – in which consciousness itself becomes the theme or object of contemplation. Non-thetic consciousness (of) consciousness is a general, non-thematic consciousness that accompanies all consciousness including thetic self-consciousness; it is therefore a prerequisite of thetic self-consciousness.

   Sartre contrasts the translucency of consciousness with the opacity of objects. For Sartre, objects are opaque in always having aspects that are not presently appearing – insides and hidden sides. Even a transparent object does not reveal all its possible appearances at once because it can only be viewed from one perspective or angle at a time. As noted earlier in the chapter, the actual appearances of an object at any one time indicate an infinite series of transphenomenal appearances that are presently hidden but which could appear.

10. As a soldier, so he tells us in his *War Dairies*, Sartre strove to achieve authenticity by accepting his being-in-situation. It was during his time as a conscript in the provinces of northern France (1939–40) that Sartre first used the phrase *being-in-situation*. The demands of war swept him away from his beloved Paris at a time when he was enjoying great success and notoriety as the author of *Nausea* and *The Wall*, and it would have been all too easy for him to bemoan the sudden change in his circumstances. Instead, he endeavoured to dedicate himself without regret to the role of a soldier, albeit a soldier with few duties who was often at liberty to read and write for sixteen hours a day. Not least because he was free from the many social distractions of Paris, Sartre's circumstances during the Phoney War (the eight-month stand-off between France and Germany) provided him with the perfect opportunity to write and hence to fulfil the destiny he had chosen for himself as a child. It was, then, relatively easy for Sartre to be authentic during the Phoney War. By all accounts, however, he remained authentic and positive and continued to embrace his being-in-situation when his situation became much tougher. That is, when the Germans captured him in June 1940 and he became a prisoner of war.

CHAPTER 3: SARTRE'S SHORT STORIES

1. Russian born Olga Kosakiewiecz was a beautiful, intelligent, proud and capricious young woman who had been a student of Simone de Beauvoir's in Rouen in the early 1930s. Sartre and de Beauvoir decided early on that their unique personal and intellectual relationship constituted a 'necessary love' that could tolerate and even benefit from the 'contingent love' of their various affairs. The passions that Olga

stirred in both of them seriously challenged this arrangement. The necessary love between Sartre and de Beauvoir was threatened above all by Sartre's intense infatuation with Olga and his jealous, thwarted desire to possess her. From 1935 to 1937, as he tried everything in his power to win her, her refusal either to accept or reject him drove him to near madness and despair. Sartre later claimed he never knew jealously except where Olga was concerned and undoubtedly his affair with her was a life-defining episode that haunted his writing for many years.

Several of Sartre's female characters have some of Olga's personality traits. Lulu in *Intimacy,* for example, and Inez in *In Camera* (see note 1, Chapter 5). The Sartre character most identifiable as Olga, however, is Ivich Serguine in *Roads to Freedom*. The ménage à trois at the centre of de Beauvoir's 1943 novel, *She Came to Stay*, is based on the ménage à trois involving herself, Sartre and Olga.

2. I have been unable to check all editions of *Intimacy*, but at least one, the 1960s Panther edition, has been censored. For example, from the story, *The Childhood of a Leader*, the censor has removed a direct reference to homosexual activity: 'Then Bergère shouted in triumph. "At last!" he said, "you've decided. All right," he added, breathing heavily, "we'll make something out of you." Lucien slipped out of his pajamas.' The censor has also removed the expression of the central character's thought that homosexual activity is an addictive and dangerous drug: '"I could never do without it, it'll be like morphine!"' Both the passage and the sentence appear on pages 117 and 118 respectively of the *uncensored* New Directions edition of *The Wall* used in writing this book.

3. *Phoney war*: The eight month stand-off between French and German troops between 1 September 1939 and April 1940. The inspiration for Sartre's *War Diaries, Notebooks from a Phoney War 1939-40.*

4. The significant increase in the number of school massacres in the USA since the late 1990s no doubt reflects the growing frustration, alienation and paranoia felt by young people growing up in a violent, gunsoaked, decadent, desperately competitive and materialistic culture. It also corresponds to an increase in the availability, speed and popularity of the internet. Websites and chat rooms preoccupied with the disturbed young men who tend to carry out these crimes continue to play a key role in inspiring an ongoing series of copycat killings. Deranged Hilbert-type characters, such as Eric Harris, 18, and Dylan Klebold, 17, who shot dead 14 students (including themselves) and one teacher at Columbine High School, Littleton, Colorado on 28 April 1999 have, thanks largely to the internet, achieved a worldwide cult status among disaffected youth. Like Erostratus, the infamy of Harris and Klebold is perpetuated in these very pages!

5. Many of the incidental details in *The Childhood of a Leader* are also drawn from Sartre's own childhood as later described in his autobiography, *Words*. For example, at the start of the story Lucien is wearing an angel's costume. '"I look adorable in my little angel's costume." Mme. Portier told mamma' (*CL*, p. 84). In *Words* Sartre writes, '... in a blue

muslin dress, with stars in my hair and wings, I went from one person to the next, offering them mandarin oranges from a basket, as they
exclaimed: "He *really is* an angel!"' (*Wo*, p. 27).
6. Maurice Barrès (1862–1923). French novelist, journalist and politician,
noted for his fervent nationalism, his anti-Semitism and his involvement
in the Dreyfus Affair. As an early influence on writers such as Gide,
Aragon and Mauriac, Barrès remains an important if controversial figure in French literature. In *The Childhood of a Leader*, Lucien Fleurier
reads Barrès' *Les déracinés* and *Jardin de Bérénice* on the recommenda-
tion of the racist nationalist, André Lemordant. Sartre clearly despised
Barrès, and even lampooned him as a model *salaud* (swine or bastard) in
his 1938 novel, *Nausea*. 'An excellent portrait, granted. Olivier Blévigne
had a little black moustache and his olive-tinted face somewhat resem-
bled that of Maurice Barrès. The two men had undoubtedly met: they
sat on the same benches' (*N*, p. 135). The central character of *Nausea*,
Antoine Roquentin, even has a dream in which he spanks Barrès until
he bleeds. 'I gave Maurice Barrès a spanking' (*N*, p. 89).
7. After World War II Sartre returned to the theme of anti-Semitism in
Anti-Semite and Jew (1946), a book largely inspired by his desire to
address the taboo subject of French complicity in the Nazi project
at the time of the widely unwelcome return to France of French Jews
deported by the Nazis. *Anti-Semite and Jew*, like Sartre's play of the
same year, *The Respectable Prostitute*, confronts the issue that the
defeat of German Nazism was not the defeat of prejudice and hatred in
those Western democracies that defeated Nazism.
8. Lucien Fleurier's fellow Fascist, Lemordant, has a moustache, as does
the Fascist *falangista* who takes himself so seriously in *The Wall*.

> The *falangista* had a moustache. I said to him again, "You ought to
> shave of your moustache, idiot." I thought it funny that he would let
> the hairs of his living being invade his face. He kicked me without
> great conviction and I kept quiet. (*W*, p. 16)

The *salauds* (Swine or bastards) Blévigne and Barrès in *Nausea* also
have moustaches (see note 6).

Sartre is obsessed with moustaches, they recur so often in his fictional writings that one loses count of them. Some of his female characters have them too, although they are excused for not having *cultivated*
them. ('She was a good-looking, buxom Marseillaise with a shadow of
a moustache' [*R*, p. 267].) He identifies them, on men, as a ridiculous,
futile gesture, as superfluous and surreal. They tend to belong to minor
characters, to unthinking men with no inner life, to characters that
exist as the Other for his main characters. A man cannot see his own
moustache, at least to the extent that others see it, so a moustache exists
primarily for others and a man with a moustache is a man who has
undertaken to exist for others rather than for himself. In so far as it is
typical of the bourgeois to strive to *be* his social role, the moustache, for
Sartre, becomes the emblem of the shallow, self-satisfied, respectable,
reactionary middle-class gentleman.

The fine gentleman exists Legion of Honour, exists moustache, that's all; how happy one must be to be nothing more than a Legion of Honour and a moustache and nobody sees the rest, he sees the two pointed ends of moustache on both sides of the nose; I do not think therefore I am a moustache. (*N*, p. 147)

9. The quotation actually refers to one of the *salauds* in *Nausea*, the late Olivier Blévigne, a deputy of Bouville, the president of the Club de l'Ordre and the orator of *Moral Forces*. His grand portrait in the Bouville museum makes him look far taller and far more imposing than the 'student terrorized by the Commune, the bad-tempered midget of a deputy' (*N*, p. 136) that he was in life. See also notes 6 and 8.

CHAPTER 4: SARTRE'S NOVELS

1. Sartre appears to have written *Queen Albemarle and the Last Tourist* mostly during his holidays to Italy in the early 1950s. Relaxing in Italy, always his favourite destination, away from the ill-humoured Parisian political scene, he was able to indulge his imagination and his craft as a storyteller. Simone de Beauvoir once described the work as the 'Nausea of Sartre's maturity' (Quoted in Cohen-Solal 2005, p. 319 and p. 379). A few pages of the reputedly 500-page manuscript were published in *France-Observateur* in 1952 and *Verve* in 1953, and later reprinted in *Situations IV* in 1964 as 'A Bed of Nasturtiums' and 'Venice from My Window'. All currently available fragments of the manuscript were published by Editions Gallimard, Paris, in 1991.

2. *Nausea*, in translation, reads at times like a poem by T. S. Eliot. There is the same economy and melancholic beauty of language, the same solitary, alienated voice lost in time and uncertainty, the same sense of the mystery of existence conjured up through the surreal juxtaposition of mundane objects. Sartre's *Nausea* and Eliot's early poems, particularly 'The Love Song of J. Alfred Prufrock' and 'The Waste Land', succeed in penetrating the skin of everyday objects and scenes.

   The sylphs all around me have been taken in: they see nothing but the thin film, that is what proves the existence of God. I see underneath! The varnishes melt, the shining little velvety skins, God's little peach skins, explode everywhere under my gaze, they split and yawn open (*N*, p. 179).

The reader is compelled to reappraise objects and scenes, while the objects and scenes themselves are compelled to indicate, indeed to *be*, the unfathomable mystery of life itself. 'I have measured out my life with coffee spoons' ('Prufrock', in Eliot 2002, p. 14). Both Sartre and Eliot recognize that the profound strangeness of existence is not something remote or occult, but rather that which is about us all the time in the 'ordinary' things we see and use but tend not to really notice. 'Objects ought not to *touch*, since they are not alive. You use them, you put them back in place, you live among them: they are useful, nothing more. But they touch me, it's unbearable' (*N*, p. 22).

Both writers also have a deep sense of the relentless passage of time and the implications that this has for our sense of ourselves and the world. Both derived their ideas on temporality from the French philosopher Henri Bergson and his major work, *Time and Free Will*. Eliot attended Bergson's lectures at the Sorbonne, while Bergson's writings first inspired Sartre to consider himself a philosopher when he was introduced to them as a student at the École Normale. Bergson distinguishes between divisible, scientific time and the continuous temporal flow that is intuitively experienced by consciousness and is so central to psychic life. *Nausea* and many of Eliot's poems are heavy with a sense of the temporal flow to which Bergson refers and with troubled reflections on that temporal flow.

3. See notes on Sartre's drug taking: note 2, Chapter 1 and note 12, Chapter 5.

4. Sartre does not equate knowing the truth with knowing lots of facts. Filling ones head with facts can be a way of avoiding seeing ones existence for what it really is. The form of bad faith exhibited by the Autodidact is also exhibited by Jacques in *Roads to Freedom*. Sartre explores this form of bad faith most thoroughly in *Truth and Existence*, a philosophical work he wrote in 1948 but which was not published until 1989.

5. After World War II Sartre came to view Marxism as the dominant philosophy of the age and existentialism as a subordinate theory the purpose of which is to function within Marxism at the level of individuals positively influencing its future development. In his vast *Critique of Dialectical Reason* Sartre ambitiously undertakes to synthesize Marxism and existentialism arguing that they are compatible theories of the human condition.

6. Ivich Serguine is based on Olga Kosakiewiecz. See note 1, Chapter 3.

7. In his major work, *The Phenomenology of Perception*, conceived to some extent as a response to Sartre's *Being and Nothingness*, Merleau-Ponty writes:

> Underlying myself as a thinking subject... there is, therefore, as it were, a natural self which does not budge from its terrestrial situation and which constantly adumbrates absolute valuations... In so far as I have hands, feet, a body, I sustain around me intentions which are not dependent upon my decisions and which effect my surroundings in a way which I do not choose. (Merleau-Ponty 2002, pp. 439–440)

8. Sartre lived through two world wars, he was a prisoner of war, he worked for the Resistance movement in an occupied country and certainly he and people he knew were regularly confronted with a choice between bravery and cowardice. It is not surprising, then, that he is fascinated with the subject of cowardice, that it is a recurrent theme in both his factual and fictional writing. *The Reprieve* and *In Camera* are just two Sartre works that explore the subject of cowardice. In *Being and*

Nothingness Sartre considers a man who, though he acts in a cowardly way, resorts to bad faith to deny that cowardice is the meaning of his conduct (*BN*, pp. 89–90). In *Existentialism and Humanism* Sartre takes the example of cowardice to illustrate the indeterminacy of the self, arguing that nobody is born a coward. People simply choose to act in a cowardly way and can choose to act in a heroic way (*EAH*, p. 43). In *Iron in the Soul* Jacques flees as the Nazis advance on Paris then manoeuvres his wife, Odette, into declaring that they fled because of her fears rather than his. In the same novel, a young soldier, Pinette, chooses to fight and die rather than surrender. He cannot bear to be thought of as a useless coward by his relatives. In *The Wall* Ibbieta wants only to face his execution bravely, in *Men Without Shadows* the prisoners fear their potential for cowardice at least as much as they fear pain and death, and in *Dirty Hands* one of Hugo Barine's reasons for wanting to be a killer is to prove to himself and others that he is not a coward. There are several other examples that could be cited.

9. *Anti-Semite and Jew*: See note 7, Chapter 3.
10. The prisoners exhibit what has come to be known as Stockholm syndrome, a psychological response in which captives and hostages bond with their captors showing them loyalty and regard. The syndrome is named after the 1973 Norrmalmstorg robbery, Stockholm, in which a five day hostage situation led to the hostages becoming emotionally attached to those who were victimizing them. Although such behaviour is common, Sartre would want to attribute it to bad faith on the part of individual captives, to a person's choice of himself in response to an extreme situation, rather than to the influences of a syndrome that supposedly compels people to adopt a certain pattern of behaviour. He would argue that in choosing to identify with their captors, captives are seeking to share in their captors transcendence so as to escape being the enslaved objects of that transcendence. By admiring German efficiency, for example, and willingly adopting German as opposed to French time, Brunet's fellow prisoners cease to feel that they are mere victims, mere transcendences-transcended by the Other, and feel instead that they are the Other, that they are honorary victors.

CHAPTER 5: SARTRE'S PLAYS

1. Inez' story echoes to some extent the story told in Simone de Beauvoir's 1943 novel, *She Came to Stay*. Sartre and de Beauvoir were intrigued by the theme of the ménage à trios and had been since their own emotionally charged ménage à trios with Russian born Olga Kosakiewiecz. See note 1, Chapter 3.
2. For Sartre's preoccupation with the theme of cowardice see note 8, Chapter 4.
3. *Men Without Shadows* is the best-known English title of this play but a more literal translation of its original French title, *Morts sans sépulture*, is *Death Without Burial*. It is also sometimes referred to as *The Victors*.

4. For Sartre's preoccupation with the theme of cowardice see note 8, Chapter 4.

5. Raskolnikov, the central character of Fyodor Dostoevsky's novel, *Crime and Punishment*. In an attempt to escape his poverty and that of his family, Raskolnikov kills an old pawnbroker and her sister with an axe. He initially denies his crime but eventually admits responsibility for it.

6. The most common English translation of *Le Diable et le bon Dieu*, the original French title of the play, is *Lucifer and the Lord*, but *The Devil and the Good Lord* is a more accurate translation. It is possible that 'bon Dieu' may have something of a double meaning for Sartre. It may refer both to God and to the central character of the play, Goetz. Goetz is a strong leader, a local god, a demigod, with the power of life and death over many people. During the play this demigod decides to do only good, thus becoming what might, at a stretch, be described as a *bon Dieu*. If Sartre did have this double meaning in mind then it is an error to translate the title of the play as *Lucifer and the Lord* because it does not preserve the double meaning.

    The English 'lord' can mean 'God' or 'lord of the manor'. In English, it seems obvious that 'the Good Lord' refers both to a benevolent God and to the benevolent Lord Goetz, but of course, Sartre could not have intended this particular English double meaning as he wrote in French.

7. Sartre blew hot and cold with communism and with the French Communist Party in particular. The section in Chapter 5 of this book on his play, *Dirty Hands*, explores some of the ups and downs of this stormy relationship. Never less tolerant or more vindictive than when politics was involved, Sartre often fell out with his contemporaries when their current political opinion happened to be heading in the opposite direction to his. Most famously, political differences ended his friendships with his fellow existentialists, Albert Camus (1913–1960) and Maurice Merleau-Ponty (1908–1961).

8. From the late 1940s to the mid-1950s, largely to further his own political career, Senator Joseph McCarthy (1908–57), one of the most vicious, sleazy and deceitful characters in American history, conducted a sustained campaign of accusing prominent Americans of being communists or communist sympathizers. McCarthy's generally unsubstantiated accusations generated such an atmosphere of hysteria and paranoia in the USA that many Americans came under pressure to denounce others as communists to avoid being denounced as communists themselves. The classic allegorical statement on what has come to be known as the McCarthy witch-hunts or McCarthyism is Arthur Miller's, *The Crucible*, a play about the Salem witch trials of 1692. Between 1953 and 1955 Sartre adapted *The Crucible* into a screenplay for the 1957 film *The Witches of Salem* directed by Raymond Rouleau.

9. *Soir à Paris* is a caricature of the popular French newspaper, *France-Soir*. Sartre had attacked the newspaper and its editor, Pierre Lazareff, the year before *Nekrassov* appeared. The unscrupulous and self-important

editor of *Soir à Paris,* Jules Palotin, is a thinly veiled parody of Lazareff. It was this that the Parisian press chose to find particularly offensive. Interestingly, *France-Soir* is mentioned in the play as a rival paper to *Soir à Paris* and Lazareff as a rival editor (*Ne,* Scene 4, p. 198). Sartre may have done this so as to have grounds, if required, for resisting legal charges that Palotin and Lazareff were one and the same.

10. The intimate link between *In Camera* (*No Exit*) and *The Condemned of Altona* is more clearly suggested by the original French title of the latter play, *Les Séquestrés d'Altona.* 'Les Séquestrés' translates as 'The Sequestered'; 'sequester' meaning both 'to remove or separate' and 'to retire into seclusion'. In both plays the characters are cut off and confined. Literally confined in the case of *In Camera,* metaphorically confined in the case of *Altona.* In both plays the characters are trapped by their sense of guilt, by their past actions and by their desire to understand and/or justify them. As *The Sequestered of Altona* would be the most appropriate and revealing English title of the play we can only wonder why it is titled *The Condemned of Altona.*

11. Franz bears some similarities to Pierre, the reclusive, inspired madman in Sartre's short story, *The Room.* See Chapter 3.

12. Sartre had a personal aversion to crustaceans, particularly after his mescaline trip of 1935. They are a recurrent theme in his writing, particularly in his 1938 novel, *Nausea.* They represent malice, blind will, base nature and naked, absurd, unjustifiable existence. See note 2, Chapter 1.

13. For information on Sartre's support for Algerian independence and the various attacks he endured in the process see note 8, Chapter 2.

BIBLIOGRAPHY

WORKS BY SARTRE

The Age of Reason, trans. David Caute (Harmondsworth: Penguin, 2001).

Anti-Semite and Jew, trans. George J. Becker (New York: Schocken, 1995).

Baudelaire, trans. Martin Turnell (New York: New Directions, 1967).

Being and Nothingness: An Essay on Phenomenological Ontology, trans. Hazel E. Barnes (London and New York: Routledge, 2003).

The Childhood of a Leader, in Sartre, *The Wall*, trans. Lloyd Alexander (New York: New Directions, 1988).

The Condemned of Altona (*The Sequestered of Altona* or *Altona* or *Loser Wins*), trans. Sylvia and George Leeson, in *Penguin Plays: Altona, Men without Shadows, The Flies* (Harmondsworth, Penguin, 1973).

Crime Passionnel (*Dirty Hands*), trans. Kitty Black (London: Methuen, 1995).

Critique of Dialectical Reason Vol. 1, Theory of Practical Ensembles, trans. Alan Sheridan-Smith (London: Verso, 2004).

Critique of Dialectical Reason Vol. 2, The Intelligibility of History, trans. Alan Sheridan-Smith (London: Verso, 2004).

Erostratus, in Sartre, *The Wall*, trans. Lloyd Alexander (New York: New Directions, 1988).

Existentialism and Humanism, trans. Philip Mairet (London: Methuen, 1993).

The Family Idiot Vols. 1–5, trans. Carol Cosman (Chicago: University of Chicago Press, 1981).

The Flies, trans. Stuart Gilbert, in *Penguin Plays: Altona, Men without Shadows, The Flies* (Harmondsworth: Penguin, 1973).

Hope Now: The 1980 Interviews (co-author: Lévy, Benny) trans. Adrian van den Hoven (Chicago: University of Chicago Press, 1996).

The Imaginary: A Phenomenological Psychology of the Imagination, trans. Jonathan Webber (London and New York: Routledge, 2004).

Imagination: A Psychological Critique, trans. Forrest Williams (Ann Arbor: University of Michigan Press, 1979).

In Camera (*No Exit* or *Behind Closed Doors*), trans. Stuart Gilbert, in *In Camera and Other Plays* (Harmondsworth: Penguin, 1990).

Intimacy, in Sartre, *The Wall*, trans. Lloyd Alexander (New York: New Directions, 1988).

Iron in the Soul, trans. David Caute (Harmondsworth: Penguin, 2004).

Kean, or Disorder and Genius, trans. Kitty Black, in *Three Plays: Kean, Nekrassov, The Trojan Women* (Harmondsworth: Penguin, 1994).

Lucifer and the Lord (The Devil and the Good Lord), trans. Kitty Black, in *In Camera and Other Plays* (Harmondsworth: Penguin, 1990).

Men without Shadows (Death without Burial or *The Victors),* trans. Kitty Black, in *Penguin Plays: Altona, Men without Shadows, The Flies* (Harmondsworth: Penguin, 1973).

Nausea, trans. Robert Baldick (Harmondsworth: Penguin, 2000).

Nekrassov, A Farce in Eight Scenes, trans. Sylvia and George Leeson, in *Three Plays: Kean, Nekrassov, The Trojan Women* (Harmondsworth: Penguin, 1994).

Notebooks for an Ethics, trans. David Pellauer (Chicago: University of Chicago Press, 1992).

Oeuvres romanesques, Michel Contat and Michel Rybalka (ed.), Bibliothèque de la Pléiade (Paris: Gallimard, 1981).

La Reine Albemarle ou le dernier touriste (Queen Albemarle and the Last Tourist) (Paris: Editions Gallimard, 1991).

The Reprieve, trans. Eric Sutton (Harmondsworth, Penguin, 2005).

The Respectable Prostitute, trans. Kitty Black, in *In Camera and Other Plays* (Harmondsworth: Penguin, 1990).

The Room, in Sartre, *The Wall,* trans. Lloyd Alexander (New York: New Directions, 1988).

Saint Genet, trans. Bernard Frechtman (New York: Pantheon, 1983).

Sartre on Theatre, Michel Contat and Michel Rybalka (ed.), trans. Frank Jellinek (New York: Pantheon, 1976).

Search for a Method, trans. Hazel E. Barnes (New York: Vintage, 1968).

Sketch for a Theory of the Emotions, trans. Philip Mairet (London: Methuen, 1985).

Situations Vols. 1–7 (Paris: Gallimard 1947, 1948, 1949, 1964, 1965). Vols. 8–9, *Between Existentialism and Marxism,* trans. John Mathews (New York: Pantheon, 1974). Vol. 10. *Life/Situations,* trans. Paul Auster and Lydia Davis (New York: Pantheon, 1977).

Théâtre complet, Michel Contat (ed.), Bibliothèque de la Pléiade (Paris: Gallimard, 2005).

The Transcendence of the Ego, A Sketch for a Phenomenological Description, trans. Andrew Brown (London and New York: Routledge, 2004).

The Trojan Women, trans. Ronald Duncan, in *Three Plays: Kean, Nekrassov, The Trojan Women* (Harmondsworth: Penguin, 1994).

Truth and Existence, trans. Adrian van den Hoven (Chicago: University of Chicago Press, 1995).

The Wall, in Sartre, *The Wall,* trans. Lloyd Alexander (New York: New Directions, 1988).

War Diaries: Notebooks from a Phoney War, 1939-1940, trans. Quintin Hoare (London: Verso, 2000).

What Is Literature?, trans. Bernard Frechtman, (London and New York: Routledge, 2002).

Words, trans. Irene Clephane (Harmondsworth: Penguin, 2000).

OTHER WORKS REFERRED TO

Beckett, Samuel, Molloy, *Malone Dies, The Unnameable: A Trilogy* (London: Everyman, 2005).

Bergson, Henri, *Time and Free Will* (Boston: Adamant, 2000).

Brentano, Franz, *Psychology from an Empirical Standpoint*, trans. A. Rancurello, D. Terrell and Linda McAlister (London and New York: Routledge, 2004).

Burns, Robert, 'Man was made to Mourn', in *Burns, Poems, Chiefly in the Scottish Dialect* (Harmondsworth: Penguin, 1999).

Camus, Albert, *The Outsider (The Stranger)*, trans. Joseph Laredo (Harmondsworth: Penguin, 2000).

Cohen-Solal, Annie, *Jean-Paul Sartre: A Life*, trans. Anna Cancogni (New York: The New Press, 2005).

Cox, Gary, *The Sartre Dictionary* (London and New York: Continuum, 2008).

de Beauvoir, Simone, *The Ethics of Ambiguity*, trans. Bernard Frechtman (New York: Citadel Press, 2000).

de Beauvoir, Simone, *Force of Circumstance*, trans. R. Howard (Harmondsworth: Penguin, 1987).

de Beauvoir, Simone, *The Prime of Life*, trans. Peter Green (Harmondsworth: Penguin, 2001).

de Beauvoir, Simone, *She Came to Stay* (London: Harper Perennial, 2006).

Dostoevsky, Fyodor, *Crime and Punishment*, Trans. David Magarshack (Harmondsworth: Penguin, 2007).

Eliot, T. S. *Collected Poems: 1909-1962* (London: Faber and Faber, 2002).

Faulkner, William, *Light in August* (London: Vintage 2000).

Gaarder, Jostein, *Sophie's World*, trans. Paulette Moller (London: Phoenix, 1995).

Hamsun, Knut, *Hunger* (Edinburgh: Canongate, 2006).

Kierkegaard, Søren, *The Sickness unto Death, a Christian Psychological Exposition for Edification and Awakening*, trans. Alastair Hannay (Harmondsworth: Penguin, 1989).

Laing, Ronald. D., *The Divided Self: An Existential Study in Sanity and Madness* (Harmondsworth: Penguin, 1990).

Marx, Karl and Engels, Friedrich, *The Communist Manifesto* (Harmondsworth: Penguin, 1985).

McCulloch, Gregory, *Using Sartre: An Analytical Introduction to Early Sartrean Themes* (London and New York: Routledge, 1994).

Merleau-Ponty, Maurice, *Phenomenology of Perception*, trans. Colin Smith (London and New York: Routledge, 2002).

Midgley, Mary, *Beast and Man, the Roots of Human Nature* (London: Routledge, 2002).

Miller, Arthur, *The Crucible: A Play in Four Acts* (Harmondsworth: Penguin, 2007).

Murdoch, Iris, *Sartre: Romantic Rationalist* (London: Fontana, 1968).

Nietzsche, Friedrich, *The Gay Science*, trans. Walter Kaufmann (New York: Vintage Press, 1974).

Nietzsche, Friedrich, *Beyond Good and Evil: Prelude to a Philosophy of the Future*, trans. R. J. Hollingdale (Harmondsworth: Penguin, 2003).

Pirsig, Robert M., *Zen and the Art of Motorcycle Maintenance: An Inquiry into Values* (London and New York: Vintage, 1974).

Rousseau, Jean-Jacques, *Emile, or On Education* (Harmondsworth: Penguin, 1991).

Ryle, Gilbert, *The Concept of Mind* (Harmondsworth: Penguin, 1990).

Salinger, J. D., *Catcher in the Rye* (Harmondsworth: Penguin, 1994).

Voltaire, François Marie Arouet de, *Candide, or Optimism* (Harmondsworth: Penguin, 2006).

Wittgenstein, Ludwig, *Philosophical Investigations*, trans. G. E. M. Anscombe, (Oxford: Blackwell, 1988).

Wittgenstein, Ludwig, *Tractatus Logico-Philosophicus*, trans. D. F. Pears and B. F. McGuiness (London and New York: Routledge, 2001).

FURTHER READING

Barnes, Hazel E., *Sartre* (London: Quartet Books, 1974).

Barnes, Hazel E., *Sartre and Flaubert* (Chicago: University of Chicago Press, 1981).

Bernasconi, Robert, *How To Read Sartre* (London: Granta, 2006).

Cox, Gary, *Sartre: A Guide for the Perplexed* (London and New York: Continuum, 2006).

Danto, Arthur C., *Sartre* (London: Harper Collins/Fontana, 1991).

Descartes, René, *Meditations and Other Metaphysical Writings*, trans. Desmond M. Clarke (Harmondsworth: Penguin, 1998).

Fell, Joseph P., *Heidegger and Sartre: An Essay on Being and Place* (New York: Columbia University Press, 1983).

Fox, Nik Farrell, *The New Sartre* (London and New York: Continuum, 2006).

Hegel, George Wilhelm Friedrich, *The Phenomenology of Spirit*, trans. J. B. Bailey (New York: Dover, 2003).

Hegel, George Wilhelm Friedrich, *Science of Logic*, trans. A. V. Miller (New York: Humanity Books, Prometheus, 1998).

Heidegger, Martin, *Being and Time*, trans. John Macquarrie and Edward Robinson (Oxford: Blackwell, 1993).

Howells, Christina (ed.), *The Cambridge Companion to Sartre* (Cambridge: Cambridge University Press, 2005).

Husserl, Edmund, *Cartesian Meditations: An Introduction to Phenomenology*, trans. Dorion Cairns (The Hague: Matinus Nijhoff, 1977).

Kant, Immanuel, *Critique of Pure Reason*, trans. Norman Kemp Smith (London: Macmillan, 2003).

Leak, Andrew, *Sartre* (London and Chicago: Reaktion, 2006).

Manser, Anthony, *Sartre: A Philosophic Study* (Oxford: Greenwood Press, 1981).

Masters, Bryan, *A Student's Guide to Sartre – Student's Guides to European Literature* (London, Heinemann, 1972).

McBride, William L. (ed.), *Sartre and Existentialism: Philosophy, Politics, Ethics, the Psyche, Literature and Aesthetics, Volumes 1-8* (London: Garland/Taylor and Francis, 1997).

McCall, Dorothy, *The Theatre of Jean-Paul Sartre* (New York: Columbia University Press, 1971).

Morris, Katherine, *Sartre* (Oxford: Wiley-Blackwell, 2007).

O'Donohoe, Benedict, *Sartre's Theatre: Acts for Life* (Oxford: Peter Lang, 2005).

Priest, Stephen (ed.), *Jean-Paul Sartre: Basic Writings* (London and New York: Routledge, 2001).

Schopenhauer, Arthur, *World as Will and Representation* Vols. 1 & 2, trans. E. F. J. Payne (New York: Dover, 1967).

Webber, Jonathan, *The Existentialism of Jean-Paul Sartre* (London and New York: Routledge, 2009).

INDEX